URBAN LIFE AND URBAN LANDSCAPE SERIES

Zane L. Miller, General Editor

COLUMBUS, OHIO
A PERSONAL GEOGRAPHY

Henry L. Hunker

OHIO STATE UNIVERSITY PRESS • *Columbus*

Library of Congress Cataloging-in-Publication Data
Hunker, Henry L.
   Columbus, Ohio : a personal geography / Henry L. Hunker.
       p. cm.
Includes bibliographical references.
   ISBN 0-8142-0857-6 (alk. paper)
   1.   Columbus (Ohio)—History—20th century.   2.   Columbus
(Ohio)—Geography.   I.   Title.
   F499.C757 H86 2000
   977.1'57043—dc21

                                                                    00-009360

Text and jacket design by Gary Gore.
Type set in Adobe Garamond by Graphic Composition, Inc.
Printed by Thomson-Shore, Inc.

The paper used in this publication meets the minimum requirements of the American
National Standard for Information Sciences—Permanence of Paper for Printed Library
Materials. ANSI Z39.48–1992.

9   8   7   6   5   4   3   2   1

For Beth, who made this journey
with me,
and for our four sons—Fred,
Kurt, David, and Erich,
all Columbus natives . . .

CONTENTS

ACKNOWLEDGMENTS

This book evolved out of fifty years of experiences in Columbus during which many within the university and the community helped to shape its message. The willingness to share time and information with me was generous, whether on the part of university colleagues and mentors or the city's business and political leaders with whom I had contact, as well as those friends I called upon to verify a fact or answer a question. But, in the final analysis, it is a personal statement—a personal geography. I have given careful attention to the facts and have attempted to minimize the biases that are a part of any such undertaking.

I want to recognize the cooperation and support that I have received from the Department of Geography and from the College of Social and Behavioral Sciences. I would also recognize and thank Mark Horner, a doctoral student in geography, who produced the maps that accompany the text; the Ohio State *Lantern* and artist Jim Kammerud for permission to use one of his cartoons; and *The Columbus Dispatch* for permission to use the terrific photo of Columbus at 2000!

It goes without saying, but needs to be said, that I thank my wife and family for their interest, support, and patience.

1

Introduction

I FIRST VISITED COLUMBUS IN DECEMBER 1946, more than fifty years ago, to attend a meeting of professional geographers gathered at Ohio State University. It wasn't a particularly memorable experience, being shaped, in part, by the miserable weather—the gray and gloomy overcast sky and the remnants of snow and ice piled along the curbs and yards; the overwhelming sense was of a city damp and bleak and cold. But then, too, I really didn't care to be at Ohio State, a school whose football team had so consistently humiliated Pitt, my alma mater. With a fellow geographer, we had traveled to the city via Route 40—the old National Road—into Columbus along Main Street, with its seemingly endless miles of motels, finally arriving at the old Chittenden Hotel at the northwest corner of Spring and High Streets. We "dined" in its coffee shop, the Purple Cow, where an inscription informed us that "I never saw a purple cow, I never hope to see one, but I can tell you anyhow, I'd rather see than be one!"

We dutifully attended meetings of our professional colleagues on campus, where, as luck would have it, I would later establish my own professional roots. As young graduate students, we were interested in seeing and hearing some of the big names in the profession and, incidentally, in meeting some of the local geographers. We knew the names of these men—yes, all men—and had some sense of their reputations. We were surprised to read in the Saturday morning paper—was it the old *Ohio State Journal* or *Citizen-Journal*?—that fire had destroyed the library of one of them,

Professor Roderick Peattie, on Perry Street, just south of the university campus. Peattie was known to us, as he was to many Columbusites, because of his numerous books that presented geography to the reader in a palatable fashion.[1]

We actually saw little of the city. There were no field trips to afford us that opportunity, nor do I recall any apparent attempt to inform the professional guests about Columbus. Thus, we left Columbus only a little wiser and not much better informed about the town than before we had made the 200-mile journey from Pittsburgh.

I didn't return—there was no reason to—until the spring of 1949, when I drove down from East Lansing, Michigan, where I held my first academic position, at Michigan State. Once again, I came to Ohio State to participate in a professional conference. This one proved to be more illuminating about the city than the first, especially since a field trip had been arranged to introduce us to a few aspects of the city.

The first was a stop at Battelle Institute, then largely housed in the original administration building on King Avenue, prior to its expansion to become one of the largest private research institutions in the world. We didn't attempt to enter (it was early Saturday morning), but we drove to it, and our guide, Professor Alfred J. Wright, told us about Battelle and hinted at reasons why it, as a research institution, might be important to the city in the future. We left King Avenue and were shown a building on Olentangy River Road where a new commercial laundry detergent, ALL, was being manufactured for the new automatic washers then coming on the market.[2] So there was some creativity here after all. . . .

Our trip took us, ultimately, out East Fifth Avenue, which at that time, 1949, was still plagued by surface railroad crossings and often by long delays for automotive traffic, as were many other streets in Columbus—a tribute of sorts to the city's importance as a rail center. But it was a major route eastward from the campus area, and it led to the airport, Port Columbus, and to the big wartime plant of the Curtiss-Wright Corporation, our destination. Here Professor Wright explained the importance of the corporation to Columbus since it had arrived in 1941, although he had to admit that it wasn't producing anything at the moment.

But space in the huge plant had been made available for an upstart post–World War II new business—the Lustron Corporation. What an idea! Mass-produced, prefabricated, porcelain-clad steel homes for the booming postwar housing market. Porcelain-clad steel walls had been used in Standard Oil service stations before World War II and in the White Castle

System here in Columbus. The postwar innovation of using this proven product as the basis for housing construction was a significant technological development. I recall walking through the almost empty Curtiss-Wright plant to get to the area where pieces for the houses were being built. The idea was to make and assemble the necessary components for the houses, including plumbing and electrical supplies, and then to load them onto large flatbed trailers—pale blue, if my memory of them is correct—to be sent off to home sites around the country for erection. It was a great idea whose time had come, or so it seemed to me then. Unfortunately, alleged mismanagement and financial problems related to funding provided by the federally sponsored Reconstruction Finance Corporation to subsidize part of the costs led to the demise of Lustron in 1950, as did the fact that building and zoning codes in many cities did not permit construction of the homes. Before this ultimate event Lustron homes had been erected in a number of cities and on sites in the Columbus area. We visited a home site on the east side, were made welcome by the home owner, and looked around in awe at this innovation.

I didn't give Columbus much more thought until I was accepted for graduate work at OSU. It was my contact with Professor Wright and his enthusiasm for aspects of the city's development that influenced my decision to accept an assistantship, despite any reservations. By September 1949, my wife and I found ourselves searching for rooms or an apartment or any kind of housing unit in the city in competition with the thousands of veterans then attending the university. And that is another story.

Desperation drove us to search the papers thoroughly for housing. More than one prospect took us to dirty and infested rooms in overcrowded rental properties in the university neighborhood. Finally, we ended up in a garage in the middle of a large vacant field somewhere east of the railroad tracks and north off 17th Avenue on what was then Duxberry Avenue. Most of the site is occupied by the Ohio Historical Society and, now, the new soccer stadium. In the fall of 1949 it was sparsely settled, with dogs and chickens rampant. We had a one-room space with a stove and refrigerator, and an attached toilet. We heated water on the stove and bathed in a tub that hung on the rear of the house. We also discovered, as autumn weather set in, that the building was in a slight depression—depression enough to capture the early morning fog, so that we awakened in our one room to what was at times easily a foot or two of fog covering the floor. Welcome to Columbus!

In due course, our housing improved, but we had no intention of staying here once I had earned my doctorate. My dissertation research in the early 1950s focused initially on the factors affecting the location of manufacturing industry in Columbus, and interviews with the CEOs of many of the firms were rewarding both for the information provided and for the contacts made with these business leaders.[3] The opportunity to continue this research at the university and to join the geography faculty served to keep us in Columbus.

It was about that time that the article "Columbus, Ohio" by George Sessions Perry appeared in the old *Saturday Evening Post* in its Cities of America series.[4] The byline read: "Broke and bewildered only a decade ago, Columbus today [1952] is a busy, comfortable, well-governed city. It's a bad town for a football coach, but a good place for a politician." Reviewing this article almost 48 years later, one wonders how much has changed.

Perry knew that Columbus was Ohio's capital city and the "home of the state university," and, not surprisingly, he knew of James Thurber, but he seemed to be more obsessed with "the unreasonable demand of town and alumni" on football and football coaches. So some things don't change too much.

His observations occurred at a time when the city was becoming more industrialized, as my own research revealed, but he recognized that Columbus was no "small Detroit or Pittsburgh." It was also a time when Columbus was widely considered to be an excellent "test city" for new products, and from that he judged that the city was fairly representative of many U.S. cities of the time. And it was a time when Columbus functioned as "one of the nation's most popular convention cities . . . [with] its downtown hotels, such as the Deshler-Wallick and the Neil House . . . usually crammed with people." Some things do change!

Perry bemoaned the commercialization of Broad Street—*the* residential street in the city—but asserted that "the town has blossomed forth in beautiful suburbs such as Bexley and Upper Arlington." He noted as well that "the latest trend in residential architecture" was taking place here, as ranch-style homes displaced the traditional "Middle Western vanilla type" so common in the past. And he noted that despite the Maramor and Marzetti restaurants, "Columbus usually eats at home." What would he say if he could see us now?

The article reviewed the city's political role in the nation and state, especially that Ohio had helped prepare seven of the nation's presidents for office. And Perry was rather impressed that our "commercial metabolism at the moment . . . [was] more or less precisely what the doctor ordered," with a widely diversified industrial base and a role as a major wholesale and retail

The Columbus skyline was dominated by the Lincoln-LeVeque Tower into the 1960s. The art deco State Office Building and adjacent parks, and several buildings of the F. & R. Lazarus department store, are prominent features above the Scioto River floodplain.

center. Recognized with enthusiasm were the city's universities and cultural institutions, modest though the latter were, as key to the city's function as a cultural center.

Perry went on to review the city's historical development. His early reference to the city being "broke and bewildered only a decade ago" was explained in his discussion of problems associated with the management of the city and region through the pre–World War II depression years. He then focused on the revival of the city under the leadership of then Mayor James Rhodes and the work of the Metropolitan Committee in successfully addressing an array of civic problems that the city faced. In a concluding paragraph, Perry suggested that Columbus, Ohio, was "almost as nearly as any in the land, the common-sense ideal of a fruitful, decent, comfortable, enlightened and well-governed city." This was praise indeed.

In retrospect, then, this is the city we had come to and in which we would spend our lives. We have been in Columbus ever since, in a town that has become a city and at a university that has become a major research

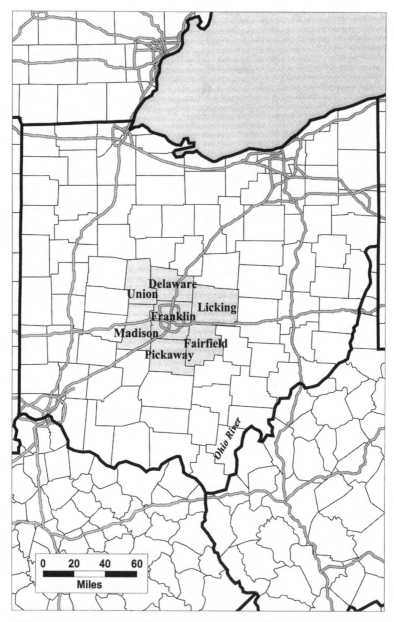

Columbus and the surrounding counties are centrally located in Ohio. The city's geographic accessibility, now enhanced by the Interstate Highway System, has been a major resource since the selection of the site to be Ohio's capital.

and teaching institution. It has proven to be a good place to live and to raise a family, although it may still not be a great place to visit. But we're working on it.

Certainly, perceptions of Columbus in this last decade of the twentieth century are anything but bleak and cold. The city is finally recognized as a free-standing entity—Columbus, without the once necessary appendage, Ohio. Even better, we know, and so do those whose business it is to study cities, not only that the image is good but that the reality is as well.

For its size, Columbus has been the fastest growing city in the north-eastern quadrant of the nation and one of the fastest growing large cities anywhere in the nation. As other cities of the midwestern heartland experi-enced the loss of their industrial bases and an associated loss of population, Columbus was expanding into new arenas of economic development predi-cated upon its historic role as a primary service center and was attracting new residents from within the region and beyond. The location of key headquarter facilities of major national firms brought not only an expanded demand for workers but new management teams and their families from outside the area. What they found here, often after initial misgivings about their moves, was a city that not only met their needs and most demanding expectations but exceeded them. They, in turn, brought a challenge to the status quo in leadership, in shopping, in real estate, and, surely, in culture, and in so doing they helped to stimulate a positive change in the commu-nity. We have benefited from it ever since.

Thus, Columbus has the look and feel of a young city as it anticipates the twenty-first century. There is a vibrancy that reflects a new focus in the economy, that responds to an aggressive demand for a more inspiring cul-ture, and that, significantly, responds to new leadership and new confidence at work, building on the foundation established by previous generations.

So this is a geographer's tale. We came here because of a geographers' meeting, and geography has kept us here for fifty years. While here, I have shared this geography of Columbus with thousands of university students, city leaders and government officials, and scores of other interested persons and groups through lectures, written commentary, and field trips. Here it is, then: *Columbus, Ohio: A Personal Geography.*

I have used the expression *personal geography* to clarify the fact that this is one man's view of the city and his experiences over fifty years. It is not a traditional geography in any sense of the term; it does reflect how I came to know and understand Columbus during these years, and this, in turn, is what I have sought to express in this work.

2

Columbus: The Physical Setting

THERE'S AN OLD SAYING THAT TELLS A LOT about a city's prominence: "It's not the site, it's the situation." In other words, the success of a community or region is driven by its relative situation, or geographic location, with respect to other cities and regions, to the state, or to the national and international arenas. On the other hand, site is also an important phenomenon worth considering because it tells us a lot about the physical qualities of our own community. If *situation* is a relative concept—that is, a relationship between places—*site* is an absolute concept, highly specific and unique in that it deals with the physical characteristics of a single place.

Both site and situation play a role in the establishment of a community and in its eventual development. Historically, site may well have been the key factor shaping the decision to encamp or settle at a specific place. In some instances—a superior harbor, the presence of a mineral resource, strategic heights that afforded protection—the physical site could be extremely important to the establishment and well-being of a settlement and, in some cases, may remain so today. In many other instances, and especially those in which the initial advantages of the site have been minimized by time and change, the situation or geographic location of the site has emerged as the force dictating its successful development.

Not surprisingly, site and situation both had quite a bit to do with the original settlement of central Ohio and of Columbus. The region west of the Scioto River was one of the first parts of the Northwest Territory opened to settlement following the Revolutionary War and the establishment of the Territory and the enactment of the ordinances associated with it. By 1784, a tract of 4.5 million acres of land lying between the Scioto River on the east and the Little Miami River on the west was granted to Virginia by the newly formed federal government in return for Virginia's agreement to drop all further claims to lands north of the Ohio River and east of the Mississippi. This tract—the Virginia Military District, or VMD—was reserved by Virginia as bounty lands to be used to reward veterans of the Revolutionary War who had fought under Virginian command. First entries for land in the District were made in 1787 by Nathaniel Massie near Manchester in Adams County, adjacent to the Ohio River.[1]

It was no accident, then, that the first land claims in the central Ohio area would be made by Virginians, nor that these lands would be situated west of the Scioto River. The survey of lands by Lucas Sullivant in the region led to the siting of a settlement in 1797 on the low west bank of the Scioto near its junction with the Olentangy River. But owing to the low-lying nature of the site and to related problems of flooding and fever (ague) linked to it, a move was made to a new site a few hundred yards further inland, which became the village of Franklinton.

Why, indeed, had these early surveyors not located their new village on the more desirable higher grounds or site on the eastern bank of the river? Osman Hooper, a local historian writing in the 1920s, answered by noting that Sullivant, a Virginian, "had nothing to do with the latter lands [eastern bank]. The limit of the tract he was surveying was the river."[2]

To the east of the Scioto, several different areas were later opened to settlement, parts of which are included in the area that makes up the Columbus region as we know it today. These are the U.S. Military District (1796), to the north of Fifth Avenue, which provided grants of land to men who had served in the military during the Revolution; the Congress Lands (1790), to the south of Refugee Road, opened for sale to pioneer settlers; and the Refugee Tract (1798), land provided by the government for Nova Scotian sympathizers to the Revolutionary cause, situated between Refugee Road on the south and Fifth Avenue on the north. As these additional lands were opened to settlement, Virginians laid claim to lands east of the river as well. When the Ohio General Assembly began to seek a new site for the state capital close to the geographic center of the state, 1,200 acres of land and other inducements on the east bank of the Scioto were offered by the Virginians and accepted by the legislature in 1812. The site was platted

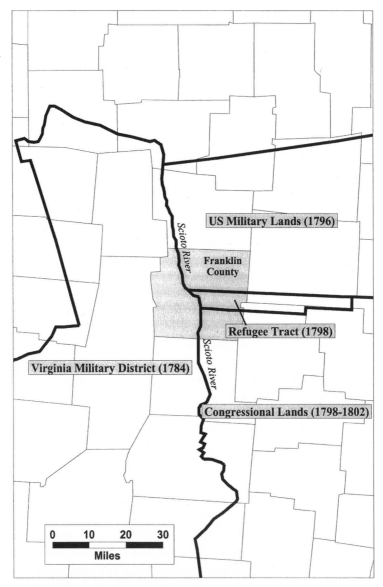

US Military Lands (1796)

Scioto River

Franklin County

Refugee Tract (1798)

Virginia Military District (1784)

Scioto River

Congressional Lands (1798-1802)

0   10   20   30
Miles

Early settlement of the Central Ohio Region was influenced by the young nation's disposition of land in the Northwest Territory. Virginia claimed and retained land in the area west of the Scioto River and east of the Little Miami River in order to provide military grants for land to its veterans of the Revolutionary War. Other grants, such as those made in the U.S. Military Lands, the Congress Lands, and to Nova Scotians in the Refugee Tract, brought settlers to Central Ohio from the eastern states.

by Joel Wright, and Columbus evolved as a planned state capital, with the first sale of lots in 1812.

In just such a way, situation and site were forces to be reckoned with in the initial settlement of the city, and speculation in land as a way of life and as a means of accumulating wealth was already established. That Columbus grew and prospered initially is testimony to the importance of each factor in supporting the successful emergence of Ohio's new capital city. We will consider both of these factors further and their impact on the growth and development of Columbus—how they helped to shape the future of the city and the central Ohio region. Attention will be directed first to the qualities of the physical *site* that have helped to shape or fashion development within the city and region. We will then, in chapter 3, examine the *situation* or geographic location of Columbus and the region as a force affecting its relationships with other cities and regions.

SITE AS A FACTOR

It's been said that "when you buy land, you buy a climate." This may be true enough: weather and climate are integral features of site. But it should be obvious that you buy much more than climate; you buy the totality of the land's many unique physical qualities that may affect the development of the city and region—or your own plot of land, for that matter.

What are these qualities? Well, they may be many and varied, but they are all features of the physical space of the city—the space that it occupies. The relative importance of that space is, as already suggested, a situational or locational factor.

The basic features of site—for Columbus in 1812 and for Columbus in the year 2000—include, in addition to its weather and climate, the specific and unique characteristics of its land surface and topography, its underlying geologic structure, the varied rocks and minerals of which it is composed, its surface and subsurface waters, and the flora and fauna. Singly or in combination, these features of site may play a significant role in the community's development because their presence or absence, and their relative usefulness, can help to shape how the society may develop them and, in so doing, assist in the development of the community. To understand the role that they play, let's consider some specific site characteristics of the Columbus region.

Geology and Topography

The observation has often been made by those who have studied Columbus's site that the city has evolved on the central Ohio till plain. This is a reference to the impact of glacial history upon the region. The relatively flat glacial till plain, cut by the several parallel north-to-south-flowing streams—from Blacklick Creek on the east to Big Walnut Creek, Alum Creek, the Olentangy River, the Scioto River, and the Big Darby Creek on the west—is a key factor in "allowing" the emergence of the low-density city that Columbus has become, with relatively easy access historically in every direction to and from the Downtown.

Till, or glacial drift, is unstratified depositional materials made up of clay, sand, pebbles, and boulders left by the glacier as it "retreated" or melted away. Glacial action in the region had the effect of smoothing the hills and filling in the valleys in the preglacial terrain, a landscape that was probably much like that found today in the southeastern Ohio unglaciated Appalachian Plateau. The till, in turn, has provided the basis for the later development of area soils.

It is necessary, of course, for engineers to know something about the subsurface geologic structure, if for no other reason than to have some measure of the stability of the bedrock and its depth. Major skyscrapers, in particular, need stability and solid footing. The 555-foot-high Lincoln-LeVeque Tower, for example, rests on bedrock some 110 feet below the surface, and bedrock is present throughout the urban core at varying depths from 100 to 200 feet beneath the surface.

The central Ohio area is also underlain by sedimentary rocks of the Devonian period, a time when much of Ohio was covered by a vast inland sea. The sediment that formed at that time gave rise to the limestone and shale beds that extend throughout the Scioto Valley north to Lake Erie. The older Columbus limestone outcrops in the western part of the valley. This is a relatively pure limestone, rich in fossil-bearing materials. Over four hundred different species of fossils have been found, although good fossil remains are harder to find today. The beds, tilting to the east, are relatively even and about a hundred feet thick.

The Delaware limestone overlays these beds throughout the Scioto Valley. This is a thin-bedded limestone averaging about thirty-five feet in thickness and lacking the rich fossiliferous materials of the older Columbus limestones. Exposures of the Columbus limestone outcrops and of some Delaware outcrops as well are visible in the quarries along the west side of

The important role of mineral resources in the Columbus economy is reflected by the numerous limestone quarries present in the Scioto Valley. In recent years, abandoned quarries have served as sites for both residential and commercial development.

the Scioto Valley, where they once formed the basis for an important mineral industry. Following extensive quarrying of these beds in the past, some of the quarry sites have been developed as residential and commercial building sites in recent years. They afford a sometimes picturesque setting, often complete with access to the quarry lakes for recreation.

East of the Scioto River, the Olentangy shale, a fairly thin bed, and the Ohio shales are the principal materials. The Olentangy shales are about thirty feet thick, contain few fossils, and are not particularly resistant to erosion. The Ohio shales are quite extensive to the east and are up to seven hundred feet thick. Outcrops of the Ohio shales may be observed in the streams that cut down into the Olentangy Valley. A characteristic feature of the Ohio shales are ferruginous (iron) concretions, spherical in shape and ranging in size from a few inches up to six or more feet in diameter. The Ohio shales are an oil shale containing, in places, pockets of natural gas.

In general, the limestone materials of the western half of the valley have provided a basis for the development of reasonably rich agricultural soils.

The shales of the eastern area provide a less satisfactory soil base and, consequently, a less productive agriculture. Certainly, the central Ohio gardener has had to deal with these variables in creating the attractive garden settings that characterize the region.

The nature of both the subsurface sedimentary rock layers and the overriding glacial deposits has provided the basis for a variety of economic activities. Central Ohio has long been important for its production of limestone, sand and gravel, and shale. Glacial deposition of the sands and gravel, combined with the underlying limestone throughout the Scioto Valley especially, is the reason for a still active quarrying industry. The communities of Marble Cliff and San Margherita have historic ties to the industry, as did the once well-known Hartman Farms south on Route 23. The farms were developed on the hills produced by an esker, the sand and gravel remains of a glacial stream. Today, the productive farm is gone, but the esker is being quarried for its sand and gravel.

In 1998, Franklin County continued to rank among the major producers in Ohio in the quarrying of limestone and sand and gravel. It ranked fifth in the production of limestone, with 5.0 million tons, whose principal use is currently in construction, particularly in road building and commercial construction. The widespread use of limestone in local homes, garden walls, and buildings is clear evidence of the utility and beauty of this resource in the Columbus region.

Franklin County and the region rank high in the production of sand and gravel as well. The county ranks second in production in Ohio, with over 5.9 million tons produced, primarily for use in construction and related industries. Some of the region's sand deposits were important historically to the establishment of a glass industry in the region. These sands and natural gas from the gas fields of east-central Ohio were the raw materials that supported a prosperous glass industry in the region beginning about a century ago.[3]

Water Resources

Glacial action also shaped the course of our surface streams and provided the fill in the preglacial stream valleys, which serve today as reservoirs of groundwater. The central Ohio region is a well-watered site, thanks to its annual precipitation and the availability of both surface and subsurface waters. The groundwater, for example, is not only a source of water for residential and industrial wells but a potential source of water for expanded development in the region. Historically, water was taken from the surface streams or from underground wells. The principal source of water was and is the Scioto River watershed. The first waterworks was established in 1871 at the junction of the Scioto and Olentangy Rivers, producing 550,000 gallons per day from a well in the gravel beds. But as population grew, the demand for water increased. By 1905, Griggs Dam was constructed on the Scioto River, and in 1925 the O'Shaughnessy Dam was built upstream in southern Delaware County. These, and minor sources from the Big Walnut and Darby Creeks, served the area well until the 1940 war years, when increased population and industrial development created expanded demand for water.

The response was the construction of Hoover Dam in 1954 on Big Walnut Creek; it has become the city's largest source of water, accounting for about 60 percent of the total. Even so, there is ongoing concern about future water supply. The city's *Water Beyond 2000* study anticipated a 45 percent increase in water demand by 2020, for example. Columbus has acquired approximately two thousand acres of land in northwestern Delaware County, on which three upground reservoirs are to be built in anticipation of future needs, and it has tapped the glacial waters in the preglacial valley of the South well field in northern Pickaway County. Other water sources may offer alternatives in the future, but undoubtedly at greater cost to society.[4]

Weather and Climate

It's a truism that "everyone talks about the weather, but no one does anything about it." True enough, for we seem to be at the mercy of those forces that shape the weather and climate of our region, and there isn't much that we—ordinary citizens and meteorologists alike—can do about it except try to understand the underlying forces a bit better and learn how to adjust to the vagaries of the weather that we experience.

What we want to know about, usually, has something to do with the four key elements of weather—temperature, moisture, air pressure, and wind. Often, we want to know what the weather will be like today or tomorrow so that we can "adjust" to it in some fashion—know what clothing to wear, for example. Our slavish following of the TV weather reports is evidence of this keen, if routine, interest. We may also want to know something about how the weather and climate may affect our long-term plans for an event such as a picnic, sports event, or wedding. More seriously, we may want to consider how weather and climate may affect our choice of where and how we want to live.

Can we capture, then, the essence of our central Ohio climate in a few sentences? Regional climatologists identify the area as having a climate described as humid microthermal or continental with long summers. That is, our weather and climate are primarily influenced by continental or land-based forces, which produce greater extremes of weather, typically, than the more moderating marine or marine-based forces affecting coastal areas. We know of the interplay of high- and low-pressure systems in the Ohio Valley, and of the related influence of polar air masses (and so-called Alberta Clippers) and tropical air masses upon the region. We've learned to live with cold and warm fronts and the associated temperature and moisture conditions that accompany them.

We know, because we may have experienced them, that we have cold winters, with the average temperature of our coldest month, January, at 26.5 degrees Fahrenheit; but there is also the potential for fairly low minimum temperatures, with the absolute minimum for Columbus set on January 19, 1994, at −22 degrees. With the continental climate, we also have fairly long and hot summers, with a July average of 73.2 degrees. July 1999 was the hottest July on record. The result is a relatively long growing or frost-free season of over 190 days in 1998, important to our farm population but appreciated as well by urban dwellers. Summer extremes are above 90 degrees and may soar to over 100 degrees, with an extreme maximum of 106 degrees. Along with these wide annual ranges in temperature, we have rapidly changing daily temperatures (the diurnal range) that reflect the continental influences.

Central Ohio is a well-watered region, with annual average precipitation of 38.09 inches, or over 3 inches per month. Typically, there is a maximum rainfall in the summer, with a July average of 4.31 inches. The summer maximum is fortunate because of the high rates of evaporation during this period. The lowest monthly average is in October, with 2.15 inches.

Of course, we can expect snow, ice, and sleet along with rain during the winter months, but the amounts vary from year to year. The average yearly snowfall amounts to 27.5 inches, with a January average of over 8 inches. But the maximum snowfall in January has exceeded 20 inches several times, the latest being in 1999, when 20.6 inches fell in the first two weeks of the month. With persistent low temperatures and cloudy skies, snow cover may remain on the ground throughout much of the winter season, but this is not the expected condition.

Much of the precipitation is frontal in origin—that is, it is tied to the interplay of warm and cold fronts passing through the central Ohio region. Precipitation associated with warm fronts tends to be lighter in quantity but may last for several days; cold front precipitation may take the form of short, heavy storms that pass through the region more quickly.

During the summer months especially, thunderstorms may be quite common and, if accompanied by high winds, may do considerable damage. The Columbus region experiences an average of forty-two thunderstorms each year. Much more violent are tornados (Ohio has an average of fifteen per year), which are an occasional threat to the region during the spring and early summer months.

With the usual abundant moisture in the summer along with summer temperatures, Columbus is well known for the high relative humidity it experiences. Clearly, there is justification for the saying "It's not the heat, it's the humidity" that we hear when locals gripe about summertime unpleasantness. The situation is made more burdensome, perhaps, by the fact that we have a fairly high percentage of cloudy days, receiving only about 60 percent of expected sunshine in our summer months and less during the remainder of the year. The days with clear, blue skies are to be appreciated.

One of the positive features of the weather is, of course, the distinctive four seasons that are so much a part of the local weather scene. Seasonal changes may on occasion be frustrating, but they are also dynamic forces affecting our daily lives and activities. To many residents, the decisive question is whether spring, with its renewal in the blossoming of flowers and the variety of budding deciduous trees, or autumn, with its magnificent range of colors, is their favorite season.

We may not have lake breezes or mountain elevations and spectacular views in central Ohio, but then again, we do not live in a desert climate where we would be fretting about air conditioning with temperatures over 100 degrees for days on end and facing water shortages, nor are we subject to the bitter cold and long-lasting snow cover that more northerly cities face.

Despite the generalizations that we have just made regarding its climate, we should recognize that within our region climatic conditions often vary from one part of the city or region to another. For example, the differences between suburban areas and the core of the city are obvious. The core is essentially an urban heat island where open space, tall buildings, downdrafts, wind corridors, sunlight and diffusion, excessive asphalt surfaces, autos and buses, and the heat generated by people, buildings, and

various systems all contribute to a buildup of heat. The suburban neighborhoods, with a lower density of housing and lots of trees and vegetation, are
usually much cooler.

Similarly, we may make residential location decisions that involve consideration of views or vistas, elevational differences, the presence or absence
of surface water (e.g., streams, pools, lakes), or other specific features of site.
Even within a specific site—a residential lot, for example—climates may
vary from place to place. These climatic differences within a limited setting
reflect existing "microclimates" or facets of them.[5] One consequence is that
the homeowner may control or respond to certain aspects of the climate by
making informed decisions with respect to individual sites. The critical
point, of course, is the selection of an initial site with respect to certain
desired characteristics. For example, on what side of a street should a house
be built, given traditional constraints and design, to maximize solar radiation? How can the house be placed on a lot to maximize southern exposure
where wanted or to gain exposure to summer breezes? What role should
elevation and terrain, the presence of trees, the presence or absence of surface water, and so on play in developing both a lot and a house—in other
words, what is the role of *site*? Here microclimates may come into play in
that buildings and walls may shade part of a site or protect it from strong
winds. Slight elevational differences may allow us to plant quite different
species of plants and increase variety within our gardens given the impact
of sun or shade upon garden plots. Even a simple move from one side of
the street to the other might require adjustments to different site characteristics that could affect decisions regarding the use of the site and construction of a home. The point is that microclimates are present and need to be
adapted to wisely.

In other words, the *site* of our city, or of our own piece of it, is the
collective set of physical resources present. The qualities of these resources
affect how they are used, but how they are used is also a product of our
needs and wants, our knowledge and technology, and how we value the site
both now and for the future.

TWO CASE STUDIES

Two examples—case studies in a way—of the effects of aspects of
weather and climate upon the city follow. The first reviews a now historic
study of climate controls in Columbus; the second considers the impact of
one climatic element—wind and wind direction—upon a specific section
of the city, South Columbus.

Case Study #1: The Climate Control Project

Columbus and central Ohio was the focus of a series of articles published in 1949 in *House Beautiful* magazine as the "Climate Control Project" and produced in conjunction with the American Institute of Architects.[6] This project still has meaning today. The purpose was to study climate and climatic control for various regions of the United States in order "to better your living." The project operated on the premise that "there must be some relation between man's having an environment he can really control and his ability to make progress—personal and social progress." This sweeping generalization—often debated in geographic literature—was based on the observation that the areas in the United States with "the most *easily controlled* climates" (italics in original) had "the highest income per capita, the best health, and the best intelligence and culture records" (p. 131), whatever these may be. From *House Beautiful*'s point of view, one's house was the best place to exercise control, not surprisingly. Thus, the question: How to produce a perfect house designed for a specific climate?

As luck would have it, the city and region that seemed to meet these qualifications was Columbus and central Ohio. The climatic data for our city and region were examined in detail, and after careful analysis and review, an "ideal" house for the region was proposed—a house that would in its exterior and interior design respond most advantageously to the climatic opportunities and constraints posed here.

The general observation was that central Ohio's climate "comes pretty close to being 'typically American'" (p. 163). Even so, five "dilemmas" were identified in the climate that the "ideal" house would attempt to respond to:

1. High heat and humidity in summer
2. Considerable sunny, windy weather in spring and fall
3. Much wintertime cloudiness
4. Little snow, but rain all year
5. Temperatures that are seldom extremely cold but that remain cold for a long season (about 40 percent of the year)

Sound familiar? Well, having identified these problems, the researchers qualified them with the observation that "despite these flaws, there's a lot of pleasant weather!"[7]

Given these conditions, *House Beautiful* called upon architects and landscape architects to propose housing that could be built or adapted to minimize the problems noted. Using detailed statistical analysis of the region's climatic characteristics in conjunction with related exterior and interior design data, an attempt was made to determine how adaptation could be achieved in the "real world." To that end, a house and its site were designed to use the controls and design adjustments that research indicated would serve Columbus, Ohio. The house was designed by the well-known Columbus architectural firm of Brooks and Coddington, which would also design St. Stephen's Episcopal Church, one of the first modern church structures in the nation. The landscape architect was Marion V. Packard.[8]

Considered in the design of this home for central Ohio were measures related to solar radiation and exposure, to protect the home from them in the summer and to maximize them in the winter. For a traditionally designed home in Columbus, the siting of a house on the north side of an east-west street—a south-facing house, in other words—is usually the best solution.

The architects felt that the design of the house should utilize the out-of-doors more extensively in the spring and fall, protecting the house from the wind, yet capturing the warmth of the sun. Solar windows were one way to overcome the high percentage of cloudy days, especially in the winter months.

Certainly, the article intended to inform the homeowner about how weather and climate would affect a home site. Two sections of the article addressed the homeowner: one, "How to *Pick* Your Private Climate," addressed the features of weather and climate that should be considered; a second suggested "How to *Fix* Your Private Climate" as the site was developed and a home constructed.

For example, the quality of building materials and how they are used could address issues related to extremes of temperature and moisture. Columbus's year-round precipitation creates problems that may be anticipated and adjusted to, for example, by providing such features as wide eaves, ample gutters, and good drainage. Temperature extremes and considerable freezing and thawing also have to be anticipated and dealt with. Obviously, house design and the quality of construction materials are factors that should be considered anywhere. This study provided Columbus and central Ohio with a scientific attempt to achieve effective "climate control."

Nearly fifty years have passed since this informative publication, but the search for the "ideal" home relative to weather and climatic forces continues, especially as environmental issues present new challenges to the architect and designer as well as to the homeowner. At the same time, new technologies and changing materials and techniques afford the opportunity for innovative response to the problems and the pleasures presented to us by the physical environment.

Case Study #2: The South Columbus Experience

Ordinarily, most of us don't give much thought to the wind or to wind direction unless a storm or, more fearsome, a tornado is reported to be approaching the area. The effects of high winds in a storm or tornado may be disastrous, of course, and central Ohio does experience them.

On the other hand, the more ordinary characteristics of wind and wind direction may have a pronounced, if not disastrous, impact upon our community, and the impact may last for decades. A clear case in point, and one with a long history, has been the role of the prevailing westerly and southwesterly winds upon the city, particularly upon South Columbus. Through "accidents of history" and bad planning, the South Columbus community has had a succession of unfortunate atmospheric-related experiences that are tied directly to the west-to-east movement of the air masses passing through the region. Today it suffers from environmental problems resulting from atmospheric pollution generated by a number of industries over time and, most recently, by the trash-burning power plant.

In fact, it could be argued that this specific aspect of our weather and climate—wind direction—may have served to shape how the South Columbus neighborhood developed. Through the years, it experienced pollution produced by railroads, industry, sewage treatment facilities, the trash-burning power plant, and a variety of other activities. The basic problem? Many of these operations have been located on the southwest edge of the city, some adjacent to the Scioto River, precisely in the path of the southwesterly winds that are the major movements of air affecting Columbus. The result? A neighborhood that has in some ways lagged behind the development of other parts of the city.

The early culprits were the railroads. With their romantic but steam-belching engines and with a web of rail nets strung throughout the city, much of Columbus was exposed to the soot and dirt and noise of the railroads. Parts of the city were adjacent to major railroad yards and to the shops necessary to the maintenance of the rolling stock. The South Columbus experience wasn't unique; several communities bore the brunt of the soot and smoke. Such conditions were accepted because there were jobs to be had in this industry (ten thousand jobs as late as the 1940s) and because society relied on rail traffic and was not yet prepared to address the problem.

South Columbus was also the early site of so-called heavy industries, particularly iron and steel, that developed in the last quarter of the nineteenth century, linked to the raw material resources of southeastern Ohio. A strong tie existed between raw materials, industry, railroads, and the resident population of manufacturing workers who lived in the area.

Problems associated with the railroads and manufacturing industries were compounded by the siting of sewage treatment facilities, a rendering plant, major waste disposal sites, and the city's trash-burning power plant on lands just west of the Scioto River and adjacent to the southwest side of the city. With statistical proof of the prevailing nature of the westerly and southwesterly winds, it is unfortunate that a private rendering plant should have been located there, and, even more inexplicable, that public facilities should have been situated with so little care given to the impact of smoke and odors from these facilities upon the residents of the larger community.[9]

These examples are intended to illustrate how one climatic element can play a role in how a community may develop and how physical forces of the environment can influence community well-being over time. But South Columbus is not the only part of the region to experience the strong effects that winds and wind direction may have upon a community. In the far north of the city, downwind from the Anheuser-Busch brewery there has been the sweet-sour smell associated with the brewing of beer. More distant and less frequent are the wind-carried odors produced by the large Mead Paper plant in Chillicothe, which, when atmospheric conditions are just right, may still find their way up the Scioto Valley.

FINAL COMMENT

We have recognized here that aspects of our physical environment—the unique physical characteristics of our region—are factors that not only affect how we perceive and enjoy our community but also help to shape the perceptions that others have of Columbus and the central Ohio region as an attractive, perhaps even exciting, place to live in and visit.

3

Columbus: Situational Considerations

WHEREAS SITE IS AN ABSOLUTE CONCEPT related to the physical characteristics of a specific place, the *situation* or *location* of that place is a relative term in that it deals with the relationships between places. Clearly, the success of a community or region, or the success of a company's location decision, is driven in large measure by its situation or geographic location with respect to the relationships it has with other places both in its own region and state and, increasingly, in the national and international arenas. If you ask a professional developer or realtor to name the three most important factors affecting the decision to establish a business in a community or region, chances are good that he or she will tell you, "Location, location, location!" And within the local community, situation may be the key factor that helps to influence the householder's decision about where to live as the realtor chants the same familiar phrase, "Location, location, location."

In this chapter, we will consider first how Columbus and the central Ohio region function and interact with places beyond the local environment: that is, the *interregional* factors that need to be reviewed as we consider our region's relationships with the rest of the world. Second, we will look at the situational relationships that develop within the context of our central Ohio region: that is, the *intraregional* interactions that are at the core of the local region's vitality.

THE CITY AND THE REGION:
INTERREGIONAL CONSIDERATIONS

The typical business firm seeks to find a generally attractive location that will help to minimize its costs of operation. Traditionally, this locational choice, especially for a manufacturing firm, responded to some quality of market location or to the firm's accessibility to its raw materials and suppliers. The Columbus Chamber of Commerce, as well as scores of professional developers, may use an old gimmick of informing us that Columbus is within "X" number of miles of some percentage of the U.S. population or of some critical subset of it, and then showing us a map with Columbus at the center of a set of concentric circles representing set distances from the city, with evidence of the population or market present within each concentric zone.

There's nothing wrong with this, especially when the city in question commands trade with as high a percentage of the U.S. population within a 500-mile market territory as Columbus does. After all, when you sense that your city has some unique quality of location, it's a natural tendency to want to broadcast that fact and so promote the city. The Cleveland Electric Illuminating Company used to claim that its market area was "the best location in the nation," and perhaps it was. But they don't say that anymore. Things have changed.

The fact is that although geographic location or situation is a natural phenomenon, it is enhanced by timing and economic circumstance—either you have "it" or you don't at a given time. At one time, for example, Ohio's location—its geographic accessibility—was called an "inexhaustible resource," and so it seemed to be. But even God-given geographic location may be changed by circumstance. It can be enhanced by good timing or diminished by changing economic conditions; by resource depletion or change; by fluctuations in market forces, ranging from a shift from local to regional to international competition, to costs associated with raw materials, energy, labor, or even environmental regulations; and, increasingly, by technology.

Thus, location is a physical factor, as when we define where a site is with respect to other sites or to markets, but it quickly becomes an economic phenomenon when we attach value to it, as implied by the degree of accessibility that our site has with respect to others. How accessible we are reflects not only the ease or difficulty in accessing the site but also the means by which it is done and the cost. Traditional location theory, whether used by the geographer, economist, or development specialist, seeks to rationalize business location decisions in terms of overcoming the distance costs associated with access to markets or material supplies and to the transportation systems between competing places.

At its simplest, improved transportation permits us to overcome the costs of space: it allows us to overcome what is sometimes called "the friction of distance." That's important, whether we are discussing shipping a product to New York or are considering the journey to work and back home again for the average commuter. The issue is whether we have the proper transportation facilities to reduce the total set of costs involved in overcoming distance. Historically, a succession of inventions and innovations in transportation served to reduce these costs and so enhanced the competitive value of Columbus's location. The progression in central Ohio from overland trails through the wilderness to canals and the National Road to the coming of the railroads to modern highways and, finally, to the vast Interstate Highway System and modern air transport attests to this. Each improvement had the effect of changing the relative value of Columbus and its location as it altered or improved the city's accessibility.

Columbus remains, today, a remarkably well-located city with excellent access to the major markets of the nation. It is readily accessible—there are really no significant physical obstacles other than distance that restrict contact—and the presence of major east-west and north-south interstate routes and the I-270 Outerbelt has encouraged the development of an expanding warehouse and distribution industry.

The relative location of a city and region may change not only with technological changes in transportation but through technological change in *communications* as well. In the last several decades, there has been a technological and accompanying social revolution of sorts that has increased the use of and reliance on communication systems based, fundamentally, on enhanced computer-generated systems. Columbus is, in a sense, a prototype community in this regard. The *Economist* has discussed the impact of the so-called communication revolution as leading to "the death of distance" and, consequently, as a factor that will influence development throughout the world.[1] Certainly, society's need to increase geographic accessibility and overcome distance led to the "transportation revolutions" that shaped the nineteenth and twentieth centuries. The "communication revolution" promises to be the force that will shape our futures in the twenty-first century, and it helps to explain the changing geography of Columbus today.

The traditional goods-producing economy in which Columbus and the nation grew and matured is no longer predominant. Goods production relies on great transportation systems to move the necessary raw materials and semiprocessed goods from their sources to their manufacturing markets and, in turn, depends upon the system to transport finished products to consumers, wherever they might be. It is a system producing and shipping tangible goods or "things." Make no mistake about it, we're still highly dependent upon this system and the manufacturing industries linked to it, as our crowded highways attest, and we seek to enhance it. But the changes that have been accruing since the end of World War II, if not before, have forced us to recognize that an increasing share of the productive economy, of the labor force, and of the market is geared to the production and marketing of *services,* or intangible "nonthings." Many of these services— probably most of them—are not transported but literally communicated, and that is one thing the Internet is about at its simplest.

Hence, dependency has more or less shifted from transportation-based factors that shape decisions about location and productivity to factors that reflect the increasing reliance on and influence of communications. If, as some have suggested, the single most important "product" of the future is information—an intangible "nonthing"—then a sophisticated communications system must be in place to engage in the production, distribution, and consumption of that information. What does this mean to us here in the central Ohio region and to the society in general? It means that where and why one locates today may be determined much more by a host of new forces than by the traditional forces of geographic accessibility and the economic justification of it. In brief, our inherent geographic location has been altered by technological change—and probably for the better.

An example that reflects the variety of forces that may shape comparisons of situational qualities at the *interregional* level is the Sun Belt–Frost Belt controversy that began in the late 1970s. Initially, characteristics of weather and climate (features associated with *site*) at the local and regional levels had a lot to do with triggering comparisons between the two regions, although in the final analysis the economic and demographic overtones became more compelling. It wasn't particularly helpful that climatologists and the media were caught up with the notion that the exceptionally low temperatures and prolonged periods of heavy snows that we experienced in the late 1970s in Ohio and the Midwest were the forerunners of the cooling off of the planet and the possible resurgence of an "ice age" in our own backyard, complete with suggestions of glaciers at the doorstep.

That kind of publicity enhanced the image of the Sun Belt and served to point up less desirable features of weather and climate in the so-called Frost Belt states. When the Midwest's industrial machine began to falter in the face of foreign competition in the production of steel and other commodities, and the quality of its traditional regional resources began to decline, both business and workers began to relocate to the climatically more attractive Sun Belt states, which apparently had the potential of being economically more rewarding and stable as well. It is difficult, therefore, to assign a value to the role of weather and climate in shaping our perceptions of the Sun Belt, but out-migration from Ohio and the Midwest was a fact of the 1980s, and most of Ohio's industrial cities can attest to the loss of manufacturing operations and businesses, as well as human capital. For reasons that had little to do with our weather and climate, Columbus, almost alone of Ohio's cities, seems to have emerged relatively unscathed from the experience.

In fairness, it should be noted that the Sun Belt offered a collective set of *amenity* resources that addressed a different kind of lifestyle whose time had come. In part, these resources were captured in the phrase "sun, sand, surf syndrome"—a way of life that promised a total environment in which life could be pursued more gracefully and, perhaps, with more fun.

The image applied especially to Florida, the Gulf states, California, and the Southwest. These regions had the ability to attract business and industry in which communications systems were more important than or at least as important as the transport system in the rationale of business location decision making. In a way never possible in the past, the amenity resources of an area became the raison d'être for relocation.

In contrast, Columbus and central Ohio do not possess a basic set of amenity resources that stir the imagination or are perceived to be uniquely attractive. Neither our land and water resources nor our weather and climate provide the means whereby a set of summer or winter experiences can offer the basis for major growth or for the expansion of a tourist industry. And the traditionally strong resource base of the region that once supported an industrial economy has weakened and become more costly. Much of our success lies, then, in the expanding emergence of an enlightened service economy and a cultural resource base that establishes our region's raison d'être.

INTRAREGIONAL CONSIDERATIONS:
THE CITY GROWS UPSTREAM

A number of different forces play significant roles in defining how the local region has evolved and in explaining the current dynamic that helps to shape *intraregional* relationships. One of the two dominant factors affecting the Columbus region's growth and development is the principle of geography that affirms that "cities grow upstream." Whether it is universally true is hard to say, but certainly the concept applies to Columbus and the central Ohio region and its historical pattern of growth. The second has been the city's annexation policy. In a sense, the policy simply followed the geography of the region—and so did a lot of developers and realtors who accepted and profited by the principle as Columbus did indeed grow upstream.

One might ask, "Why does a city grow upstream?" Historically, it probably made more sense than it does today: one moved upstream from one's neighbors to tap the purer waters of the stream first and to avoid contamination by the wastes that might be dumped in the stream by an upstream neighbor. Over time, with increasing urbanization, there was need for some kind of regulation both to ensure access to pure water and to protect downstream neighbors from pollution. Today's water supply in central Ohio still comes largely from upstream, and simple geography explains the location of our sewage treatment facilities on the downstream side of the city and region. Obviously, both water and sewage flow downhill!

Given the propensity to grow upstream, it follows that growth in the suburban counties has not occurred equally in all directions or in population and economic matters (e.g., jobs, new business and industry, taxes). Much of what has taken place is linked strongly to the transportation system that evolved in the region in the post–World War II years.

It was not until 1963, for instance, that the Census Bureau, responding to a request by the Columbus Area Chamber of Commerce for a special review of the region's population given a decade of annexation, determined that the Columbus Metropolitan Statistical Area (MSA) should be enlarged from a one-county MSA (Franklin) to a three-county unit, with Columbus the "Central City" of the region. (A full discussion of the census classification of population follows in the next chapter.) The critical factor affecting the census decision was the movement of commuters and residents outward from the city to the north and to the south along Route 23. As the smaller cities of Delaware and Circleville attracted new industrial jobs, the movement increased. The Census Bureau, in its wisdom and using the various statistical measures it invokes, identified sufficient interaction between Columbus and the two counties, Delaware and Pickaway, to declare them part of the Columbus MSA.

With growth continuing, four additional counties were later brought into the Columbus MSA—Fairfield, Licking, Madison, and Union—as the interstate highways I-70, I-71, and I-270 provided increased access to the suburban counties and consequently increased commuting. This was important, of course, but the limited access policy of the interstate system then in practice restricted the potential impact.

Equally or more important to the entire region was the completion of the fifty-five-mile Interstate 270 Outerbelt around the perimeter of Columbus. William Habig of the Mid-Ohio Regional Planning Commission (MORPC) called the Outerbelt "a job base," and, in a sense, that is what it is. The Outerbelt has attracted scores of new businesses, especially in the warehousing and distribution industries, as well as new manufacturing plants and office complexes. And once a job base is in place, residential growth most surely follows. I-270 filled in some of the open space between the city and the adjacent counties, contributing further to Columbus's sprawl, especially to the north. Before anyone was aware of it, extended commuting was established, and the city side of the suburban counties experienced rapid residential expansion and the conversion of agricultural lands to suburban development. An unwelcome side effect has been traffic congestion associated with the expanded highway system. In effect, the *interstate* highway system, in Columbus and in other cities as well, has become an *intracity* transportation network. This, an unintended consequence of public policy, has tended to corrupt the original purpose of the interstate concept.

Quite clearly, then, growth has continued upstream. The southern portion of the Columbus MSA has grown much more slowly, and that portion of the I-270 Outerbelt has not captured new business opportunities or residential growth on a scale typical of other sections of the Outerbelt. In the mid-1990s, however, attention focused on another form of transportation as a generator of growth, the old Rickenbacker Air Base, now organized as the Rickenbacker Port Authority with its Air Industrial Park. This site may result in new annexations by the city of Columbus. Even if not, its development, with its air service and accessibility to the interstate system, is a major spur to expanding growth in the southeastern part of the MSA.

Of course, other forces led to the areal expansion of the city and region. What was happening here was happening in many other parts of the country

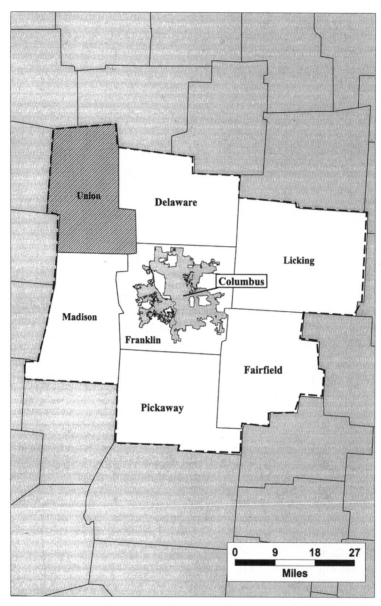

Columbus is the Central City for the Columbus Metropolitan Statistical Area (MSA). The MSA has grown from a single county in 1950, Franklin, to include by 1990 the six other counties shown on the map. Since then, the census has removed Union County from the Columbus MSA, although the Columbus Chamber of Commerce still includes it in its definition of "Greater Columbus."

as well. The location and relocation of manufacturing industry during and following World War II was, in many ways, the forerunner to the suburbanization of other activities. Following the war, residential construction and the movement of retailing from the downtown to suburban sites furthered the process. The older urban centers and their core areas (or "downtowns"), which historically were home to manufacturing activity and to the blue-collar workers who made up the labor force, had became overcrowded with people. Traffic was increasingly congested, space was limited and costly, and many manufacturing industries faced the aging and eventual obsolescence of their plants and plant sites.

Furthermore, both private sector initiatives and government policy, intentionally or not, created an environment in which the outward movement to the lower density suburban areas of the region by manufacturing, commercial businesses (especially retail trade), and the residential population was encouraged. Key factors that contributed to the suburbanization movement included the increased number of automobiles and trucks in the postwar society; federal support for new highway construction, some of it geared specifically to relieve congestion in the urban core area; federal policies that encouraged suburban relocations under the federal mortgage lending programs and the G.I. Bill; the lower costs of space and related service costs to manufacturers and some business institutions; and residential expansion, especially the trend of building single-family homes on relatively larger lots, tied to increased population.

By the 1950s, major new industrial plants had either already located on or beyond the city's fringe or planned to—General Motors and Westinghouse to the west and the revitalized aircraft industry under North American Aviation and the Western Electric plant to the east are examples—and suburban residential expansion was well underway. Coincidentally, the migration of retail business from the Central Business District, or Downtown, to the suburbs began, prompted by traffic congestion and overcrowding in the core on the one hand and the suburban relocation of the residential market—the consumer—on the other.

At the time, as we have already noted, Columbus was less than fifty square miles in land area and still had room to grow in all directions: it stood alone on the central Ohio till plain, with relatively few small suburbs and, further out from the city, what were then called satellite communities. Much of the county was made up of unincorporated agricultural lands in several townships.

Under the dynamic and charismatic leadership of former Mayor Maynard D. "Jack" Sensenbrenner, Columbus embarked on an ambitious program of territorial annexation. Mayor Sensenbrenner recognized then, as we do today, that the well-being of the political city of Columbus was essential for the growth and well-being of the larger region. At the heart of the annexation program was the issue of how to capture for the city some of the growth in industry and business and, yes, in residential population that was taking place, especially in the unincorporated areas lying beyond the city's political jurisdiction.

Consistent with his expressed goal of making Columbus the best city in America, Sensenbrenner sought through the annexation process to avoid many of the problems confronting America's cities, such as the loss of urban residents, businesses, industries, and their tax bases, as a result of frozen political boundaries that were a reflection of the existing annexation law. The experiences of both Cleveland and Cincinnati, cities that already in the 1950s were hemmed in by smaller political units and had no opportunities for expansion, were familiar to the mayor, encouraging the aggressive annexation movement here.

The Columbus annexation policy recognized that this single large city in the region had an extensive water and sewer system already in place and that the growth areas in unincorporated agricultural lands in the several townships that lay beyond the city's limits in the 1950s did not. Annexation promised such services to those areas that chose to attach themselves to Columbus; for many communities, annexation was a more reasonable way for them to acquire these necessary utilities than to attempt to go it alone or to continue to use well water and septic tanks. Over time, the bits and pieces, large and small, of these areas were annexed. The aggressive annexation program met its initial goals, and the suburbanization of the region was underway. Success, of course, gave rise to the need for an enlarged water and sewer system for the expanding region.

In 1970, the Arthur D. Little consulting firm completed a study dealing with future annexation as part of *The Columbus Plan: 1970–1990*.[2] By then, annexation had gone on for almost twenty years, and the city's area had increased from about 40 square miles to 173.2 square miles. The Little study led to recommendations that future annexations and strategies should support a policy that anticipated vital economic development, but within an area that could be served efficiently by government. Even though growth was the goal, further annexation would mean lower residential densities and greater distances involved in journeys to work and other travel, with significant impact on the regional transportation network. A "priority area" was targeted for annexation outward to the Outerbelt.

In the mid-1970s, the Mayor's Economic Development Council (MEDC), organized to produce the Overall Economic Development Plan for the city, considered the issue of limiting growth. Talk about "limits to growth" had become popular at that time thanks to worries about the depletion of world resources and damage to the environment. In due course, William Habig, director of MORPC, raised the question of how much growth is good in a given time period in a given region, noting that the limit to growth lies in determining government's ability to service that growth. Some twenty-four years later, Habig and others are still trying to resolve the issue.

Of course, growth and expansion in the region were not without cost, especially to the traditional political alignments more common to the earlier agricultural society. One hundred years ago, there were eighteen townships in Franklin County, and the township form of government was seen to be "the closest to the people." Columbus's annexation policy swallowed up many of these townships, whose numbers had already diminished because of urban encroachment. Today, only a few townships continue to function in the county, with most providing one or two basic services, such as fire or police, and their existence continues to be threatened by annexation.

The annexation process not only served to expand the area base of political Columbus but resulted in important changes in the distribution of the city's population. From 1950 to 1970, for example, overall growth in population for the expanding city increased by more than 50 percent, but the "older city" (as defined by its 1950 corporate limits) grew by less than 10 percent. Growth was in the suburban communities *within* political Columbus. Between 1960 and 1990, this pattern continued: Columbus gained a total of 161,942 people as the "older city" of 1950 lost 116,938 and suburban Columbus gained 278,880 people. Population growth increased in virtually all of the surrounding suburban municipalities, such as Worthington, Westerville, Gahanna, Grove City, Hilliard, Dublin, Reynoldsburg, Obetz, and Canal Winchester in Franklin County. Similar experiences were characteristic of many older political centers across the nation as the uneven migration of the more affluent citizenry to the suburbs—often referred to as "white flight," especially if school desegregation and busing were involved—left behind the less fortunate in the urban core.

Today, suburbanization and low-density urban sprawl, brought on by annexation and by various other forces in the post–World War II years that encouraged outward expansion, have overwhelmed the central Ohio region, much as they have the nation. Columbus, with an approximate area of two hundred square miles, is now the Central City for the extensive six-county metropolitan area. The region as a whole has been confronted with the continued loss of its rural character as the development interests continue their relentless drive into virgin territory, bringing, at almost any cost, suburban living to the region. It is not only the "too big" houses, often on "too large" lots, that are the problem but also the traffic congestion that commuting has encouraged. The anticipated pleasant suburban lifestyle has too frequently given way to crowded schools, crowded highways, and crowded egos. In a nutshell, both the city proper and its suburban neighbors are confronting the specter of growth, and given our apparent incessant need to grow in order to feel fulfilled, we are probably getting what we deserve, even if it is not always quite what we asked for.

As society continues to increase its reliance on the computer and on increasingly sophisticated communication systems, it is expected that populations will spread over geographically larger space. Even now, individuals can operate electronic "cottage industries" from their homes in relatively remote sites yet be actively involved in the day-to-day life of the region.

Continued growth thus raises interesting questions. With Columbus clearly the dominant and most heavily urbanized unit in the region, and with its annexation policy still in place, if moderated, what will be its future impact upon the suburban counties and their principal communities, their county seats? Can the counties and communities remain politically and economically independent of Columbus while still dependent upon their ties with the core city?

Like it or not, managing a growing urban-suburban metropolitan region today creates problems that did not exist historically. Trying to deal with issues that transcend political bounds raises questions that are linked directly to political and economic power. What are the options? Are regional organizations, such as MORPC, the answer? Can we plan adequately for the water and sewer needs of this large geographic area without all the parties involved? Can the transportation system be developed effectively without regional input? More liaisons between city and county governments appear to be essential to the well-being of the region. Certain functions lend themselves to regionalization. Clearly, decisions relating to sewage and water, the highway system, the courts, and, perhaps, economic development, given the unfortunate competitive use between communities of tax abatements and incentives, might benefit from cooperative input from government units that may face outmigration of population and the subsequent loss of leadership and tax revenues and, at the same time, increased suburbanization and what that entails.

What has occurred within the region is not unlike some visions of the future city, a city no longer dominated by a single large urban core but one with a series of nuclei, each providing most of the services and functions of the core at accessible points on and within the regional transportation network. These expanding nuclei need not reach the size of the core nucleus, Columbus, but they will provide most of their citizens' needs in an environment that is presumably more attractive and productive. The core city, Columbus, may continue as the major business and cultural resource center, even while it loses segments of its population and business base to the suburban areas. In one sense, Columbus may well serve as the hub of a "wheel" of a well-developed regional economy.

Within such an economy, *intraregional* relationships affect most of us at the individual level as homeowners or renters. At this level, our interests are usually concerned with the location of our residence—our home or apartment—with respect to our jobs and friends or to schools, church, shopping, and our other activities. It is usual for many of us to decide where to live on the basis of these relationships as we try to minimize a set of costs in terms of dollars, time, and energy in the effort to overcome distance. In the movement to suburbia, we have complicated our lives because of the demands placed upon us. One reason for the traffic gridlock that we encounter today is that the place where we live and the place where we work are no longer related.

The above model characterizes the central Ohio region today. Encouraged in part by the transportation system and by revisions made in it to accommodate growth, residential and commercial expansion has burgeoned in the upstream northern segments of the region, from Hilliard to Dublin to Worthington and Westerville to the New Albany and Easton complexes where upscale residential units and shopping facilities predominate. The southern parts of the region are experiencing increased growth and expansion as well. At the other extreme, the low-income populations tend to be increasingly isolated in the urban core, removed from the upscale communities and thus from the economic opportunities they offer.

In a sense, this reflects a resegregation of the area's population that has taken place, not on the basis of race and ethnicity necessarily, but on the basis of income and social class. The upwardly mobile are, obviously, socially mobile, and this is revealed in their choice of residential community. This carries over in terms of housing choices, educational opportunities, and even job opportunities. To the extent that the flight to the suburbs is a major movement in the region, it leaves the central core of the region, where mobility is much more limited, poorer and older.

SUMMARY

Any community is affected by its geographic location and by changes in the society that modify it. Columbus and the central Ohio region have benefited from their location in the heart of an expanding U.S. society, from the opening of the frontier to settlement two hundred years ago to the present. Although our geographic location was not an inexhaustible resource, it was and remains a key resource shaping the growth and expansion of our economy. The geography of our location has changed through time, primarily because of technological changes, first in transportation and more recently in communication. One consequence of the communication revolution has been the reorganization of our economy into a dynamic service economy with international dimensions. Our *interregional* relationships have expanded from ones dependent on Ohio and the Midwest to ones reaching not only national players but international players as well. At 2000, Columbus is a city-region well prepared for the future.

At the local level, our *intraregional* relationships are more complex than in the past, in terms of both political realities and socioeconomic conditions. How these play out cannot necessarily be foreseen, but the region's economic health is strong, and there exists the potential for the emergence of a more united regional identity.

4

Population and Demographic Change in Central Ohio

"T HE CITY IS THE PEOPLE!" THE 1990 CENSUS count revealed that Columbus was the sixteenth-largest city in the United States and, for the first time, the largest city in Ohio after enjoying a 12.0 percent increase in population from 1980 to 1990 that brought the city's population to 632,910.[1] With an additional 5.9 percent increase to 670,224 between 1990 and 1998, Columbus became the nation's fifteenth-largest city.[2] These data are for the "political" city of Columbus—that area lying within the defined legal political bounds of the city.

Of the twenty-five largest cities in the country in 1990, only seven had increased their populations in the decade at a higher rate than Columbus. All seven were Sun Belt cities, ranging from San Diego, with a high 26.8 percent increase, to Los Angeles, with a 17.4 percent gain.[3] This was heady company! In its growth, Columbus reflected, and still does, a "model" for one set of growth centers in the United States in the 1990s: the state capital with a major state university at its heart. Columbus is one of the larger cities supporting this model.

Equally impressive is that within Ohio the state's other large cities continued to lose population. In the 1980 to 1990 decade, Cleveland, with a −11.9 percent loss, ranked sixth in percentage loss among all large U.S. cities. Other Ohio cities with losses were Akron with −6.1 percent, Toledo with −6.1 percent, Dayton with −5.9 percent, and Cincinnati with −5.5 percent. Further losses are projected for each of these cities by 2000, although at a lower rate.[4] But among Ohio's six largest cities, only political Columbus has displayed population growth that belied the region's position in the heart of the so-called Rust Belt.

Another measure of city size, and perhaps the simplest, is *spatial*—the areal size of the city, usually measured in square miles—although the land area of a city may change over time, just as population does. The vitality of Columbus reflects the impact of almost fifty years of annexation that added to the political city the rapidly growing unincorporated township and rural areas that surrounded it. Columbus's ability to increase its political area from approximately fifty square miles in 1950 to over two hundred square miles today has had a lot to do with the vitality of the political city. Both political Cleveland and political Cincinnati were larger than Columbus in 1950, with each at just under seventy-five square miles. But these two cities experienced suburbanization beyond their political limits earlier in their development, resulting in the incorporation of independent cities that have served to encircle and hem in the larger and older political units, thus limiting their physical growth.

Thus by the mid-1950s, when Columbus launched its intensive campaign to annex land in the surrounding unincorporated townships, neither Cleveland nor Cincinnati had that option readily open. Currently, whereas Columbus has expanded to approximately 200 square miles in land area, Cleveland has a land area of only 77.0 square miles and Cincinnati only 77.2 (1996 data). Measured by land area as well as population, Columbus is the largest city in Ohio. Generally, we measure the political city in terms of area—the number of square miles within its boundaries—and by number of residents. We also want to know population density, or persons per square mile.

It is important not to oversimplify a complex set of relationships, but it is safe to suggest that the success that Columbus has had in avoiding some of the urban problems experienced by other Ohio cities relates in no small way to its successful annexation efforts. This is not to say that further annexation should be the order of the day.

In addition, it must be recognized that the Columbus economy has been dynamic, capturing many of the qualities of a growth society. Many of the cities experiencing continuing population loss, including those in Ohio, are ones in which major manufacturing industries played a significant role in their earlier history. These cities have witnessed an outmigration of population not only to their suburbs—often a manifestation of so-called white flight—but to other parts of the country, where the blue-collar labor force sought to find better job opportunities. These trends, often cited in descriptions of the Midwest as the Rust Belt, have been tempered more recently as the region has shown renewed strength. Columbus has attracted newcomers with its expanding mix of service-based economic activities, ranging from government to money and banking to research and development.

THE CHANGING POPULATION

To the uninitiated, it may appear that the Census Bureau occasionally is confusing when discussing population and demographic data within a region. What it really does is define cities in several different contexts and label them accordingly. Consequently, depending on what definitional unit is used, different claims may be made for our community or for any other in terms of growth and change.

Clearly, how a city is defined will be reflected in the statistical data associated with it and how these data are used. For example, when we use the term *city*, just what do we have in mind? The Ohio Constitution defines any political unit with a population of five thousand or more as a city. (This definition, incidentally, does not necessarily apply elsewhere in the United States.) The term *political city* refers to that area lying within the legal or corporate bounds of the city. It has legal standing as defined by charter or statute and may be measured by the number of residents and by the land area within these legally prescribed bounds, as already noted.

The Census Bureau introduced the term *central city* to describe, at its simplest, a political city of fifty thousand or more population that is the largest political unit in population in its county. As such, that city is the central city of a *Metropolitan Statistical Area*, or *MSA*, which is defined as "a large population nucleus, together with adjacent communities having a high degree of economic and social integration with that nucleus."[5] An MSA consists of at a minimum one county, the county in which the central city is situated, but it may include additional counties that are socially and economically integrated with the central city county. Hence, today the *political city* of Columbus is the *central city* of the six-county *Columbus Metropolitan Statistical Area*.

The Census Bureau is just as much interested in what happens in the geographic region lying adjacent to and beyond the political city—in our case, the six-county MSA—as it is in the city itself. It recognizes that many people who work in the city live in the adjacent suburbs and even in outlying rural areas. And it recognizes that some people who live within the city commute to work outside its political limits in the normal course of their workday. This matter of commuting between home and work and back—that is, the daily journey to work—from different geographic areas and political units is characteristic of the American way of life. The Census Bureau is interested in this activity because of the way in which it affects both the political city and the adjacent areas with respect to differentials in urban and suburban lifestyles in income, employment, education, social mores, and other socioeconomic factors, and also with respect to racial and ethnic diversity and potential polarization of the city and region. What is clear is that our lifestyles may change dramatically in the future given changes in family size, housing preferences and costs, mobility, and increased diversity.

The Columbus MSA has changed over time with the continued growth and interaction of the population of central Ohio. In 1950, for example, the Columbus MSA consisted of the Central City of Columbus and Franklin County—a one-county MSA. As political Columbus grew in both population and land area, the social and economic interaction between the city and its larger geographic region increased. Gradually, other counties became more closely integrated with Columbus and Franklin County, most notably Delaware and Pickaway Counties, as noted earlier. By 1963 the Columbus MSA was defined as a three-county MSA. The expansion of population both north and south along Route 23 and the increased commuting to and from home and workplace between these areas further expanded the socioeconomic interaction taking place. Whatever the changes, however, what remained obvious was the dominant place Columbus occupied as *the* primary urban center of this geographic region.

With the completion of the interstate highways through the Columbus area and the development of I-270 (the Outerbelt), the population became even more subject to commuting. The expansion of suburban and rural nonfarm communities, coupled with the growth of new businesses and industries adjacent to or near the expanded highway systems, led to further integration of previously rural areas with urban Columbus. By 1973, the Census Bureau included Fairfield and Madison Counties in the Columbus MSA, thereby creating a five-county metropolitan area. With the later additions of Licking and Union Counties, the Columbus MSA was a seven-county MSA at the time of the 1990 census (see map on p. 30). In 1992, Union County was deleted from the Columbus MSA by the Census Bureau as it became more independent of ties with Columbus and as commuting was reduced. At present, the Columbus MSA is defined as a six-county area,

Suburbanization has been underway in Columbus and the surrounding Central Ohio region since the post–World War II years, as this 1974 photo to the west illustrates. The city's aggressive annexation program gave rise not only to an increase in area but to an increase in development throughout the region.

although the Columbus Chamber of Commerce, now officially called the Greater Columbus Chamber of Commerce, may include Union County and other geographic areas in its definition of "Greater Columbus."[6]

In essence, the Columbus MSA is a mix of activities with a dominant urban center, Columbus; numerous expanding suburban residential and business communities; a growing rural nonfarm population; considerable land area in which the major economic activity remains productive agriculture; and recreational and open space. Thus, Columbus's social and economic "action space" is today a larger spatial area responding to residential relocation in the area and the outward expansion of economic activity.

This is, at once, a vital and expanding residential environment and an increasingly complex economic region with expanding businesses, industries, and public sector institutions. Within much of the region, relatively low-density development is characteristic, considerable open space and recreational activity are evident, and rural lands remain in agriculture as one moves farther from urban Columbus. But the combination of rapid growth and change within the larger region has been the essence of Columbus's successful emergence as a key urban region not only in the northeastern quadrant of the United States and the Midwest but in the nation as a whole.

The census population count for 1990 for Ohio and its major urban areas reveals that both Columbus and its metropolitan area grew at rates significantly above those of the state as a whole and of other major urban areas as well. This trend has persisted into the late 1990s. Ohio's population of about 10.8 million had virtually stagnated by 1990. Since then, the years of stagnation appear to have been reversed, with an increase of 3.0 percent in population from 1990 to 1996 to a total of approximately 11.2 million people. Projections for Ohio's population by 2025 suggest relatively modest growth to 11.7 million people. Columbus's growth continues to the present, with Columbus and Franklin County reaching a combined population of over one million by 1994 for the first time in history.

It is only when the *metropolitan area* population is examined in comparison with other Ohio MSAs that Columbus fares less well. This reflects the fact that Columbus is the only large city within its six-county MSA; no other community in the region has a population in excess of 50,000. As the Central City of the MSA, political Columbus is the focal point for the six counties in central Ohio, counties with about 1.5 million residents. Despite the recent sharp increases in population in these counties, the Columbus MSA lags behind the Cleveland and Cincinnati metropolitan areas in both number of counties and population.

From 1980 to 1990, the seven-county Columbus MSA registered an overall 10.7 percent increase in population of 133,592, for a total of 1,377,419 (1990). (These figures included Union County.) Growth among the seven counties varied from a 24.3 percent increase for Delaware County, the state's fastest growing county, to a 6.0 percent gain in Licking County. Since 1990, the MSA has continued to grow. Again, Delaware led Ohio with a 30.6 percent increase between 1990 and 1997; Union, with a 20.8 percent increase, and Fairfield, with a 17.4 percent increase, also ranked among Ohio's top counties. Growth was based primarily on in-migration and the relocation of population, not on higher birth rates. Madison (11.9 percent), Pickaway (10.3 percent), and Licking (8.7 percent) Counties all showed impressive gains.[7]

Of the 1.5 million people living in the MSA, approximately 70 percent live in Columbus and Franklin County. The political city of Columbus alone accounts for about 45 percent of the total metropolitan population. This is evidence of the city's strong role in the region, if a bit of a surprise given the expansion of residential developments in the suburban counties. Clearly, the Columbus MSA is the premier growth area in Ohio.

DEMOGRAPHIC CHARACTERISTICS

It is difficult to argue with growth, whether it is measured in terms of population, economic development, or physical expansion. As Americans, we have grown accustomed to growth and are uncomfortable if we lag behind others in statistical comparisons. It's a part of being American and, for us, part of an ethic that probably goes back to the initial opening and settling of the Ohio Country. It is most apparent in our desire for constant economic growth, but it is also obvious as we worry over the consequences of changes in population and in our peculiar demographic mix.

There are some characteristics of the population's growth and change that need to be examined a bit further. So far, we've considered recent changes in population as a basis for understanding what's happened to the region in terms of numbers and as a way of briefly comparing the Columbus MSA with other metropolitan regions in Ohio. This examination has provided us with measures of attainment and of comparability—and that is good and proper.

It has been said that "demography is destiny" in the sense that current demographic data tell us a lot about the future.[8] If we go a step further and consider some of the demographic characteristics of our population and some of the recent changes and trends in these characteristics, we may gain a richer understanding of the region and its potential. Included here may be such features as the ethnic makeup of the population and its age structure, as well as the various socioeconomic measures, such as employment opportunities, housing, income, and poverty, that help us to identify issues that affect our community and region, whether positively or negatively. These are issues and measures that cannot be ignored, and for the good of the region's long-term vitality, they should not be.

One of the principal changes occurring across the nation relates to the *ethnic composition* of an area's population. Over time in central Ohio, the dominant ethnic groups were those associated with western Europe, and both early and later settlement in the region reflected this dominance. The Ohio historian George Knepper noted that "Columbus was Ohio's least ethnic city" in 1900, with only one-third of the population so defined. At the same time, he indicated that "the capital city had the largest percentage of blacks (6.5 percent) among the state's principal urban areas."[9] In contrast, many of the major industrial cities, especially in northern Ohio, attracted waves of migration from eastern and southern Europe in the last quarter of the nineteenth century, so their populations were much more ethnically diverse than those of the Columbus area. In response to the two world wars, migration out of the American South, particularly from Appalachia, brought white Appalachians and black migrants to Ohio's urban centers. Columbus shared in this experience, especially during World War II, when the in-migration of these groups provided needed labor in wartime industries.

More recently, migrations from Latin countries and from the Pacific Basin have served to alter the ethnic composition of our populations in the nation as a whole, by state and by region, and within states. In Ohio, for example, whites accounted for almost 90 percent of the population and blacks for 10 percent in the 1980s. By 1990, the population was 87.8 percent white, 10.6 percent black, and a small proportion, 1.8 percent, from some other ethnic group. But the minority populations in the "other" category currently have higher birth rates than either native whites or blacks. Thus, whereas the absolute growth of these groups was not large in Ohio, the Asian population had a 90.7 percent increase and the Hispanic a 6.5 percent increase in population from 1980 to 1990. The black population experienced a 7.3 percent increase, and the white population declined by 0.8 percent in the same time period.[10]

As we can see from these statistics, the old ethnic mix is undergoing rapid change, and the principal contributors to the change are the Asian and Hispanic subgroups. Even as black and white populations in Columbus grew at 14.3 percent and 9.4 percent, respectively, in the last decade, the "new" minorities, Hispanics and Asians, who accounted for only about 3.5 percent of Columbus's population, were growing at a faster rate, raising important questions about the changing diversity of our population and labor force.[11] Some projections for the United States suggest that the racial mix will have changed by 2015 so that the white share of the total will be about 66 percent, the black share 13 percent, the Hispanic share 15 percent, and the Asian share 5 percent. American Indians, Eskimos, and others would have a 1 percent share of the total.[12]

These changes address the issue of increasing cultural diversity both in the nation as a whole and in our own region. The impact of this is far-reaching and may include changes in the education system to accommodate differing cultural histories and languages. In addition, the new cultures may bring about changes in the marketplace in response to different attitudes toward housing, entertainment, and other activities as the region acclimatizes to the diversity.[13]

Nonetheless, data for Columbus in 1990 reveal that whites still account for nearly three-fourths of the total population of 632,910 and blacks for about 22.6 percent. Figures for Franklin County, including Columbus, show a greater dominance of whites, at 81.5 percent compared to 15.9 percent for the black population, as expected.[14] And when data for the six other metropolitan counties in the MSA are considered, the ratio is even greater. In short, the black population tends to be urban, and the suburban populations are predominantly white. This situation may lead to polarization of groups by ethnicity and race within a society, a trend that often reflects wide disparities in the economic well-being and social mobility of the individual groups.

The Columbus MSA is not unlike the nation with respect to other demographic measures. The *age structure* of the nation's population is changing as the baby boomers of the 1946-to-1964 generation mature and age. The fact that they began to turn fifty in 1996 portends a different future for society. The median age of the U.S. population is now thirty-six years, the oldest ever. This group will define society in the future, since it will account for half the population. With this aging population, U.S. population growth would have soon stabilized were it not for immigration and the higher birth rates among immigrant groups.

In the Columbus region, ours has been a reasonably young population, with, for example, 20 percent in the 20 to 30 year age cohort in 1980. But it is aging too! By 2000, the cohort will drop to 15.7 percent of the population. In contrast, the 50 to 60 year group, which accounted for 9.8 percent of the population in 1980, is expected to account for 11 percent by 2000.[15] As the population ages, a drop in birth rates and slower rates of growth can be expected. In turn, the aging of the population gives rise to changes in the labor market and in the marketplace for goods and services as demands shift from those affecting the young to those affecting an older population group. Included, of course, are social services: for example, a younger population may require expanded educational and recreational facilities, whereas an older population will need increased health and care services. In addition, the type of housing desired may change.

Changes in *housing* and *house size* in the Columbus MSA reflect national trends as well. In general, house size—that is, the number of persons residing in a home—has been decreasing since the 1960s, reflecting, among other things, a change in the lifestyles of the citizenry. For instance, in the

Columbus MSA in 1970, there were 3.11 persons per household; by 1990, the household size had dropped to 2.54 persons. But the decrease in household size, along with population growth, has led to an increase in the number of households in the region from just over 354,000 in 1970 to 525,000 in 1990, thus stimulating the market for housing and for products for the home.[16] In the course of these changes, the definition of a *family unit* and the very nature of family formation has changed. It is generally recognized that the typical family of the post–World War II period has been displaced by a variety of living arrangements that reflect not only population changes but also changes in traditional social values and institutions.

Another demographic measure, and one related to the quality of life in a society, is that associated with *poverty*. Central City Columbus has a disproportionate number of those in the MSA who are poor, whereas the suburban growth areas are, in a statistical sense, underrepresented by this group. On the other hand, in many ways, the so-called power structure of the community is located in the suburbs, which are distanced from the urban core in a way that was not quite true in the past. Suburbs were once considered to be "bedroom communities" of the urban core; the trend now is toward the increasing economic and political power of these areas, although they are usually dependent on the Central City as the dynamic heart of the region.

Further, employment in entry-level jobs in the growing service economy is often to be found in suburban locations, although the potential labor force for many of these jobs remains within the Central City, particularly in the so-called inner city, where poverty persists among both whites and blacks and where job opportunities are limited by distance and often poor transportation. These conditions contribute to the polarization of the population by social and economic measures, in that "distance" may be measured not only in terms of physical distance with respect to miles, travel time, and the costs associated with overcoming distance but also in terms of social distance, with respect to education, job skills and training, social mobility, and the quality of services provided. In the modern American city, geography tends to isolate the poor.

A 1983 *Columbus Dispatch* article, "Inner City—Without Change, Future Bleak," noted that within the 1950 boundaries of the city of Columbus, the poverty rate was set at 22.5 percent of the population and was increasing.[17] At the same time, the poverty rate in the remainder of Franklin County had declined. The term *inner city* was used initially by urban specialists to denote that part of a political city in which poverty was concentrated. Its usage here identifies the 1950 city of 50 square miles as an "inner city" and compares it with the remainder of the county and, when used currently, with the present political city of 200 square miles.

Recent studies indicate that the trends noted here continue. In fact, the number of poor living in census tracts defined as "extremely poor" (i.e., with a poverty rate over 40 percent) is increasing.[18] In addition, the poor, whether black or white, continue to experience limited mobility. For one thing, living in isolation in segregated and poor neighborhoods limits exposure to other types of people and thus compounds the problems.

The point is that we tend to isolate ourselves from others both geographically and socioeconomically. The poor have limited choice in terms of where they will live and work, and being impoverished and disadvantaged, they find the larger society inaccessible. In effect, they become spatially isolated in the urban core, where social contacts and economic opportunities are limited. Well-intended government measures to provide low-rent public housing have had the effect, both in Columbus and nationally, of encouraging the concentration of poverty.[19]

Those with more choice have moved to the suburbs, seeking more attractive residential housing and neighborhoods and a social setting more satisfying in terms of meeting their expectations. In the past, the out-migration of the white population was provoked, at least in part in Columbus, by school busing and desegregation. Continued development of upscale residential suburbs may be a positive economic force in the region but may encourage and exacerbate further deterioration in social and economic conditions and job opportunities in the older urban core. As populations continue to live in isolation in the core area with their job opportunities elsewhere, the potential is strong for concentrations by race, income, housing, and even education to occur, which may lead to a "culture of poverty" in this area.

It is not by chance that the growing suburban communities represent a culture distinctive from that of the older urban core and free of many of the problems confronting these areas. A different set of values apply, values of a predominantly white population that has enjoyed economic success, is essentially conservative in its political and social beliefs, and has had the chance to exercise choice.

SOME OBSERVATIONS

Ours is a dynamic area in a state and region whose prognoses for the future in the last quarter of the twentieth century were not always encouraging. But census projections in the 1990s suggest continued strong growth into the new century. More important than growth, perhaps, is the direction that the growth will take and the related character of the employment structure of the Columbus region. As noted, it is clear that demographic changes are underway in terms of both spatial reorientation and characteristics of the population. The continuation of an aggressive annexation program may need to be tempered by an understanding of trends in family formation and size, space needs and related housing and energy costs, lower population densities and numbers, and the social and economic activities conditioned by these trends, including job generation, educational needs and skill requirements, technological innovation and resulting economic expansion, business relocations, and changes in commuting patterns.

Although Columbus is the state's largest political city in terms of land area and population, it still ranks as the third-largest city-region when the metropolitan populations are the criteria, and that is an important difference.

So, other than "bragging rights," what implications of size might there be? A general assumption is that the larger the city or region, the larger its potential for growth, for innovation and new developments, for varied and more sophisticated services and markets, for a wide-ranging set of cultural attributes, and so on. As a community strives to achieve prominence and "respectability" and, perhaps, competitiveness with its neighbors, the "numbers game" may be important. For we recognize that a certain threshold of population—a *critical mass*—must exist in a community if it is to achieve first-rate status in terms of national recognition and in its cultural institutions, whether these include a symphony orchestra, an outstanding art museum, opera and ballet companies, or, yes, professional sports teams. There has to be an audience—a market and accompanying financial support—capable of demanding and supporting these activities. This is not easy to come by.

In the sense of a critical mass, it has to be recognized that historically Columbus lagged behind both Cleveland and Cincinnati. Both cities draw upon a richer heritage of financial support than Columbus, and both have larger regional and metropolitan populations and larger geographic television markets to draw upon to finance, sustain, watch, and attend their cultural events. Columbus is simply not yet in—dare we say it?—the same ballpark.

There is another closely related factor. Columbus's markets have been, traditionally, to the south and southeast, areas that have not enjoyed the industrial success and related wealth associated with other parts of the state. When Columbus reaches out to attract people to the city, it is in direct competition with Cleveland to the north and Cincinnati to the southwest. This is especially true when the television market is considered. This "cultural trade area" is restricted and more geographically limited.

These are key factors—the critical mass of people capable of supporting major activities in the region and the quality of the geographic trade area that the city serves. But as our metropolitan population grows—and we *are* a major growth region—so will the critical mass necessary to allow the Columbus region to claim preeminence in Ohio.

5

The Columbus Area Economy

FROM ITS CREATION AS THE STATE CAPITAL IN 1812, the gradual evolution of the Columbus economy was dictated primarily by the city's chief function as the center of state government and by the opportunities provided by the geographic environment. The central location of the Columbus site within Ohio was a key factor affecting its selection as the capital city. Overland transportation routes, usually following earlier Indian trails, were soon in place to accommodate limited local trade as inns, hostelries, and other service undertakings necessary to support government functions evolved. With settlement, the need for simple manufactured goods led to a highly localized handicraft or manufacturing industry based primarily upon agricultural raw materials and forest products. There was limited water power available along the rivers for sawmills, grist mills, flour mills, and distilleries; there was only modest commerce on the rivers.

HISTORICAL OVERVIEW

Despite its being the capital city, Columbus remained a small community; at its incorporation as a city in 1834, there were 3,500 residents, and it reached a population of only 17,882 by 1850. By then, however, overland transportation had been enhanced. Local "turnpikes" were constructed as early as 1816, and by 1833 the National Road passed through the city. The eleven-mile Feeder Canal from Lockbourne to Columbus, connecting the city with the Ohio and Erie Canal (Portsmouth to Cleveland), was opened in 1831, and by the 1850s early railroads were in place. These improvements in transportation opened the central Ohio region to increased regional trade and commerce.

Small manufacturing firms evolved, catering not only to the commercial market but to the needs of farmers, miners, and others in the emerging region. There were foundries: Joseph Ridgeway & Company began operations in 1822, producing agricultural implements and, by 1848, steam engines; and the Hayden Iron Works, underway in the mid-1830s, produced a variety of iron products. Carriage and wagon shops were in operation fairly early on, and tool companies, such as the Ohio Tool Company and the Ohlen, Drake Company, were producing planes, saws, and other items by the 1850s. No truly large-scale manufacturing operation developed until later in the century, partly because of the limited market but more because of the conservatism of local capital, which was more interested in land speculation—even then—and in transportation, with investments in both stagecoach lines and railroads.

In the late 1860s, the government, federal and state, expanded activities in the area. A federal arsenal was established here in 1864, with an accompanying military training center. After the Civil War, the state completed construction of the Deaf and Dumb Asylum, on Town Street; the Blind School, whose building still stands on Parsons Avenue; and a State Lunatic Asylum, on West Broad Street. In these endeavors, the state of Ohio was among the leaders in the states in providing the necessary care and social services for its citizenry. These operations were important factors contributing to the area's growth, and Columbus's political role was enhanced by this expansion of government activities in the city.

1870–1900. By the end of the Civil War, Columbus was still predominantly a political and commercial center, with a population of 31,274 in 1870. In the years following, the city grew rapidly, as did other Ohio cities in this period of urban industrialization, reaching a population of 125,560 in 1900 as Ohio's third-largest city. Contributing to the growth was an expanded interregional transportation system. By 1890, for example, fifteen railroads, some with large shops here, came into Columbus, many of them hauling coal from southeastern Ohio to Columbus and to markets beyond the region. The rich mineral and timber resources of the southeastern counties provided the basis for a new and expanded manufacturing industry and reduced reliance upon agricultural raw materials as the basis for industry. The direct ties to the region's mineral resources were evident in the development of the Columbus Iron Company and the city's first blast furnace in 1870, in the establishment of what was to become Buckeye Steel Castings in 1886, and in the location of steel-making facilities in the city by Carnegie Steel in 1894. In the 1880s, local boosters optimistically dubbed the city the "Birmingham of America," reflecting their confidence in the richness of the mineral raw materials of southeastern Ohio and the development of the local iron and steel industry.

Local inventions and innovations were often a key factor in industrial development and led to the growth of other industries linked to mining activity. With the invention of a coal-mining machine, the Lechner Manufacturing Company, the forerunner of the Jeffrey Manufacturing Company, was in business by 1877; Kilbourne & Jacobs was organized in 1881 to manufacture equipment for the mining industry; and the discovery and use of natural gas, as well as the presence of such nonmetallic minerals as sand and lime in the region, stimulated the opening of glass manufacturing plants by the 1890s. Timber resources remained vital, especially to the growth of the carriage and buggy industry. Columbus emerged as one of the largest producers of carriages, wagons, and buggies in the United States, if not in the world, by the end of the nineteenth century. As many as twenty buggy companies functioned here in 1900, including one of the largest in the world, the Columbus Buggy Company.

Despite this burst of industrial expansion, which was occurring in many American cities in the latter quarter of the nineteenth century, Columbus remained true to its initial role as a government center, with associated trade and commerce of continued importance to its economic success. In addition to the new facilities to care for those in need, the Ohio State University was located in the city in 1870. But even with Columbus's historic commitment to a service economy, there was recognition that expansion of manufacturing was a necessary ingredient in the process of growth for the city. What was then the Columbus Board of Trade encouraged the attraction of new business and industry to Columbus as a stimulus to further growth.

1900–1940. These efforts to attract new business and industry continued into the post-1900 period, and the community assisted by raising funds to promote and assist the effort and to develop promotional literature to publicize the city. Columbus was recognized as a conservative community with

The Buckeye Steel Castings plant in South Columbus traces its origin to the late nineteenth century and the mineral resources found in southeastern Ohio. It remains an integral part of the South Side community even as other manufacturing operations have been lost.

little risk capital available to support new industrial endeavors; on the positive side, it was judged to be a low-wage city that had excellent labor relations, which usually meant the absence of any organized labor initiatives.

"Home-grown" industry, often resulting from local inventive genius or technological innovation, also continued to develop and grow. Some of the organizations that emerged were eventually claimed to be the largest of their type in the world, such as Jeffrey Manufacturing (mining machinery), Jaeger Machinery (portable cement mixers), Buckeye Steel Castings (railroad castings), Ralston Steel Car Company (railroad freight cars), Seagraves (fire engines), M.C. Lilley (regalia), and Peruna Drugs (patent medicines).

Some significant changes were reflected in the increased, although still relatively minor, role of outside (national) firms in Columbus. From 1917 to 1920, for example, Ford Motor Company established a branch assembly plant here, consistent with its plan to decentralize production; the American Zinc Oxide Company located a major facility on Joyce Avenue; and Timken Roller Bearing built its large plant at Fifth and Cleveland Avenues.

The location of the huge federal government military depot on the city's east side in 1918 not only stimulated the local economy but proved to be a stabilizing force in the large service sector.

In 1921, Roderick McKenzie, an Ohio State sociologist, identified three major industrial communities in Columbus: the group of plants adjacent to the New York Central tracks north of the Downtown and centering on the Jeffrey plant on North Fourth Street; the cluster of plants adjacent to the Olentangy River and extending northward to First Avenue from the Jaeger Company plant to the Columbus Coffin Company plant and others; and the South Columbus industrial area south on Parsons Avenue to Marion Road and beyond, where the steel and glass industries were located.[1]

Before World War II, both the economic depression of the 1930s and the dominant role of local businesses in setting policy led to a period of only limited growth. By many observers, the Columbus Board of Trade, ostensibly organized to attract new business and industry, was viewed as an organization that more effectively discouraged new initiatives. Dominated by representatives of major local firms, the organization seemed to be intent on protecting the competitive advantages existing companies reaped from the prevailing low wage rates, the lack of competition for labor, and the general absence of effective unions. These qualities were consistent with the paternalistic relationship that some firms developed between the company and its workers and the community. But World War II and its long-term impact challenged this traditional system of industrial relations and changed the nature and character of manufacturing and business in Columbus in general.

1940 and the Postwar Years. During the war, investment in new manufacturing operations and in the expansion of others led to unparalleled growth in manufacturing activity. Employment in manufacturing reached an all-time peak, and manufacturing's share of the total labor force was at a high point. The decision by the federal government in 1941 to locate in Columbus a $14-million aircraft plant, the Curtiss-Wright plant, helped to re-shape the existing industrial economy and also brought into play forces that were to have a profound long-term effect upon the city. The decision, made to some extent over local opposition, was primarily a response to three considerations: the availability of labor, drawing upon surpluses in southeastern Ohio, Appalachia, and the South; an available site adjacent to Port Columbus on East Fifth Avenue; and national defense policy. Once underway, the aircraft plant, which at its peak employed 25,000 people, supported scores of subcontracting businesses in the city, notably small machine shops, as well as others engaged in servicing and supplying it. In addition, and perhaps more important in the long run, the plant, with its national scope and relatively high-wage, union labor policies, brought a new concept of manufacturing to Columbus. Simply put, it had the effect of reducing the influence of old-line firms and of opening Columbus to a different set of industrial challenges.

With the end of the war, there was what might be termed a "nationalization" of the Columbus economy.[2] It brought with it a recognition of the city as a place where national firms might thrive. The Curtiss-Wright plant set the stage for postwar expansion. After the war, national firms, attracted to the city by its favorable geographic location and its surplus pool of trained industrial labor, located branch plants here. The Curtiss-Wright facility was unable to convert effectively to civilian aircraft production, but for a short period it housed the newly formed Lustron Corporation to mass-produce porcelain-clad steel homes for the postwar market (see chap. 1). Later, with the beginning of the Korean conflict, North American Aviation moved into the building. National firms that built large new manufacturing plants, usually on the outskirts of the city, included General Motors (the Ternstedt plant, 1946) and Westinghouse (1952) on the west side, and Western Electric (1959) on the east side.

If Columbus did, indeed, emerge from World War II with a new manufacturing focus, it had not shown either a willingness or a desire to become a blue-collar industrial town. Promoters of the city argued for expanded manufacturing, especially as the automobile industry grew, but in the late 1950s, when both Ford and International Harvester proposed the city as a site for branch plants of their operations, residents of concerned neighborhoods banded together to turn them down. Later still, when Volkswagen began its search for a plant site for its first expansion to an American base, Columbus proved to be, at best, a casual competitor for the plant. Were these mistakes? Or did the ordinary citizenry understand better than some of its leadership that there were not just benefits but costs associated with bringing in more industrial jobs, and that the costs might well exceed the benefits? In a way, this reaction to expanded industrialization reflected the ongoing conservatism of Columbus just as much as the lack of aggressive leadership by the community's "big guns" did. It wasn't wrong to suspect, as some did, that Columbus's leadership made their decisions felt more by what they chose *not* to support than by what they did support—a suspicion that remained in place through the 1990s.

In retrospect, Columbus was rarely mistaken for a "smokestack" city, even in the days when it had a more active industrial economy than now. For no matter how large or how successful the industrial economy, it did not support the typical heavy industrial firms characterized by the steel, chemical, rubber, and automobile manufacturing industries of the Midwest. Nor did local industries generally produce the problems, real or imagined, often associated with the so-called heavy industry firms—environmental issues, labor-related problems, union dominance, high wages, and the cyclical nature of such firms. One consequence is that Columbus has not suffered the same fate since the 1960s as have other Ohio cities in which heavy industry dominated the economy—that is, the loss or relocation of major industries such as steel, rubber, and chemicals, the loss of jobs and resident populations, and the related urban decline associated with Cleveland, Youngstown, Akron, and Dayton, for example.

1960–2000. In the 1960s in Ohio, more than 35 percent of the labor force in the large industrial centers was employed in manufacturing, and in some of the smaller industrial towns, over 50 percent of the labor force was so employed. Approximately 1,285,000 Ohioans were employed in manufacturing in 1960, representing 41 percent of the labor force. By 2000, the number had declined to just under 1.1 million, representing less than 20 percent of the labor force. In the Columbus MSA, just under 30 percent of the labor force in 1960, or 73,300 workers, was engaged in manufacturing; by 2000, even though the industrial labor force stood at 94,000, manufacturing's share of total employment had declined to only 11 percent. In many of Ohio's other cities, the loss of manufacturing activity was devastating to the economies. In Columbus, while the loss was pronounced, it was buffered by the continuing growth of employment in the service sector, in which employment increased from 283,000 in 1970 to over 730,000 by 2000, for an increase of more than 155 percent.[3]

These conditions led the *Wall Street Journal* as early as 1980 to comment that Columbus "perks along on what people here call its 20 percent economy—a mix of government, trade, service . . . and manufacturing sectors."[4] It's true that these figures suggest a certain balance in employment and give rise to a local assertion that the city is "recession proof," but upon closer examination they reveal and support the contention that Columbus was becoming a larger and more diversified service economy and that change in the productive sectors, especially manufacturing, was continuing. Table 1 lists the twenty-five largest employers in the Columbus area in

TABLE 1
Largest Employers in the Columbus Area, 1981

1.	State of Ohio	28,300
2.	The Ohio State University	17,700
3.	Federal Government	11,100
4.	F & R Lazarus	7,600
5.	Columbus Public Schools	7,300
6.	Western Electric Company	6,500
7.	City of Columbus	6,400
8.	Franklin County	5,400
9.	Ohio Bell Telephone Company	4,800
10.	Sears, Roebuck & Company	4,500
11.	General Motors Corporation	4,300
12.	Defense Construction Supply Center (federal government)	4,300
13.	Nationwide Insurance Company	4,100
14.	Consolidated Rail Corp. (CONRAIL)	3,500
15.	Ranco, Inc.	3,000
16.	Borden, Inc.	2,800
17.	Worthington Industries	2,800
18.	Mt. Carmel Medical Center	2,700
19.	J. C. Penney Company	2,600
20.	Riverside Hospital	2,600
21.	Battelle Memorial Institute	2,500
22.	BancOhio National Bank	2,300
23.	Big Bear Stores	2,200
24.	Columbus Products Company	2,000
25.	The Timken Company	1,850

Source: Columbus Area Chamber of Commerce, 1981.

1981. The list illustrates the importance of the services to the local economy and especially of government at all levels. Of the top ten employers, nine are services, including six government units. Only one manufacturing firm (Western Electric) falls into the top ten category, but there are six others among the twenty-five.

In this period, many of the old-line manufacturing firms attracted national investors who acquired the companies, with the result that either they were removed from Columbus through mergers and absorption or they closed their doors and shut the manufacturing operations down. Examples include the Ralston Steel Car Company on East Fourth Street and its "company town," which emerged from World War II in a noncompetitive position and whose assets were sold off in 1954. The Jeffrey Company, once the city's largest manufacturing firm, was ultimately acquired by Dresser Industries, and its extensive buildings on North Fourth Street were torn down, marking an end to much of the industrial character of that area. Jaeger Machinery, founded in 1903, filed for bankruptcy in 1978, and its various parts were sold off. Federal Glass ended production on Marion Road in 1979 when a proposed merger failed. Seagrave, the Ohio Malleable Iron Company, and other companies in which local inventions, initiative, capital, and leadership had played a major part in their development disappeared from the scene.

Present Decade. The Ohio Bureau of Employment Services projected the Columbus Metropolitan Statistical Area (MSA) "to be the fastest growing metropolitan area in Ohio" in employment in the 1990s. Employment in the Columbus MSA exceeded 730,000 workers by 1990, for a gain of 41.7 percent since 1980, and continued to increase in the 1990s. But by 1995, manufacturing employment dropped to 93,000 workers, and its share of total employment fell to 12.5 percent, continuing its relative decline. The point must be made, however, that manufacturing became increasingly capital intensive in this period even as manufacturing employment, if not production, declined locally and nationally.[5]

Projections by the Ohio Bureau of Employment Services of employment growth from 1996 to 2006 estimate that employment in the state will increase by 11.9 percent. Among the eight largest metropolitan areas, the Columbus MSA will enjoy the second-largest increase: more than 111,600 workers, for a 14.0 percent gain. The largest increase, 116,100 workers, for a 14.1 percent gain, is for the larger Cincinnati metropolitan area, and the lowest is a projected increase of 8.6 percent for the Youngstown-Warren MSA.[6]

In Columbus, most of the growth will occur in the service sectors. Three service sectors each accounted for a large share of employment in 1990: wholesale and retail trade employed 190,000 workers, or 26.0 percent of the total; the general services sector had 182,000 workers, or 24.9 percent of the total; and government employed 129,000, or 17.7 percent of the total. The combined sectors of transportation/utilities, finance/insurance/real estate, and construction employed 129,000, or 17.7 percent of the total. By 2000, 85 percent of the workers in the Columbus MSA, or 730,700 of the 862,200 total, were employed in the service economy.[7] Co-

TABLE 2
Largest Employers in the Columbus Area, 1999

1.	State of Ohio	28,015
2.	Federal Government	16,500
3.	The Ohio State University	15,707
4.	Honda of America Mfg., Inc.	13,000
5.	Bank One Corporation	10,992
6.	The Limited Inc.	10,000
7.	Columbus City Schools	9,124
8.	City of Columbus	9,112
9.	Nationwide Insurance Enterprise	9,100
10.	Kroger Company	7,500
11.	Mount Carmel Health System	7,000
12.	Grant/Riverside Methodist Hosps.	6,328
13.	Franklin County	6,300
14.	United States Postal Service	6,149
15.	National City Bank	4,200
16.	Ohio State University Hosps.	4,189
17.	Consolidated Stores	4,040
18.	Schottenstein Stores	3,900
19.	Lucent Technologies, Inc.	3,890
20.	Abercrombie & Fitch	3,800
21.	Wendy's International, Inc.	3,634
22.	Huntington Bancshares, Inc.	3,586
23.	Big Bear Stores Co.	3,500
24.	American Electric Power Corp.	3,300
25.	Defense Supply Center, Cols.	3,000

Source: Columbus Area Chamber of Commerce, 1999.

lumbus's future—and that of the nation—is clearly in the service sector, and continued expansion is expected there. In this respect, Columbus's experience resembles that of the nation rather than that of the Ohio economy generally.

A list of the top twenty-five employers in 1999 (table 2) confirms this observation. Only one manufacturing firm, Honda, is in the top ten, and only one other, Lucent Technologies, Inc., is among the twenty-five largest firms. Government units, including education, account for eight of the top twenty-five employers; other service activities in the top twenty-five include seven retail establishments, four financial or insurance companies, three hospitals, and one utility.

Here, again, the city's history has had a lot to do with it. For even as an

The State Capitol is in the heart of downtown Columbus surrounded by other government and private sector buildings, as well as the ubiquitous parking lots. To the south is the Ohio Theatre and the built-up area that would be cleared in order to develop the City Center mall. The Capitol building and grounds have been renovated and restored in recent years.

industrial economy flourished in the early postwar years, the city remained well rooted in what was to become its growth sector, *services*. At its heart, Columbus remained a government center, and the basic governmental function encouraged over time the development and expansion of a host of other economic activities reliant upon government. Few other state capitals have grown to the size of Columbus or have evolved the complex economy that has developed here. The key issue was the direction that the city's service economy would take and *how*, not whether, the city would evolve as a predominantly service economy.

Perhaps nothing did more to awaken Columbus to this possibility than a comment to Columbus Rotarians in 1975 by Sherwood Fawcett, then president of Battelle, to the effect that Columbus ranked with Washington and Moscow as one of "the great centers for scientific and technical information." A few years later, Rowland Brown, then president of OCLC, the Online Computer Library Center, which was, in effect, a modern-day local

Battelle Memorial Institute, south of the university campus, is one of the largest research institutions in the world. It has broadened its research interests and facilities widely since 1950.

invention, affirmed this observation, citing in particular the presence here of Battelle, Chemical Abstracts, Ohio State University, and his own organization. He noted at the time (1981) that "Columbus, with its many on-line computer centers, may easily rank first in the nation as the storer, retriever and disseminator of information that goes beyond scientific and technical areas to encompass the vastness of the human experience."[8] In 1992, the city's role in the new information technology was enhanced when the United Nations identified Columbus as the only North American "trade point" or "info port" in an international technological electronic data network for global trade connecting with other designated sites throughout the world. It is worth noting that Columbus has developed a role that is not dependent upon manufacturing the equipment essential to the growth of the information industry—the computers and software—but rather is directed toward the production, use, and distribution of information.

Modern, computer-based communications are essential, of course, as has been amply illustrated by the presence in the city of CompuServe and by the roles that local insurance and financial industries, such as Bank One and Nationwide, play nationally. In the 1960s, Bank One initiated electronic banking with the new Bank Americard (now Visa) and expanded it with the introduction of automated teller machines (ATMs) in 1971. Later, it began to process transactions for Merrill Lynch and by 1988 was processing credit card transactions for firms in every state. In addition, Bank One began to expand its banking operations in the 1970s by buying other Ohio banks and by 1985 was making interstate banking purchases. In recent years, it ranked among the ten largest banking institutions in the United States, merging in 1998 with First Chicago NBD Corporation.[9] Bank One's history provides a good example of how the service economy may generate "exports" and the related "multipliers" in the local economy.

In other ways, as well, the city's service functions have expanded. The completion of the extensive interstate highway net in central Ohio buttressed Columbus's traditionally strong locational advantages, as illustrated by the subsequent growth of both the wholesale and retail sales sectors. Early on, Sears and J.C. Penney built large distribution centers adjacent to the Outerbelt. And the expansion of The Limited organization, initially firmly situated in Columbus, has brought not only its corporate offices and stores to the area but extensive warehousing and distribution facilities as well.

These qualities, and the perceived high quality of life in the area, served to attract the headquarters of national organizations. Firms such as American Electric Power and the Borden Company relocated out of the New York metropolitan area and chose Columbus as a desirable site for their business operations and as a place attractive to their employees.

In brief, the service economy here has the ability and the potential to market its services beyond the local region, attract dollars and investments from other parts of the nation and world, and thereby serve to stimulate growth, create jobs, generate income and wealth, and develop an improved quality of life for our citizens, which appears to be the long-term promise of the new social and economic revolution that has occurred, whether it is defined as a postindustrial revolution, as an information revolution, or by some other term. In any case, it recognizes that "knowledge is power" and hence that an educated labor force is critical to its continued success. *Business First* reported on a study of 1990 census data for eighty MSAs, ranking them on the basis of the percentage of residents twenty-five years or older who had earned at least a B.A. degree. The average for the eighty MSAs was 20.3 percent. The Columbus MSA ranked twenty-third, with 23.3 percent of residents so defined, but was outranked by such cities as Washington, D.C., San Francisco, San Jose, and Raleigh-Durham; on the other hand, it outranked the other large Ohio cities.[10]

UNEMPLOYMENT

A closely related phenomenon is the unemployment rate for the Columbus MSA. Throughout the last decade or longer, this region has enjoyed a lower unemployment rate than any other major metropolitan area in the state. As of December 1999, Madison County had the lowest unemployment (2.0 percent) of any Ohio county, followed by Delaware and Franklin Counties (2.1 percent). The other counties in the Columbus MSA had unemployment of 2.8 percent or lower.[11] Ohio generally has fared well compared to the nation, reflecting improved economic conditions in the state, but in recent years the Columbus MSA, in contrast to other Ohio cities, has rarely experienced the challenging problems that unemployment brings.

Clearly, part of the reason for this success is the makeup of the labor force in central Ohio, with the area's strong emphasis on expansion in the service sectors and the stability and even decline in the manufacturing sector. The benefits of such a situation do not, unfortunately, apply to all citizens. Those with limited educations and job skills, or those older members of the labor force who have lost manufacturing jobs, continue to face problems, but fortunately they represent a small proportion of the total labor force of the region. A more recent problem is that low unemployment has its downside as well, since many businesses find it difficult to meet their employment needs given the competition for labor in this environment.

SUMMARY

In the last decade of the twentieth century, then, ours is a healthy service-based economy. At the same time, it has consistently refuted the contention that such economies are simply those that take in one another's washing and thereby fail to generate income and growth. If ours were a highly localized service economy, we might have cause to worry. But the Columbus experience reveals a service economy built upon the same economic premises as those associated with the industrial economy of the past.

Traditional economic development theory in a local or regional context was predicated upon the ability of the economy to generate "exports" to other regions. Manufacturing was viewed as the principal means of producing a tangible good or "thing"—the potential "export" product. The successful development of a manufacturing base in a community depended in large part upon its access to markets and material supplies. In other words, the *geographic location* of the community and the *transportation systems* that served it were key factors affecting growth and development.

Considerable evidence was developed over time to support the notion that a new industrial firm would increase jobs and regional revenues. That is, associated with the manufacturing plant was the prospect of new jobs in both manufacturing and services, as well as increased income from sales. Clearly, in addition to the direct benefits generated by manufacturing in employment and tax revenues, for example, there were presumed indirect benefits involving other manufacturing and service activities. This is the so-called multiplier effect that helps to create expanded benefits in the community.

Service industries or businesses were seen as less effective producers. After all, their product was a service, an intangible product or "nonthing," and hence was presumed to be less effective in generating an "export" and, consequently, in creating a multiplier effect. But service industries are less dependent upon geographic location and transportation; the postindustrial service economy is premised upon the evolution of a highly productive *communication* system that permits the flow and transfer of information, one of the service economy's major products, across space with minimal costs. In this sense, Columbus may well be a prototype of what Jean Gottmann, who earlier created the concept of the "megalopolis," called the "transactional city," the city in which telecommunications sustains the growth of a dynamic service-based economy.[12]

Of course, there has been pressure locally not to disrupt the traditional structure of the economy in the face of overwhelming change, especially with respect to jobs in manufacturing and alternative employment opportunities. But the expansion of the service industries in the Columbus economy has benefited the city. With the advanced communications net present here, local service firms have demonstrated the capability of developing a productive service economy in banking, communications, information generation and transfer, research and development, medicine and health, and education. Furthermore, these are the very activities in which the postindustrial or information society may anticipate growth well into the next century.

6

The Matter of Image

A NEWCOMER TO COLUMBUS SOME TIME AGO asked my wife what it was about Columbus that made it a reasonably pleasant place to live and work. Her response? "It's easy." He said, "Yes, that's it!"

One might well wonder what she meant by that, but the newcomer had no problem with the response. He agreed enthusiastically, although he admitted that he had never thought of Columbus in that way. But "she was right," he said, "It's easy."

I know from having lived with her for many years that my wife knew just what she meant by the term. She found Columbus to be a remarkably "easy" place in which to find one's way when we arrived here in 1949 from Pittsburgh, a city that is no easy place even for a geographer. There was the "ease" of operating in a city whose major north-south and east-west street pattern conforms to the classic rectangular grid and where a Broad Street and a High Street, such "easy" names, provide the base lines for directions. And it hasn't hurt one bit that Columbus is essentially flat, so that one's way isn't obscured or interrupted by steep hills or deep valleys. Furthermore, the basic structure of the city's commercial activities made things "easy" as well. There was historically the single strong F. & R. Lazarus department store in the core that dominated the city, and even as the shopping centers evolved, there was a certain pattern to them that one could count on (after all, at that time they were virtually all designed by the Don Casto organization), and that made it "easy" too. People seemed to be reasonably well satisfied with local government; government officials were accessible to the public, and so in their own way were the city's CEOs, most of whom were native sons. Obviously, the city's image has been a pretty good one to those of us who live here.

So it has been an easy city to come to terms with, but the good old easy days may be over as we begin to pay some of the costs of increased growth and, perhaps, of increased "sophistication." Much of the ease of travel around the city or through it, of daily or weekly trips to work or shopping, of simple communication with one another, seems increasingly to be a thing of the past, a nice memory of what once was, in a city where our way of life has undergone considerable change and where we still struggle to define our image.

Early in my stay here, I heard references to "good old Columbus town," suggesting a city that hadn't really changed much or, perhaps, hadn't really kept pace with the "big boys." And just to remind us of that a bit more pointedly, one all too frequently heard references to "Cow Town, USA." That too seemed to stress Columbus's rural heritage and suggested that the city just wasn't keeping pace. Several years ago, the actor Robert Redford, staying in the area for a short time to film a movie, was surprised to note that "they are into lawn mowers" in central Ohio! In today's slang, it's been suggested that Columbus needs to "get real," and maybe so. But we have green grass and don't apologize for it.

It infuriates some locals that national newspapers will on occasion still identify Columbus as "Columbus, Ohio," assuming, apparently, that the reader may confuse us—the fifteenth-largest city in the nation—with some other Columbus. Aren't we capable of standing on our own? Why the negative image? Why these sobriquets? Maybe we deserved them in the past, but the point is that we don't deserve them now. Columbus has indeed come of age, and it is not just a matter of size, although we're proud of that; it is also a matter of the city's ethos and its widening culture and sophistication as a city interacting on a world stage.

THE IMAGE CHANGES

As late as the 1950s, Columbus was accused of having "a small town image . . . slow moving, soft, and mellow" but experiencing little dissatisfaction or a desire for bigness.[1] It was perhaps these qualities and the region's demographics that explained the city's national reputation as a "test city" for consumer products. But the truth was that the Downtown was a bit dowdy, having lost retailing and shopping to new suburban shopping centers. No new high-rise had been built to challenge the Lincoln-LeVeque's dominance on the skyline, nor would any be built until 1963.

In the middle 1960s, an elderly gentleman, a retired New York banker and utilities expert, walked into my office seeking to leave his estate to the university. He didn't intend to stay because, he said, "I can't stand this city. The weather's lousy, and there's no recreational facilities around here." He wasn't alone in his assessment. In 1965, the *Wall Street Journal* identified Columbus, a city that boasted of its favorable geographic location, as "this relatively out-of-the-way city," and the *Atlantic Monthly,* focusing on a different "climate," noted that "Columbus is one of the . . . most reactionary cities in the U.S." It went on to say that the city was "not really urban," that Columbus had "a very tightly controlled power structure consisting of a few families, a few banks, and one newspaper," and that it was the state capital and "home of one of the largest educational institutions in the world."[2]

Certainly, the city's skyline and perhaps its image began to change rather dramatically in the 1960s and 1970s with the construction of new high-rise buildings, several of which were corporate headquarters for major companies. In the early 1960s, a spate of new construction marked the beginning of the revitalization of Downtown. A new hotel and two major high-rise office buildings at or near the intersection of Broad and Third Streets were the basis for optimism.

Even so, by 1976, a *Dispatch* article carried the headline "Columbus Growing Rapidly, But Direction Unknown" and cited a Battelle executive, Clyde Tipton, who asked, "What do we want Columbus to be like when it grows up?"[3] No matter how hard it tried, the city just couldn't shed the feeling that it was content to be "the largest small town in America" and, depending on which civic leader one cites, "an oasis in the middle of the desert"[4] or "an island in a rough sea."[5] Those comments, and the admission by another leading Columbus executive that "in the past, we probably haven't set our sights high enough," suggested an absence of dynamic leadership in the community.[6]

In an article bemoaning the lack of venture capital in Columbus, the *Citizen-Journal* reported that Battelle's Sherwood Fawcett had said that "Columbus has the option of becoming a world science center and if it does, it will be riding the wave of the future. But the city must want it to happen." This was an exciting idea and challenge presented by a knowledgeable man, but two years later and after little response to his challenge, he observed, "Right now, I have the impression there isn't anybody in the community who has great dreams for the community."[7]

An article in *Columbus Monthly,* "Columbus's Inferiority Complex," suggested that "the city has more than its share of dreamers" but also asked, "Are we as weak as we think we are?" Clearly, the article said, Columbus has a continuing "whopping inferiority complex," especially as compared with Cleveland, Cincinnati, and other large cities. As one person expressed it, "I have a feeling everything here is average," and another said that "the blood doesn't rush in Columbus." One remark summed up these feelings: "It's a great place to live and good place to raise kids, but I wouldn't want to visit here."[8]

Perhaps in response to these sentiments, the community rallied to promote itself in 1979 with an image-enhancing $300,000 campaign, "Columbus, We're Making It Great."[9] Supported by both business and government, the campaign was upbeat and positive, seeking both to remind the city's residents of the good life here and to attract outsiders to the city. Jerry Jarrett, then president of Cleveland Trust, recognized that economic growth, vitality, optimism, and prosperity were evident in Columbus, which he called "truly a Sun Belt city flourishing in the heart of the Frost Belt." He noted the city's potential as a site for corporate headquarters (the Borden Company and American Electric Power had both relocated their corporate offices here from New York), a site for advanced services, and a center for research and development.[10] Early in the 1980s, Columbus captured the attention of both the *Chicago Tribune* and the *Wall Street Journal.* The *Tribune,* using a picture shot from the university farms with a cow in the foreground and the city skyline in the distance, called the city "quintessentially Middle American" and "an excellent place to explore the condition of the nation's heartland." The opening sentence quoted Mayor Tom Moody as saying, "We tend to do everything in this city at about a B- grade level," suggesting that we may not be first class in anything but that we're not third class either. The article called Columbus "neat, smug, provincial, and slow to accept change" and criticized the fashion sense of Columbus women and a power structure that failed to encourage new development.[11]

The *Journal* article, "Hello, Columbus: Thriving Ohio Capital Seeks to Shed Its Image as a Country Bumpkin," was more upbeat, recognizing that there was a perception of Columbus as an overgrown hick town but arguing that whereas it may not be a glittering cosmopolitan city, "it's no cow town either." The quality of urban life was judged to be good, and the growth and expansion of both the economy and the cultural milieu were identified as positive features.[12]

In 1981, Charles Lazarus and Dean Jeffers, two prominent civic leaders, were asked to share their perspectives on Columbus. In a discussion about the city's cow town image, Lazarus stated, "I don't care what they call Columbus, what I care about is what Columbus really is." Jeffers felt that the issue wasn't very important but that there were some strengths in a cow town that we might not want to lose, such as the tendency for people to care for each other.[13] Regardless of image, Columbus was changing, and both men recognized that. It had become a major center for the service economy, with Battelle, Ohio State, Chemical Abstracts, and OCLC helping to build a "critical mass" in the information and R&D fields. By 1982 the city had gained recognition "as one of the information capitals of the world."[14]

By the mid-1980s, Columbus was ranked between ninth and sixteenth as the best place in the nation to do business,[15] depending on the year and the rating organizations, even though others had ranked the city seventy-fifth in "quality of life."[16] And when the city was visited again as part of the Rust Belt by the *Chicago Tribune* in 1986 in an article entitled "America Discovers Columbus," we were declared to have "a rustproof economic climate."[17] Despite it all, a Chamber of Commerce official, still concerned with image, noted that "it's not that we had a negative image to overcome, [it's that] we had no image." And this after a marketing campaign organized to "sell" the city![18]

It's possible that Dean Macris, the planning director for San Francisco, was on target when he suggested in 1988 that "the national image of Columbus is nothing like what reality says it is. The people of Columbus underestimate their city." He stressed that this *is* a big city and that its "leadership needs to think of itself in big-city terms."[19]

By the end of the decade, the city had been listed as one of the top ten "Hot Cities—America's Best Places to Live and Work," and even though it had "never acquired a sharp public image, . . . [the] lack of an image hasn't kept Columbus from flourishing."[20] But it was discouraging when a group of New York art patrons who visited this "little known city" thought it an attractive city but one in which there was "nothing to do."[21]

By 1990, however, *Fortune* had determined that Columbus was one of the top ten cities—number six, in fact—for business in the country, although the *Economist* continued to see us as a "conservative, rather boring,

A May 31, 1985, cartoon in OSU's student paper, the *Lantern,* captured some sense of the frustration felt in the city over its failure to project an image exciting enough to attract visitors. There was no question of Mayor Buck Rinehart's enthusiasm, but relatively little was accomplished in the ongoing effort to sell Columbus. (Reprinted with permission of the Ohio State *Lantern* and Jim Kammerud.)

former cowtown."[22] Even a *Dispatch* article questioned, "Where Is Columbus Anyway?" and insisted that we face the fact that "outsiders are still a little hazy on who, what, and even where, we are."[23]

In a return visit in 1990, the *Wall Street Journal* encountered, instead of "Blandsville, U.S.A., a town of cornfields, cheerleaders, and Rotary Club dinners[,] . . . an anomaly in the middle of the Rust Belt, a booming center of banking, insurance, and other service industries."[24] That was a bit better. Even a major figure in urban revitalization in the United States, James Rouse, was impressed, noting, "What strikes me about Columbus is the energy and vitality of the city. And it doesn't have the conspicuous deterioration of other cities."[25]

So whether we're "the largest small town in America" or "quintessentially Middle American," Columbus has survived and improved as one of the best places to live and work in America. With its excellent geographic location and the dynamic development of its information- and knowledge-based organizations in education, banking, R&D, and related activities, Columbus is indeed one of the nation's "hot cities."

But we do worry about our image, and especially our corporate image, when a majority of national CEOs admit that they have no "top-of-mind image" of Columbus, even though they know that Ohio State football is played here;[26] we worried when we suffered the loss of Bank One and its national status; and we worry that Jack Nicklaus's Memorial Tournament will be tarnished once again by Columbus weather. Ratings and image—it's an ongoing battle that probably can't be won, but we want to be sure that we're not losing either.

IMAGE AND THE SKYLINE

The changing image of the city is based primarily on perceptions of Columbus held over time both by national media and by local civic leaders and ordinary citizens. But another force helps to fashion the city's image—the city's urban profile or skyline.

The image of a city may often be reflected in its skyline, the city's profile that distinguishes it from other urban areas and in every direction. An OSU urban geographer, Eugene Van Cleef, argued that the "towers, spires, sky-scrapers, and other edifices [may] stamp upon the public mind an image symbolic of a particular trade center." That is, the urban profile or skyline may tell us a lot about a place and inform us of changes in the city's culture and economy, and it certainly helps to shape the city's *image* for the public.[27] In a sense, the skyline reflects the city's *icons*, which may be a visual "measure" of a city's success. Mark Feinknopf, a local architect, seemed to agree when he noted that "a skyline defines the city, but it is only an image."[28]

Long before the American skyline was dominated by the skyscraper, individual cities had unique characteristics that helped to establish the image of the place. In the great cities of Europe, the dominant feature was, invariably, the cathedral or great church. Reaching to the heavens on the one hand and rooted in the religious culture and fervor of the people on the other, the cathedrals and churches provided not only a strong religious presence but also landmarks that were often identified with the dominant center of a cultural region.

Later on, with the rise of great commercial centers, activities associated with ports and the intercourse between nations marked those dynamic cities engaged in world commerce. In America, the water tower and the grain elevator were often the principal "markers" for the small towns that emerged as agricultural wealth and an expanding transportation system forged a bond between the two.

But more to our point are those structures and images that have emerged in America in the last hundred years. Often, to be sure, they were the courthouses or churches of our larger cities, where different ethnic cultures were represented by the steeples, onion domes, crosses, and other architectural styles of the buildings that rose above the two and three stories of business and residential structures. With the pressure for competitive locations in the community, the "downtown" soon became identified both by higher land values and by the increasing density of buildings and massing of larger and, ultimately, higher structures. Opportunistic businessmen placed a value in publicizing their presence with buildings that in one way or another stood out from the crowd. If the courthouse had once dominated, increasingly it was the palace of the entrepreneur that became the focal point of interest.

Once technology was available in the last quarter of the nineteenth century to build a truly high-rise structure—the steel frame, curtain walls, elevators, and internal systems to move water, wastes, and air through a building—the new tall buildings of ten floors, and later fifteen, twenty, or more, began to mark the site of important new activities that dominated a city's development. In many cities, these new structures were identified with major industrial firms located in the area. The physical structure and the commercial and industrial enterprises became linked and were represented by the high-rise new building or skyscraper where corporate headquarters were located.

In New York, the prototypical skyscraper city, such early buildings were associated with commercial development, such as the Woolworth Building, dubbed "The Cathedral of Commerce." Often, the dominant buildings reflected the power of individuals or the firms that they controlled. In Pittsburgh, for example, the Mellon family's dominance was manifested by the smokestacks of the steel industry in the Monongahela Valley and by high-rise buildings reflecting the family's role not only in iron and steel but also in oil, aluminum processing and other industries, and banking.

Thus, the presence or absence of a dominant city skyline tells us something about the city, about its entrepreneurs, and about how it thinks of itself. The "timing" of events leading to the skyline in 1910, 1930, or today may reveal much about a city's economy as well as something of its past and, yes, its future.

Think about it. What are the "visual signs" that let you know you are approaching a city? For most of us, and certainly for the visitor, it is the city's skyline, its vertical profile often visible from every direction.

Historically, Columbus's skyline was dominated by the State Capitol. Begun in 1838, it was not completed—if that's the right word, given the controversy over original plans for a dome that was never built—until 1860. Today, it stands rather pristinely as a restored capitol building with most of its exterior intact and the interior restored to historical periods of significance. Later, with increasing industrialization, smokestacks and furnaces of the manufacturing establishments would have been symbols of change, along with the occasional public building and perhaps a hotel (the Great Southern comes to mind). By 1920, modest high-rise structures, like the Atlas and Wyandotte Buildings, had been erected.

Even today, for many older residents of the city, the dominant image of Columbus remains the Lincoln-LeVeque Tower, constructed in 1927 by the American Insurance Union or AIU. In the now classic volume *Ohio Art and Artists* (1932), Edna Clark captured the essence of this building's impact on Columbus. She noted that "the capital city has the American Insurance Union Building, whose tower dominates the horizon from whatever point one views Columbus. Its construction marks a milestone in the growth of the city . . . it signalizes the transition from a large overgrown country town to a city. It stands out against the sky line so sharply that it cannot be ignored."[29]

Locally, the AIU building was occasionally humorously referred to as the IOU Tower, a reflection of the financial difficulties that the AIU faced at that time. As the then highest building between New York and Chicago, at 555 feet, it was a landmark used by pilots to sight the city and to confirm their directions, and it was considered by many to be the principal distinguishing feature of the Columbus skyline, the symbol of the city—its icon!

Not much changed from 1930 until the early 1960s, when a new wave of construction led to the evolution of a new skyline dominated by buildings associated not with manufacturing industry but with the city's expanding life as a commercial center—insurance firms, banks, hotels, and the ubiquitous government structures. A number of firms established their headquarters here: American Electric Power and the Borden Company,

The Columbus skyline in the 1990s from the confluence of the Scioto and Olentangy Rivers. The buildings reflect not only the presence of state offices but also representatives of the banking and insurance industries.

which moved their corporate offices into new high-rise offices here, and the representatives of the local banking and insurance industries, such as Bank Ohio, Bank One, the Huntington Bank, and Nationwide Insurance. Major state government buildings are an important presence as well, including the art deco State Office Building of the 1930s and the more recent Rhodes and Riffe buildings on Capitol Square. The stretch of buildings along High Street from the courts on the south to the Nationwide Center and Convention Center on the north, and the insurance offices east along Broad Street, are evidence of the changing skyline and, perhaps, of the city's changing image. As one observer noted, "The thing Columbus has now—and didn't have when I was a kid—is a skyline."[30] And Lamar Hunt, the Texas oilman, who came to Columbus to assess the city's role in professional sports, commented that "you have a major population base . . . no major league sports, . . . and I'll be corny enough to say that I liked the skyline."[31] In any case, the Columbus skyline is today a clear representative of the American city of the late twentieth century.

7

Leadership and the Power Structure

THE IMAGE OF A CITY HAS A LOT TO DO WITH how the city is projected both to the local citizenry and to outsiders by its political leaders and by those in the private sector. Mayor Tom Moody, who was noted for his "quiet efficiency," agreed that Columbus deserved the "B" rating given to it in the 1980s. The point is not whether the rating was correct but rather that it was generally accepted as being so, and worse, that it was perfectly good enough for "good old Columbus town." Was our leadership once content with this kind of image, and is it now? If not, what can be done about it?

One can make a fairly good case for the argument that leadership was satisfied with the city's stature in the past and did not want to stand up and be counted. In fact, many critical decisions in Columbus have been made *not* to do something—the decision not to pursue a World's Fair for 1992 springs to mind—rather than to do it. There was an earlier time, after all, when powerful interests in the city actively discouraged new growth and development so as not to upset the labor market and, probably, the perceived political stability. Since World War II, however, there seems to have been a positive response, or at least lip service paid, to the idea of growth. Growth appeared to be inevitable in the past and appears to be so today, but how we are to grow is by no means determined. Columbus has earned the reputation of being "a developers' city." It concedes that growth will occur but is inclined to ignore the consequences—not for the developer but for the community at large in terms of both social and economic costs. Who are the leaders, then, who have shaped our recent past?

Interest in this question and in the structure of community power and influence has been around for years, especially in the fields of sociology and political science. Defining power, influence, leadership, authority, and related concepts is essential to understanding what the power structure of a community may actually be and how it functions.

C. Wright Mills, in 1956, discussed power at the macro level in his book *The Power Elite,* which considered the power structure of the nation.[1] Others, including Floyd Hunter of Atlanta, used similar techniques to study the power structure of individual communities. Usually, some form of research such as "positional, reputational, and issue-decisional methods of identifying influential leaders and decision-making processes" may be employed by the researcher.[2]

Most formal studies use such survey methods to help identify potential leaders in communities large and small. The critical issue is how the leadership is defined in the survey and then, obviously, who in the community meets the criteria. As suggested earlier, leaders may be identified by the positions they occupy in the community or by their reputations. Obviously, those whose positions and reputations are viewed as among the more important should garner strong support, and this may provide a basis for ranking leaders.

Once members of the leadership group are identified, research may reveal not only their apparent public appeal but also the nature of their relationships with others in the leadership group and in the community via club and church memberships, service on community boards and on boards of directors, and other affiliations. Such information may at least provide insight into relationships that may, in time, affect decisions, actions, and support. Sociologists use "sociograms" to identify relationships among and between presumed leaders to understand and to visualize (or illustrate) the network of contacts and relationships in the group.

No such formal study of the power structure of Columbus has been undertaken. Rather, the *Columbus Monthly* published in 1976 the first in a series of reviews of leadership in the city at different intervals of time continuing to the present. Lacking an academic basis for its "research," the magazine identified and ranked potential leaders according to an undisclosed methodology, although the results suggest that selected individuals in the community were consulted. In addition, it has occasionally identified "People to Watch" or similar groups based on their potential roles in the community.[3]

National and regional writers have also had a certain fascination with the Columbus power structure. Part of that fascination stems from the fact that for the better part of a hundred years, one family has had inordinate power and influence in Columbus—the Wolfe family. Their power is reflected even today in the organizations that they continue to influence and control, as well as in their influence on the political and private sectors in the region.

John Gunther, in his *Inside U.S.A.,* wrote that "one of the strangest and least-known stories in America is that of the Columbus Wolfes. Talk about the self-made man, or men! The Wolfe dynasty . . . was for many years the greatest single force in Columbus politics, journalism and business, and its political influence seeped widely into the state at large."[4] This in 1947! He went on to comment about the family's "holdings" in central Ohio, mentioning the Wear-U-Well Shoe Corporation, started by an early family member at the turn of the century, which by 1947 was "one of the biggest and most successful in the country," as well as the family's role in the media, with an entry into publishing as early as 1903 and the eventual "control [of] the *Dispatch,* the *Ohio State Journal* and several radio stations including WBNS." By 1929, "the Wolfes organized *BancOhio,*" soon to become the basis for the family's extensive involvement in and control of banking in central Ohio. These various holdings gave rise to the assumption that the letters *WBNS* were an acronym for *W*olfe *B*anks, *N*ewspapers, and *S*hoes. Gunther also noted that the family had large land holdings in Columbus and was a major landowner in the eastern United States.

Linked to this was the family's influence on the political life of not only Columbus but Ohio as well. It was assumed in some quarters, certainly, that the Wolfes' interests ran Ohio and that their summer place, the Wigwam, "was a kind of Republican headquarters." Gunther ended his commentary about the family by noting that "there was nothing sinister in any of this. But that a single family should have set the tone and pace of an entire capital city, almost without opposition or qualification, for more than a generation, wasn't quite what you would call pure democracy either."

By 1971, the Cleveland publication *Point of View* wrote that "it's said in Columbus that without the cooperation of the Wolfes nothing moves. 'Which way will the *Dispatch* go?' is a question meant to indicate whether some venture will be backed by the Wolfes . . . or whether it will not get the backing and probably fail." Of course, the Wolfes' control of the principal newspaper in town, plus control of other media such as WBNS Radio and TV, virtually ensured that their points of view would shape how an issue was treated in Columbus and hence influence support for or against an issue. The article went on to say that "more than any other Wolfe power is the death-tight vice the Wolfes apply on the media of Columbus."[5]

According to the same article, the family control of the Ohio Company and the Ohio National Bank, "one of the largest bank holding companies in the U.S.," provided a preeminent position for the family and the kind of power that could indeed shape the development and well-being of a community. In addition, the close ties that many of the city's power elite had, in the early 1970s, to the Wolfe family interests furthered the influence of the family in key Columbus organizations through interrelationships on various private and public boards. With respect to government, the Wolfes, *Point of View* wrote, not only have the ability to influence the political process in Columbus and Ohio, if not the nation, but "are in a position to benefit *from* [italics added] government, state and local." The dominant role of the Wolfes in the life of this city continues today, although with a different set of the principal actors, now a fourth generation of the family.

There were of course other business and political leaders in the city, even if none had the power of the Wolfes at their disposal. The strong role of the Lazarus store in the Columbus economy ensured that the family was involved, but their role in community affairs was usually modest and restrained. Leadership in other organizations, especially in the set of strong Columbus-based, home-grown manufacturing industries such as Jeffrey, Jaeger, Buckeye Steel, and Columbus Coated Fabrics, was directed more often to issues related to economic development, particularly issues linked to the labor force.

In a 1984 review of the first hundred years of the Columbus Chamber of Commerce, it was admitted frankly that resistance to new business development, and especially to new firms in the industrial sector, was a characteristic of management in many local firms. The Chamber often encountered opposition from members when it sought to attract new manufacturing industry and other businesses to the community. Local firms, enjoying the benefits of a relatively low wage rate and minimum unionization, feared potential competition for labor if new businesses were to locate here. And it is highly likely that there was concern that such new businesses might upset the political stability of the community as well.[6]

World War II brought about a set of developments that would serve to change this attitude and shape the city's economy profoundly. Wartime decisions, such as that of the federal government to locate the Curtiss-Wright plant here in 1941 and to extend subcontracts for the production of war-related goods to numerous Columbus firms, helped alter the traditional character of Columbus industry.

The "industrialization of a commercial center"[7] was a phrase used to reflect the fundamental change that took place with the movement of national manufacturing industries into the Columbus area in the post–World War II years. Notable among these were General Motors (Ternstedt plant), Westinghouse, and Western Electric. One result was the investment of outside capital in the local economy and thus some measure of influence by the corporate managers of these firms. Although they did have an impact on the city through their support of various local activities and organizations, few of these businessmen became active in the community, and none reached a position in the leadership elite.

When the *Columbus Monthly* launched its series "Power in Columbus" in 1976, it noted that "a powerful person is someone who can make something happen . . . or, if he chooses, can keep it from happening."[8] Surveying the community at that time, the magazine identified three powerful families—the Wolfe, Lazarus, and Galbreath families. It recognized John W. Wolfe's traditional role but suggested that "the Wolfe Family's grip may be loosening" and that a transition to increased community power from the ranks of banking, insurance, and retailing might be forthcoming. A telling argument was that there were certain groups in Columbus with no real clout—labor, blacks, women, and even politicians. Columbus mayors, in almost all assessments of the power structure, did show up in the rankings, but often *not* because they had personally used power frequently or effectively; usually they were listed simply in recognition of the mayor's role. An exception to this was Mayor Sensenbrenner, surely one of the most charismatic of Columbus's recent mayors, who related well to the citizenry as a man easy to meet and talk to and who defined a style of leadership that helped to "sell" his annexation program to the community. In Tom Moody's case, the article argued that "he could and should be more powerful, but he just doesn't seem to have a taste for it." That seems clear in retrospect. It also recognized that although Columbus had three local members of Congress—Chalmers Wiley, Samuel Devine, and John Glenn—they exerted no real power in the city. As the decade of the 1970s closed, it was generally accepted that the absence of strong leadership was a question not of age but of vigor and enthusiasm. The old leadership still dominated but there were "new people to step into the power structure" in the future.[9]

Two articles in *Columbus Monthly* in the late 1970s dealt with this to some extent. One, entitled "Corporate Gunslingers," identified a group of business leaders who were, in effect, the public presence of their organizations in community affairs.[10] They represented their organizations on public issues, cultural affairs, and, if successful, image building. Some were

identified as the spokespersons for their companies: Trent Sickles and later
Jerry Gafford of Lazarus, Will Hellerman of Nationwide Insurance, Nor-
man Folpe of Huntington Bank, Carl Graf of Bank One, and others. A few
went on to positions of corporate leadership, but over time, their corporate
roles were often restricted by the very fact that they were so involved in
community committees and action groups.

A later article, "The Directors," considered the role of another group
with power and impact—those serving on various community boards and
boards of directors of local businesses.[11] It was not at all uncommon to find
the same set of individuals on several boards. A few were, simply, professional board members, including the occasional university professor; others
were business leaders who brought expertise to other local boards of directors. In these positions, the directors are usually not involved in the daily
business of the firm or organization but are there to bring their knowledge
and influence into the corporate mix. Certainly, there are civic leaders in
this group, but their leadership role is contained within the context of the
company or community organization they serve.

For both groups—"gunslingers" and "directors"—rarely did a true
leader emerge, nor should it be expected. Strong and forthright leadership
was still limited in Columbus.

Into the 1980s, the Wolfe-Lazarus-Galbreath triumvirate continued
atop the leader list. The *Chicago Tribune* stated that "the Big Three clearly
dominate Columbus. And nobody complains, because it is a benign sort of
rule that seems to keep everything on an even keel."[12] The March 1980
issue of *Columbus Monthly,* in its lead article entitled "Power: The More
Things Change," agreed.[13] The leaders remained John W. Wolfe, the Gal-
breaths, Charles Lazarus, Dean Jeffers, and, reflecting his organization's role
at that time in corporate giving to the community, Sherwood Fawcett of
Battelle. Several leaders were nearing retirement—Jeffers, Lazarus, and
John G. McCoy, for example—promising some changes in the near future.
But many locals as well as the national press were concerned that the "even
keel" was too even, that Columbus leadership had failed to encourage new
development and initiative. The *Tribune* suggested that there was a disdain
for mavericks, noting that mavericks did not survive if ignored by the
Wolfe media.

Through the years, new entrepreneurial talent was being honed locally,
and one could find a maverick or two in that group—the obvious example,
of course, is Leslie Wexner, owner of The Limited, local boy who made
good in a very big way. Other local entrepreneurs—if not mavericks—

included Dave Thomas of Wendy's, John McConnell of Worthington Steel, and Cheryl Krueger with her cookies. The presence of new companies which had relocated their headquarter offices here helped to bring new leaders into the community. In addition, many older, well-established Columbus industrial firms were acquired in this period by outside capital, leading to reorganization of the leadership structure in these firms, often with the displacement of local leaders.

In 1989, *Columbus Monthly* identified what it called "The Titans: Six Men Who Rule Columbus."[14] There were some familiar names and faces, but new ones as well: John W. Wolfe and, for the first time, John F. Wolfe, Leslie Wexner, John Fisher of Nationwide, Frank Wobst of Huntington Bank, and John B. McCoy of Bank One. The article also identified some "Future Titans" and "the Allies"—the latter a reference to the Wolfe interests and the Wexner interests, who, it was presumed, would be at war over the future development of the city. The article said that the independent Wexner had "shaken Columbus' power structure like no one else before him had," and of course this raised the issue of who could exert control and, it was hoped, provide leadership for the city's future.

It is useful to consider several comments regarding potential competition between the Wolfes and Wexner. In an interview in 1986, John F. Wolfe argued that the family's intention in Columbus was "to enhance the quality of life in the city and be a positive influence. . . . That's been our goal for three generations."[15] Although he insisted that the family did not have disproportionate influence, it does of course have immense power, based on considerable wealth accumulated through the years and on control of much of the Columbus media. In the same year, the *New York Times* reported that Wexner's net worth exceeded that of the Wolfes.[16] But it is *what* the Wolfes control in the media and financial areas that continues to ensure their effective power and influence. Despite this, Wexner is seen as independent in his plans and actions for Columbus and in his commitment to the public good as opposed to personal influence and power. In his independence and with his considerable financial resources, he has emerged as a major power in Columbus and one who is willing to provide forceful leadership to, as the *Economist* noted, "use his wealth to make Columbus a finer city."[17]

Change in a city's power elite usually happens slowly over time. But in the 1990s, several prominent Columbus families were faced with major disruptions. In 1991, Daniel Galbreath saw much of the family's real estate fortune disappear when market values for some properties declined sharply and internal family problems resulted in further financial stress.[18] Although he has never been as prominent or as dominant as his father, John, he has been a major player in the Columbus and national real estate and financial markets and in the exerting of family influence in the life of the city.

In June 1994, John W. Wolfe died. *Columbus Monthly* proclaimed it the "Death of the Titan . . . The End of an Era."[19] His death precipitated a change in the power structure even as John F. Wolfe assumed leadership of the family. The magazine noted that for two decades John W. "did what he wanted to do as the city's Titan among Titans. . . . What distinguished Wolfe was his love of power and control." He was "a fascinating figure, who used power in both extremes to improve the community and to cause pain." The last is a reference to Wolfe's response to individuals with whom he disagreed or who had fallen out of his favor, such as Kline Roberts (former director of the Chamber of Commerce), Will Hellerman (Nationwide Insurance), and Buck Rinehart (former mayor). His death suggested that the leadership base in the community would be broader in the future.

More recently, in October 1998, another kind of change helped to reshape the power structure. The merger of Bank One Corporation of Columbus with First Chicago NBD Corporation meant not only the shift of corporate headquarters from Columbus to Chicago but also the departure of John B. McCoy and family, a family that had been involved in banking in Columbus for over 60 years. The impact of the loss of Bank One, highly ranked among national banks, may lead to a loss in terms of national image and leadership as well as in local employment and philanthropy.

In its latest evaluation of the power structure, *Columbus Monthly* pictured Leslie Wexner on the cover; the lead article, entitled "Power Shift," suggested that there was "a new man at the top."[20] John W. Wolfe had been succeeded in this position, not by his cousin, John F. Wolfe, but by Wexner. Others in the "top five" included, as had been the case in recent years, the CEO of Nationwide Insurance, Dick McFerson, and the heads of two key banking establishments, John B. McCoy of Bank One (the article appeared in 1996, before the merger with First Chicago) and Franz Wobst of Huntington Bank. The absence of political leadership in the top group is not uncommon. Unlike many other U.S. cities, political leadership in Columbus does not necessarily provide dynamic civic leadership, due in part to politicians' historically close ties to the Wolfes.

Wexner, with his home in Columbus and with his obvious commitment to the city, has surely raised the ante, pushing the city toward new horizons. He has made his presence felt not only in the location and expansion of The Limited headquarters and distribution facilities but in his commitment to the community in his support of the United Way, the Columbus Foundation, the Children's Hospital, and other charitable organizations and to such cultural institutions as the Wexner Center for the Arts and COSI. In addition, he has taken an active role with respect to the Downtown and the Scioto Peninsula and with respect to suburban residential development in New Albany and the Easton shopping complex as well as the Tuttle mall in the northwest.

All of this may not please everyone in Columbus, representing as it does quite a different approach to civic leadership in town. A lengthy review of his career in the *New York Times* argued that Wexner is "undoubtedly . . . one of the great merchant princes of the late 20th century" but worried that a "distraction seems to be his concern with his legacy in Columbus . . . a second mayor shepherding cultural projects downtown while using his personal riches (his Limited stock alone is worth $1.25 billion) to develop an exclusive residential enclave nearby."[21] His penchant for urban planning is reflected in the New Albany development and the still evolving Easton mall, which Wexner, dubbed "the Merlin of the Mall" by the *Times,* has viewed as a reinvention of the concept of the mall that "will serve as a model for retail development in this country—if not in the world."

It is apparent that there are other new "actors" in the community who haven't, as yet, shown up among "the Titans," including members of the Schottenstein family and the Pizzuti interests. Even so, the evidence suggests that the two key figures remain John F. Wolfe and Leslie Wexner and that they may be able to share aspects of leadership for the long-term benefit of the city.

SOME FINAL THOUGHTS

Can Columbus remain the "easy" city that many of us appreciate and yet shed its "cow town" image to become something more than simply the fifteenth-largest city in the United States? Certainly, it has become a more cosmopolitan community, and it has evolved a culture that embraces a wide range of the arts, from symphony orchestra, ballet, art museum, and science center to a more diversified sports culture, both amateur and professional. It has become a major center for the "Information Age" and for activities associated with it.

One cannot help sensing that the city now has a healthy self-image, an image bolstered by its strong and growing economy and its place in one of the dynamic urban regions in the northeast quadrant of the nation. These qualities are reflected, of course, in the skyline, where the high-rise buildings of its service economy integrate nicely with the Capitol and other governmental structures. And there is evidence of potentially new and dynamic leadership prepared to take us into the twenty-first century. To borrow from an old and trite phrase, it may be that America has finally discovered Columbus—or that Columbus is discovering itself.

8

A Love Affair with Shopping Centers

S HORTLY AFTER WE ARRIVED IN COLUMBUS IN
the fall of 1949, friends from Pittsburgh came to town for the Pitt-
OSU football game. They were a lot better informed about the city than
we were and so introduced us to the then new concept of a shopping center,
the exciting Miracle Mile Town and Country Shopping Center newly
opened in 1948 on East Broad Street in Whitehall—and still there, fifty
years later!

In our excitement about something new—and almost every innovation excites in its own way—we hardly thought about the potential impact
of the shopping center upon the traditional downtown, with its retail stores,
abundant shoppers, congestion, and overall urban dynamic. But in the immediate post–World War II period, most residents of large cities were becoming aware of overcrowding, aging, and obsolescence in their downtown
areas and of increasing traffic congestion. Few could have foreseen the dramatic changes that were to occur in the next few years. In a sense, the fall
of 1949 marked a turning point not only in the development of Columbus
but in the trend to retail decentralization that was soon to capture the nation and change the way we thought about shopping.

Certainly, the new Town and Country Shopping Center reflected a
direct response to the problems faced in the Downtown, and it served to
initiate a series of actions that have helped to reshape the American city
ever since. This center strip unit, built by the Don Casto family interests,

replicated the Downtown main street, or at least one side of it, with its stretch of retail stores extending 3,000 feet along the length of the center—almost literally a "miracle mile"—and fronted by "a sea of parking," as it was often called. It was innovative and daring, with upward of a hundred stores, including a key "anchor" store, in this case the first suburban J.C. Penney store, and with the introduction of evening hours by one of its tenants, Kresge's. The Casto organization pioneered this type of shopping center and called it "the first properly balanced suburban Shopping Center to be built in the United States."[1]

Wonderful as it was, it wasn't the Castos' first venture into the development of shopping centers outside the urban core. As early as 1928, Casto built the Bank Block Building in Grandview Heights, a then new linear suburban commercial strip that attempted to accommodate the automobile. The strip, identified as a "taxpayer strip," provided space for a variety of commercial activities in sixteen street-level storefronts, with businesses and apartments on the second level and with curbside parking and a large parking lot for 350 cars at the rear of the strip.[2] The center's advertising emphasized convenience and safety for the increasing number of persons who chose to drive to the site to shop and transact business, noting that "wives and mothers might shop in safety" while at the center. The *New York Times,* in an article titled "An American Original: The Evolution of the Shopping Mall," identified the Bank Block as the Grandview Avenue Shopping Center and called it one of the earliest such facilities in the nation. Certainly, it was a forerunner of the larger automobile-based shopping centers of the post–World War II period and, eventually, of today's shopping mall.[3]

With the Casto family's base in Columbus and its initial success with the linear strip mall, the development of the Town and Country Center responded both to the problems of congestion and age in the urban core and to the outward expansion of residential development to existing suburbs and beyond in the post–World War II period. With the Town and Country Center, Casto established a prototype center that would be reproduced during the next ten years in similar but smaller centers built out in all major directions from the core: Central Point (1952), Graceland (1954), Northern Lights (1954), Great Eastern (1955), Great Western (1955), and Great Southern (1957). Each of these was patterned on the commercial strip concept, with the "sea of parking" space available for the shopper. The Lane Avenue Shopping Center, with a similar format but built by other interests, was opened in Upper Arlington in 1950.[4] These centers captured the local trade and drew customers in from the larger regional net that they reached through advertising and marketing. Accompanying their growth was the steady decline of the Downtown as the retail heart of the city.

Today, it is difficult to remember that each of these centers was constructed on the urban fringe of an expanding Columbus. Graceland Shopping Center, for example, is on the site of Graceland Farm and is less than a quarter mile north of the city's former northern boundary at Morse Road and the then northern limit of the High Street transit system. In the early 1950s, the land east of the High Street intersection on Morse Road was essentially farmland or land awaiting development, with several major low-density uses in place such as an airport, a golf course, a church summer campground (sold for development to other interests in 1997), and suburban residential properties, usually occupying an acre or more of land. A farm home still occupied the northeast corner of the High Street intersection in the early 1950s. Other early shopping centers were built in similar sites.

For example, The Great Southern Shoppers City, as it was originally called, was "located in virgin trading territory" on the southern edge of the city but abutting acreage associated with the Hartman Farms, which was then converting much of its farmland to other forms of development. The siting of the center anticipated the expansion of the city's market potential to the south.[5]

As the centers evolved, there was often considerable controversy over the necessary rezoning of the proposed sites from residential/apartment or agricultural zoning to commercial zoning, and there was concern among some local urban scholars that a "ring" of such facilities might serve to strangle growth in the city. In fact, as the new centers were developed and opened, it was apparent that existing traditional retail operations did experience market competition, forcing some to close their doors, perhaps prematurely, and leave the area. Within a relatively short time, however, the centers proved to be magnets not only for the consumer but for new retailing opportunities on streets adjacent to them. The net effect was an expanded set of retail activities both in the center and in the surrounding neighborhoods.

THE SHOPPING CENTER VERSUS DOWNTOWN

The phenomenon of the emerging and growing suburban shopping center in competition with the retail core of the Downtown in the postwar period caught the attention of sociologist Christen Jonassen at Ohio State University. He undertook a study of the consumer in Columbus in which

he measured consumer practices and attitudes in both settings, using interviews and questionnaires to gather data. He was interested in how such
measures as age, sex, marital status, race, education, home ownership, and
community size affected attitudes and were motivating factors that affected
the practices of consumers as they shopped in the Downtown or in the
suburbs. The study argued that "the consumer himself is the final arbiter
of the fortunes of the central business district and the suburban shopping
centers," and history has shown this to be correct. In his research, Jonassen
sought to determine the advantages and disadvantages of the two different
shopping areas as reflected in the shoppers' behavior, and this is the focus
of our interest in this section.[6]

What was occurring, of course, was the reorganization and restruc-
turing of the urban community resulting from the decentralization and
deconcentration of activities, ranging from manufacturing to the retail services initially and to other services eventually. In the retail field, there is
no better illustration of this point than the mainline department store. In
Columbus, the large Lazarus store dominated not only the Downtown but
the region as well and was the focal point for shopping, primarily owing to
its accessibility, convenience, range of goods, and sophistication.

Jonassen's research identified three major perceived "advantages" of
Downtown shopping as compared to shopping in the suburban centers,
"the most important being a larger selection of goods . . . , the second . . .
that people thought that they could do several errands at one time, and the
third that prices were cheaper downtown." At that time, these advantages
clearly outweighed the perceived disadvantages revealed in Jonassen's findings: "The most important was difficult parking; next in importance was
the crowded conditions found there, and the third traffic congestion." Over
time, as centers expanded, the advantages of Downtown shopping diminished, whereas the disadvantages loomed even greater.[7]

The key advantages perceived in the suburban shopping centers of the
early 1950s are not too surprising. The major advantage of the suburban
center, as noted by Jonassen, "was that it was nearer home, the next important was easy parking, and the third was that people considered the suburban stores kept more convenient hours." The research shows that "the
number one disadvantage of the suburban shopping centers was their lack
of a large selection of goods, the second that not all kinds of businesses were
represented there, and the third that prices were too high." The second
point, "that not all kinds of businesses were present in the centers," was clearly
evident in the initial development of the centers. After all, the Downtown
was more than a retail service center; historically, it had offered virtually all

of the services available in an urban region, including entertainment, theaters, restaurants, medical offices, banking and legal services, and government offices, in the most accessible part of the city region. Given this, it is interesting that Jonassen's research showed that "distance *under certain circumstances* was not a very important factor in determining shopping satisfaction with the downtown section of Columbus, . . . [but] parking was important in determining shopping satisfaction."[8]

The heart of Columbus has always been the intersection of the major east-west and north-south routes passing into and through the city—the Broad and High Streets intersection. The importance of accessibility as a factor shaping the development of urban centers in the United States, and of Columbus in particular, cannot be minimized. A recognition of the advantages of a central point of access led to urban development, and most urban theory supports this.

Historically, accessibility to the city was limited. Major changes in accessibility began before World War II in many larger communities, but in Columbus and most American cities, the more significant changes were felt in the postwar years. Automobile ownership and the expanded investment in highway systems that were intended to relieve congestion in the urban core helped to spur change. For example, in late 1949, Mayor James Rhodes and the City Council proposed building a 750-car deck over the Scioto River at Broad Street and an underground garage beneath the State House to help resolve problems of congestion in the Downtown.[9] And in 1950, the *Columbus Dispatch* carried an article, "Plans for Redevelopment Launched," that focused on the potential urban redevelopment of the Goodale Street area but also argued that the plans "must be co-ordinated with the Innerbelt system," which was still in the planning stages, a further response to traffic congestion and overcrowding in the core area. What was called "the huge Innerbelt highway . . . [was] planned to circle the Central Business District" and, in doing so, to "attract investment money" to the area.[10] At that time, of course, there was no interstate highway system in place. The Innerbelt concept was a bit of a novelty as a first step in trying to reduce core area congestion, but it remains a functional part of the city's highway system.

Residential populations were encouraged to move to what have become our suburbs, following the outward movement of manufacturing industries as they shifted from multiple-story and increasingly obsolete plants in the congested Downtown area to large, horizontal one-floor structures beyond the city's limits, where large tracts of land could be obtained at relatively low cost and where new postwar industries had also located. Federal policies encouraged suburban residential relocation under the federal mortgage lending programs, including the G.I. Bill, then in effect. Retailing and other core area consumer activities soon followed, with the shopping center being the prime example. The Downtown core, no longer the force controlling accessibility, began to lose its functions and even its form.

It's rather difficult in the late 1990s to recall the dynamism of the High Street shopping strip from Spring Street south to the big Lazarus store—a half-mile distance—that was Downtown's "anchor." For many, door-to-door window shopping was part of the excitement of the Downtown. The Lazarus store was a model of the successful old-line department store that carried virtually every product needed to maintain a home and that provided a variety of services to the public, including free home delivery of any purchase. Important, especially in the post–World War II years, was the provision of low-cost parking in several different Lazarus garages and valet parking, especially for women who were becoming drivers for the first time—services that allowed Lazarus to resist a move to suburbia for a number of years.

With one overwhelmingly dominant department store in place, the High Street area was resplendent with small specialty stores—women's and men's clothing, jewelry, luggage, furniture, and more—and larger stores providing a wider range of goods, such as Moby's, J.C. Penney, the Boston Store, The Union, Morehouse-Fashion, and others. Several hotels were still present along High Street, including the Chittenden at Spring and High, the Deshler-Wallick at Broad and High, the Neil House west across the street from the Capitol, and the Great Southern south of Lazarus. Good restaurants were there as well, with Seafood Bay, Kuennig's, Marzetti's just off High, Mills Cafeteria, and others, as well as seven movie theaters and one legitimate theater, the Hartman.

It might be useful to consider what has replaced or displaced the larger stores along High from north to south. Moby's site is occupied by the Federal Building; the Boston Store's building now houses federal judicial offices in a totally renovated building; The Union's building at Long and High has lost its retail activity at street level and has offices above; J.C. Penney's building houses offices; and, on South High, Morehouse-Fashion's store gave way to the construction at City Center. The hotels didn't fare much better: the Chittenden site is now home to the new high-rise building of the Workers' Compensation Bureau, the Deshler-Wallick has been replaced by the One Columbus office building, and the Neil House site is home to the Huntington Bank Building. Only the Great Southern survives, benefiting from historic restoration a few years ago. The retail activity once so important has been replaced with government buildings and other offices.

But there was more to the Downtown than High Street. East of Third Street along Broad was a small, upscale women's specialty fashion hub focused at Montaldo's store and the Maramor Restaurant. Lawyers' offices were to be found along East Gay and, to a lesser extent, East Long. The latter was also home to several pawnshops and a mix of other shops. Many of the other streets east of High Street were crammed with small retailers, often with apartments on upper floors. And the Central Market was still functioning between Third and Fourth Streets before urban renewal cleared that area and much of the land to the east of it.

At the time, the Downtown could still be called "the cradle of industry" and, as such, was the site for many small manufacturing operations just getting underway, often located in the upper floors of the retail shops along Downtown streets. There were large manufacturing firms, as well, in their own multistory plants. In fact, the case could be made for the Downtown as a major center for manufacturing in Columbus at this time.[11] Where and when did it disappear? Why haven't we noted the loss—or have we?

THE REGIONAL SHOPPING CENTER

By the 1960s, much of the retail activity associated with the Downtown had found its way to the suburban shopping centers. The Chamber of Commerce identified thirteen shopping centers operating in the Columbus metropolitan area at this time. With the outward expansion of the city through annexation and suburban growth, and with a net of interstate highways in place, the demand for expanded retail shopping encouraged the development of larger shopping centers. These were, in effect, *regional* shopping centers that typically had one or more "anchor" stores and a larger array of specialty stores offering a more diverse range of services to a larger retail shopping region. These were not strip shopping centers but rather a clustering of shops along an interior spine, often with anchor stores at either end of the spine. When first built, the centers or malls were uncovered.

A prime example of this experience is the story of Sears' attempts to enter the Columbus retail market, a market they had previously tapped only through mail-order outlets. As early as 1953, Sears had proposed to locate a huge retail and regional distribution center in the city near the intersection of Olentangy River Road and Dublin Road, but the project never materialized. Later, Sears planned a retail store for the northwest corner of Broad Street and Hamilton Road. But before construction was underway, Sears and Lazarus agreed to join in the development of one of the city's earliest regional shopping centers or malls, Northland, on Morse Road. The

center brought together two major retail organizations: Sears, essentially
new to Columbus, and Lazarus, for whom it was to be one of its first major
ventures outside of the Downtown. Lazarus had been committed to the
Downtown and had reinforced its decision by constructing several large
parking garages with low hourly rates to attract shoppers.

The Northland area had been the focus of a thorough review and planning effort prior to the development of the shopping center. The Northland
Study provided a rationale for full-scale social and economic development
of the area, including recommendations affecting schools, parks, residential
development, commercial development, and road and highway access.
Much of the planning was bypassed in response to pressure from development interests. One result has been that a reference to Morse Road is usually
to the problems that overdevelopment has created and to issues that should
be avoided.

The Northland Regional Mall, opened in 1964, had a larger purpose
and a larger market in mind than had previous shopping centers. With a
full panoply of stores and with two major anchors—Sears at the east end
of the central spine and Lazarus at the west—to attract the shopper, Northland hoped to reach a much larger geographic market territory than had
the earlier and smaller centers. The relatively new interstate system encouraged such thinking. Interstate 71 North was just a mile to the west, and it
was fully expected that Northland would tap the Mansfield market, an
hour's drive to the north. The Northland Regional Mall did achieve a much
greater market territory than the older shopping centers, but it never attracted a significant market from Mansfield. In 1969, Lazarus located a
store in Mansfield.

Northland's geographic location was considered quite good at that
time, and the center was the major shopping mall in Columbus as late as
1989. But in recent appraisals of the mall's future, it has been argued that
the "geography" has changed and that a mall would not be built on the site
today. The site is judged to be hard to get to and inconvenient given Morse
Road traffic and the nature of competition, especially from the new Polaris
site but from the Tuttle and Easton malls as well.[12]

One might review to what extent a regional center of this type served
as an economic stimulus to its neighborhood in earlier years. By the mid-
1960s, Morse Road, the major east-west artery for Northland Mall, was
already overcrowded with strip retail development on both sides of the road.
For example, from the interstate on the west to Cleveland Avenue on the
east, a distance of two miles, the following commercial operations were
present:

  8 service stations, usually occupying intersections
20 franchised carry-out food services
  8 department or discount stores
  5 banks, including Huntington's Operations Center
  4 automobile agencies and related lots
  5 office buildings
  5 homes and 2 churches (holdovers from an earlier day)
  7 "other" commercial land uses
      Northland Mall and three small convenience shopping
      centers of 3 to 12 stores

Even today, the Morse Road mix of stores and traffic—the "visual clutter"—frustrates and amazes. In an article in the *New York Times Magazine,* the writer Molly O'Neill, a Columbus native, discussed the colorfully revived features of New York's Great White Way. In so doing, she noted her brother's comments upon seeing Times Square: "'Hey, Morse Road!' exclaims my brother who is visiting from Columbus, Ohio. To him, Times Square looks like miles of Midwestern strip malls, only brighter and more densely packed." She went on to say that "once upon a time, New York was the mother lode. I couldn't wait to get out of Columbus and taste the city. So you can imagine my dismay to awaken, 15 years later, to find Columbus in Times Square."[13]

The large regional shopping center was the essential model for further suburban retail expansion, both nationally and in Columbus, with Northland, Eastland, and Westland centers constructed and opened by 1970. These larger and more attractive centers began to dominate the market, and many of the smaller and older strip centers lost key stores as they began to show their age. Nonetheless, there was a concomitant modernization of some centers and expansion of small strip centers and other retail outlets as suburbanization continued.

DOWNTOWN REVITALIZATION

In the same decade, the Downtown emerged from the doldrums of the 1950s, especially with the construction of several new high-rise buildings—the City National Bank Building (now Bank One), Sheraton Hotel, and the Reliance Insurance Company office building—at or near the Broad and Third Streets intersection. These were the first high-rise structures erected in the city since the Lincoln-LeVeque Tower. None of these replaced the retail outlets once typically part of the core area, but they were forerunners

Broad Street looking west in the mid-1970s. The Rhodes State Office Building dominates in the distance with insurance company offices, churchs, and cultural organizations, such as the Columbus Museum of Art and COSI, in the foreground.

of the kind of new growth that the Downtown might experience. Promotional efforts by the city and the Chamber of Commerce to attract the headquarter offices of national firms as well as local companies to the Downtown were ultimately successful. The new buildings in the mid-1960s—the high-rise Nationwide headquarters on North High, the Borden Company's national headquarters on East Broad, and those of the American Electric Power Company at Front and Long—were welcome additions to what had been a rather bleak Downtown. But even as these companies identified with Columbus in their new buildings, there was concern about how Downtown might be saved or revitalized. Clearly, the missing ingredient was a strong retail base that would attract both local and regional shoppers to the city's core.

In 1972, Mayor Tom Moody established a task force to study the Downtown for sites for potential growth. By 1974, the focus was upon the three blocks immediately south of Capitol Square. Development there "was arguably engendered by the effort to restore the historic Ohio Theatre . . . [which] preservationists successfully shielded . . . from demolition over 2 decades ago." The area proved to be the site "for the core of what was hoped would be a downtown renaissance."[14]

The Capitol South project got underway in 1976 after the city acquired the land in the three-block area south of State Street, and federal development grants were made available for retail development. Private investment financed most of the new construction in the area. City investment was to be recouped with funds from the leases that had been let to developers of the area. Eventually, most of the old buildings in the three-block area were demolished. Plans were rather optimistic, anticipating up to two million square feet of office space and up to 800,000 square feet for retail activity, a hotel, and residential space. A garage for as many as 5,000 cars was to be part of the package. It was estimated that with development between 5,000 and 8,000 new jobs and millions in new taxes would be generated. It was argued that "Capitol South is an essential element in the total plan to revitalize downtown Columbus," and no doubt it was.[15]

The initial effort in developing a site was construction of the Centrum in 1979 at the southeast corner of High and Town Streets to create a setting for social activity and thus to attract or keep people in the Downtown. The Centrum, which included a fountain and a rink for skating, was also intended to be a site where a variety of special events could be held. It was modestly successful initially but was closed by 1986. More important were plans in the early 1980s by the Galbreath interests for an office building and new hotel, the Hyatt, to the east of the Ohio Theatre.

In 1981, the Taubman Company, with ties to Leslie Wexner, came on the scene after two earlier development efforts, including one by the Rouse Company, had failed to materialize. Taubman was initially committed to build 200,000 square feet of retail facilities in the first block south of Capitol Square and later added over 500,000 square feet in the second block. Three major department stores and a host of retail shops, restaurants, and other activities were planned. The department stores, Lazarus, Marshall Fields, and Jacobson's, would be the anchor stores so essential to such a retail effort. The third block south was to be the site of a large garage topped with a residential unit.

By 1983, the Hyatt Hotel and Galbreath office building, the restored Ohio Theatre and its addition to the east, and the Beggs Building formed the southern edge of Capitol South; to the west on High, the Huntington Center was under construction on the old Neil House Hotel site; and to the north was the James A. Rhodes State Office Tower, completed in 1975. Capitol Square was the focus for core area development that was to be finally realized with the construction of the City Center mall, which opened in August 1989. With its major anchor stores and with anywhere from 120 to 150 shops, restaurants, and other activity centers, City Center renewed and refocused interest in the Downtown as a major shopping area.

Everyone wasn't necessarily pleased with the mall, but it did provide a much needed and reasonably dynamic retail center not only for Columbus but for the larger region as well. Those who were displeased regretted and opposed the displacement and loss of the small shops that had lined the east side of High Street between Town and Main Streets, and others had argued for the integration of some older buildings, such as the Morehouse-Fashion building opposite Lazarus, into City Center. William H. Whyte, architect and urban critic, had commented, while visiting Columbus in 1987, that "good downtown malls have a lot of glass that opens them up to the outside" but that if they are sealed off they may be disorienting to the consumer.[16] On a return visit at the opening of the City Center mall on August 18, 1989, he praised the mall but continued to lament the absence of windows and window displays and confessed that he didn't like blank walls such as the western wall of City Center along High Street, where small and varied retail shops had once lined the street.[17] Some critics were concerned that with the concentration of retail activities under one expansive roof and virtually none on the streets, the streets would be deserted and would lack vitality. Their concerns have been borne out as retail activity beyond City Center has steadily declined, with the closing of the old Woolworth's store in 1997 being symbolic of the trend. Nonetheless, the Downtown continued to add new high-rise office buildings to replace the retail sites, including the Riffe Center and the Workers' Compensation Bureau Building, the renovated Beggs Building, and most recently, the Fifth-Third Bank's new building at State and High.

After almost ten years, the City Center mall remains, not surprisingly, the principal shopping unit in the Downtown. There have been changes in the mall, and stores come and go, but it has had the ability to attract both local shoppers, especially Downtown professionals and office workers, and business and convention travelers from well beyond the region.

City Center mall and the three older regional malls—Northland, Eastland, and Westland, owned by the Richard Jacobs Group of Cleveland— each with in excess of one million square feet of space, clearly dominated the central Ohio market at the beginning of the 1990s. Among the latter three, upgrading of the centers with new stores and an occasional new "anchor," such as the J.C. Penney store in Northland in 1980, kept them competitive. But experts in retail marketing long argued that the Columbus area was undermalled and consequently" underserved, even as it was well served by strip malls. In comparable cities such as Cincinnati, Cleveland, and Indianapolis, more than one-third of the total retail space was in regional malls, whereas in Columbus only about one-fifth was so situated. This issue was addressed by the early 1990s with announcements for three large commercial undertakings planned for the northern part of the city-region—the Tuttle Crossing mall, the Polaris project, and the Easton Complex.[18]

THE MILLENNIUM AND BEYOND

These new developments—the Tuttle Crossing mall, the Polaris project, and the Easton Complex—have suggested to some observers that a new era in shopping is about to begin in Columbus. They promise the latest in retailing and, to an increasing degree, in entertainment and sports-related activities and a host of other services. They represent part of the continuing movement of commercial and retail activity northward, or upstream, in the region as they seek to satisfy the growing upscale residential consumer market. On the way, somewhat smaller centers have opened at Mill Run and in the Sawmill area, with a mix of retail stores aimed at this suburban market in the northwest and relying on the I-270 Outerbelt as an integral part of the planning.

When the plans for the Tuttle Crossing mall and Easton mall projects, both ventures of the Wexner and Taubman interests, were confirmed in 1992, the Polaris site lost its initial mall component and switched its focus to office and entertainment facilities. The Mall at Tuttle Crossing, as it was originally called, is a traditional mall of 980,000 square feet with adjacent extensive parking for thousands of cars. It has highway access from a privately financed interchange at Tuttle Crossing Boulevard and I-270, where Dublin, Hilliard, and Columbus meet, that opened in 1989. With its more than 125 stores, including four anchors (Lazarus, Marshall Fields, J.C. Penney, and Sears), it has defined its purpose as an upscale mall in an expanding upscale market. The Tuttle mall opened in July 1997 to generally enthusiastic reviews and scores of shoppers. Les Wexner has described it as "probably the standard garden variety [mall]" but on a larger and grander scale.[19]

On the other hand, the Easton Complex is what Wexner has called a "21st century village" of over ten million square feet on former farmland that had been assembled for development since 1986. It is planned to have not only the Easton Market shopping center but a leisure-time retail,

entertainment, and sports complex in its Town Center. Other retail stores
are in the HQ Plaza on the north side of Morse Road, developed jointly by
the Casto and Taubman interests, and there is an extensive office park and
a series of residential neighborhoods in the complex as well. It is, in a sense,
a planned community development project that some have compared to
Reston, Virginia. Like Tuttle mall, Easton is located on I-270, but at a re-
configured and redesigned Morse Road interchange in northeastern Franklin
County. To the north and east are the new residential communities and
recreational sites in the countryside associated with the expanding New Albany area.[20]

Meanwhile, the Polaris Centers of Commerce site of 1,270 acres in
southern Delaware County, with its own I-71 interchange in place since
1991, has evolved as a major office and entertainment center with an am-
phitheater and other activities. In 1994, Bank One initiated plans for a
400,000-square-foot office complex at the Polaris site to open in 2000. Not
without controversy, Polaris is completing an upscale mall project with five
anchor stores planned, Saks, Lord & Taylor's, Kaufmann's, J.C. Penney,
Sears, and its own Towne Center.

Even in the planning stages, these developments faced some of the
same challenges that shopping center developers had faced in the past. Major issues involved the assembling of the necessary land for development,
most of which was agricultural land ripe for development on the edge of
the urban area. Then they had to gain approval for the rezoning of the land
from agricultural use to commercial and/or residential. The zoning battle
in the Tuttle mall case ended in a referendum that challenged the vote of
Columbus City Council permitting rezoning. The referendum, which lost,
reflected local residents' concern about the impact of the proposed mall on
property values and neighborhood safety and on the well-being of already
existing small shopping units and other community facilities. And of
course, the question of highway accessibility to and from the sites, both for
local residents and for outsiders, had to be dealt with, if not resolved, before
development could occur. Unfortunately, the sprawl of development and
highway congestion go hand in hand, not only in central Ohio but in most
large urban regions, and the issue continues to confront society, with little
hope of resolution.

SOME CLOSING THOUGHTS

The shopping center has come a long way both in Columbus and in the
nation since the opening of the Miracle Mile Town and Country Shopping

Center on East Broad Street in the late 1940s. The Casto organization played a critical role in the development of the mall concept, as we have noted, and they remain "players" in the retail market today, with interests in eighteen local shopping centers.[21] The first centers are now almost a half-century old and show their age. No matter how well maintained they may be, they have inevitably lost out to the competitive challenges of the latest waves of development, just as the ordinary retail store had to face the competitive challenges posed by these early centers. Today, even the regional malls recognize that their markets are no longer secure as they lose anchor stores and other units and as the Easton Complex, Tuttle mall, and Polaris projects seem to threaten their survival.

Currently, Columbus wrestles with the problems associated with sprawl and congestion, even as additional new privately financed interchanges, which effectively alter the concept of the interstate highway, are sought, and as experts in the retail merchandising field question whether the area is now *overmalled,* especially in the northern sector of Columbus, and ask what the consequences might be.

Nonetheless, shopping centers have been an active force that has helped to reshape the downtowns of America and to support and sustain the suburbanization that began in the post–World War II years and continues, almost unabated, to this day. With the pressure to look inward to the city core—to the downtown—one must ask whether the Columbus Downtown can again generate an environment that can compete successfully with the new mall projects and stimulate and attract the consumer, whether local resident or tourist, rich or poor, urban or rural. How this will all play out in the retail sector with a new COSI opened on the west bank of the Scioto River, as the Short North extends its reach southward into the northern part of Downtown, as the Convention Center expands, and as a Downtown arena becomes a reality, remains speculative and is a challenging question as we enter the millennium.

9

Neighborhood Vignettes

WHEN WE FIRST ARRIVED IN COLUMBUS IN the autumn of 1949, the only "neighborhood" that I knew or cared about was that associated with the university. In due course, I established the geographic bounds within which we would find an apartment within walking distance of campus. Without thinking about it, we had found a community of—it would be nice to say "scholars"—but in fact a community of students in which we began our Columbus sojourn.

This led, ultimately, to some serious considerations regarding future residential locations and the geographic bounds that affected them. In finding short-term housing, our major considerations were cost and convenience to the campus. Later, when looking for a permanent home, I decided that my options lay within a space defined on the south by the university, on the west by the Olentangy River (Upper Arlington was clearly beyond our means), by the railroads and, ultimately, the interstate to the east, and by the city boundary to the north (then at Morse Road). This rational decision was based on the distance from home to work and on the range of housing stock in this area and its price, the latter a key factor. Within this context, we also considered a set of cultural qualities such as education, church, shopping, and recreation that one could associate with individual neighborhoods. Almost fifty years later, we continue to live within these bounds!

Obviously, neighborhoods evolve differently and change differently over time, but each has its own unique history and geography and, potentially, its own future. My purpose here is to consider several different neighborhoods in the region and to gauge the characteristics that gave rise to them and that continue to affect them.

By the early 1950s, I had come to learn a great deal about the geography of the city and about some of its neighborhoods, primarily through my doctoral research, which took me into many of the industrial neighborhoods of the city. This chapter considers several neighborhoods, all part of the Columbus whole, in which I have had specific interest as a result of my research and writings and the field trips that I have given through the years.

FRANKLINTON: GEOGRAPHY AND HISTORY

Franklinton is a classic example of how a community's history and geography may have shaped its development. Some of the same factors that influenced the area's past may also play a key role in its future.[1]

Franklinton was the first community of settlers in the central Ohio region, and it remains, two hundred years later, with the ongoing development of the Scioto Peninsula, the focal point of development, certainly in the city but in the region as well. Quite early on, it earned the nickname "the Bottoms," a reference to the fact that it was settled in 1797 in the floodplain of the Scioto River. That reference is still valid two hundred years later as the area remains concerned about the potential for flooding and as the impact of new developments on the "Peninsula" continues to shape decisions affecting its future.

We noted earlier that Lucas Sullivant, a Virginian, explored the land on the west side of the Scioto River and established the Franklinton settlement. The land lay between the Scioto and Little Miami River to the west within the Virginia Military District, the area set aside to provide grants to Virginian veterans of the Revolutionary War. As such, it was the first part of Ohio opened to permanent settlement (see map 2, p. 10).

Since the initial site in the floodplain of the Scioto caused many problems for the community—including frequent flooding, uncertain water supply, impure water, and the various fevers, ague, and other ailments associated with low-lying areas—the Franklinton settlement was soon moved to higher lands a short distance to the west. Later, when the land east of the river was opened to settlement, a group of Virginians acquired title to the land and, in 1812, offered land and a pledge to the legislature to construct several government buildings for the capital. The offer was accepted, and Columbus was established as the site of the state capital.

As government business expanded in Columbus, the new town soon

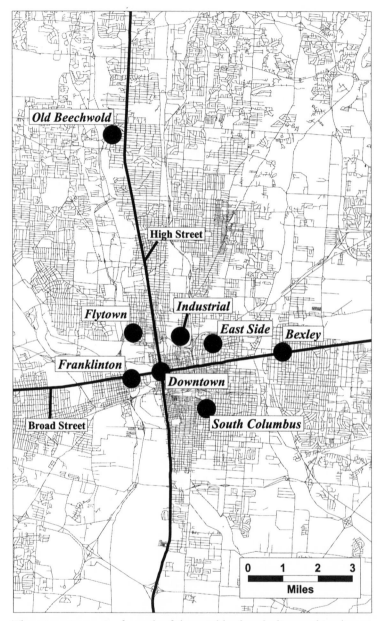

The approximate site for each of the neighborhoods discussed in chap. 9 is shown here. All are within city limits—Bexley is an enclave of Columbus—and each is illustrative of the different histories and characteristics that typify individual neighborhoods.

took precedence over Franklinton, which was destined to develop in the shadow of the new capital city. By 1824, the county court was moved to Columbus, and the city assumed the functions of a county seat. With the opening of the twelve-mile Feeder Canal from Lockbourne to Columbus in 1831 and the National Road, which reached Columbus in 1833, the predominance of Columbus was reinforced. The canal's terminus was at the foot of Broad Street on the east bank of the river; Franklinton did not share directly in canal traffic, although it did carry on barge trade with the south. Westward-moving travelers on the National Road stopped before crossing the Scioto River, and Columbus blossomed as the commercial center catering to the travelers' needs.

In a sense, Franklinton, virtually in the heart of the city, remains geographically isolated. It is bounded on three sides by the Scioto River, and to the west, on its fourth side, is both a physical and a political boundary: the physical boundary lies where the floodplain meets the uplands of the Hilltop; the political boundary—every bit as strong a boundary as the physical one—is represented by the state-held land and properties that restrict private investment initiatives. In addition, the community is crossed by transportation arteries that suggest accessibility but often serve as barriers—railroads and railroad overpasses, I-70, and Route 315. What remains on the floodplain is a historically interesting but hardly spectacular older community of mixed land uses, but one without well-established bonds with adjacent areas, including the Downtown.

The river, despite its relatively minor size and frequent bridging, remains a barrier rather than a connective corridor to the Downtown. Turn-of-the-century plans that called for an imaginative linking of the east and west banks of the river in a governmental complex might have produced an exciting solution to the problem, but they were never carried out. The existing Central High School, now modified as the site of the new and grander COSI, is a reminder of those plans. Today, efforts to revive the area with COSI and other public activities in the "Scioto Peninsula" area promise a more exciting future.

Vital to developments in Franklinton is, of course, the completion of the Franklinton flood wall. The threat of catastrophic flooding is less ominous than in the past—the flood of 1913 took 93 lives and left 20,000 homeless, and in the flood of 1959, over 10,000 were made homeless—but it is clear that an extended flood wall is an essential ingredient to any development plan for the community. Plans call for the extension of the flood wall from a point near I-70 and the Hilltop south to Frank Road, a

project scheduled to be completed by 2002. The wall will open considerable acreage for new housing and commercial development and promises
opportunities for economic growth in the area.

Somewhat more than 15,000 residents live in Franklinton today. They
are part of what one community leader once identified as "a low-income,
high-crime, high-dropout, integrated, mostly Appalachian, residential
neighborhood with declining population and the cheapest houses in
town."[2] Today, many of these same traits remain: housing costs are low, but
only 30 percent of the homes are owner occupied; unemployment is almost
four times the county average; and 50 percent of the population lives below
the poverty level.[3]

Yet there is strong pride among the community's residents, as represented by the long battle undertaken to save the Central High School building, an important community symbol, and the related development of the
Scioto Peninsula as the site for major public institutions. The battle may
have been only partially won, but it was a victory for the community's spirit.
Today, building on its sense of history and on its meager base of a few old
historic buildings, such as Harrison House, the Franklinton Cemetery, and
the Toledo & Ohio Central Railroad Station (once reputedly described by
the distinguished Yale architect Paul Randolph as "the most fascinating
thing I've ever seen!"), Franklinton encompasses in the Peninsula what has
been one of the most valuable pieces of undeveloped urban real estate in the
nation. Perhaps the community's history and geography will finally work to
its benefit.

EASTWARD MOVEMENT AND
NEIGHBORHOOD DEVELOPMENT

My interest in the different neighborhoods that make up Columbus
was sparked even further when, as a young faculty member, I attended several seminar meetings under the direction of Professor Christen Jonassen of
the Department of Sociology. In 1955, he held a seminar dealing with urban research issues facing the Columbus community. Each seminar meeting
featured a reasonably distinguished public figure who presented his ideas to
the group for discussion. Professor Jonassen invited me to attend the seminar whenever I could, and it was my good fortune to hear then Mayor
Maynard "Jack" Sensenbrenner discuss his visions for the city and region.
At a second seminar, I heard Rabbi Jerome Folkman discuss his ideas about
community and neighborhood growth, in general and as experienced by

his congregation, Temple Israel, in particular. At that time, after a survey of the congregation, a decision was made to move from the temple's historic location on Bryden Road to a new site on the far east side at what is now the junction of East Broad Street and I-270, a move that occurred in 1958.

Given this recent experience with the congregation's move, Rabbi Folkman asserted, not as a "principle" but as a general observation, that "Jews move eastward in American cities." He noted that they tend to locate to the east of the older urban core and to move further eastward over time. Certainly this has been true for Columbus, and a quick recall of several other cities—Cleveland and Pittsburgh sprang to mind—seemed to support the idea. Further investigation revealed that there were, however, many exceptions to the "rule," but the idea had merit and challenged this geographer to further consider it. In addition, it prompted numerous other questions about how cultural differences may help to explain the geographic spread of populations by neighborhood. In so doing, it provided the basis for a doctoral dissertation on the topic by Charles W. Minshall, "A Model of Residential Site Selection: The Jewish Population of Columbus, Ohio."[4]

The opening sentence of Minshall's dissertation explained the geographer's interest: "The most unique spatial characteristic of the Jewish population in American cities is its concentration in specific areas." There is a "pattern of spatial cohesion" that reflects the importance of certain institutions, such as the temple, the synagogue, educational activities, social institutions, shopping facilities, and other organizations, and an absence of restrictive covenants and other social constraints in the residential choices that Jews may make.

Clearly, the residential movement of Jews in Columbus has been to the east. The older settlement was east of High Street in the urban core and historically extended eastward on Broad Street and related streets into Bexley. Minshall notes that "in almost every other city of comparable size and age, Jewish movement toward the periphery has been motivated in no small measure by pressures exerted by both Negro and white migrant groups moving outward from the inner city." This was true in Columbus initially, but the presence of physical barriers, such as the raised Norfolk and Western Railroad tracks to the west of Alum Creek and the creek itself, helped to create "an interstitial buffer zone along the sides of the Jewish sector."[5] The residential movement continued eastward and continues today, having extended to Eastmoor, Whitehall, and Berwick over time.

The movement has been sectoral in that accessibility between the urban core and the residential sites eastward on Broad Street was a critical factor shaping the choice of where to live. A "sector theory" of urban growth was proposed by Homer Hoyt in the 1930s, based on property values in a hundred American cities.[6] Hoyt argued that the highest income families in American cities, regardless of their religious affiliation, lived in a pie- or wedge-shaped sector of the city which was on relatively high ground that was highly accessible to the core but had access as well to parks and country clubs on the periphery. Such an area was free of factory noise and smoke and removed from the poorer sections of the community. It was, in effect, the high-rent district, where newer residents pushed outward within the sector to areas on the fringe commanding higher prices. And, Hoyt argued, this high-rent sector effectively determined where and how the other sectors of the city evolved.

In Columbus, well-to-do Gentile families had earlier established such a pattern of residential site selection east on Broad Street from the urban core to the edge of Columbus in the mid-1800s and to the new community of Bexley in the late 1800s. Minshall noted that "a small group of upper-class German-Jewish families who could trace their years in Columbus back to the middle of the 19th century" had made similar moves. But by the late 1930s, Bexley remained predominantly Gentile.[7] After World War II, the eastward movement of the Jewish population was greatly accelerated as part of the larger suburbanization movement occurring in the central Ohio region.

Today, as one moves eastward on Broad Street from the urban core, one sees intermixing of large old homes of the past—many of them themselves now converted to a commercial function—with commercial buildings and a variety of institutional structures. At the southeast corner of Broad and Fourth Streets is the Columbus Club, occupying and preserving a mid-nineteenth-century home built by a railroad magnate and once a governor's mansion, a reminder that the street was once the site for the homes of successful businessmen. Further east, the Columbus Foundation occupies a lovely mansion—it, too, was formerly home to a governor and, before that, to a Columbus industrialist—that reflects the character of the street earlier in this century. And until her death in 1994, Lucille Taylor lived in the family's mid-nineteenth-century home at 1400 East Broad, the last surviving private residence on East Broad Street west of Alum Creek.

By the end of this century, Bexley may no longer be, as Minshall suggested in 1971, the "deeply buried enclave within Columbus."[8] Alum Creek and the parkland to the east provide a clear separation from the older communities to the west, and here the eastward-moving elite built their fine homes, if not quite the huge estates common to Cleveland and Pittsburgh. But Bexley's paramount role as the community in which the city's "old money" lives has been challenged through the years, first with the growth and expansion of the Arlington area in the 1920s and later, and currently by the relatively new communities in the Dublin, Worthington, and New Albany suburban areas.

A STREET CALLED HOME

Probably no community has been captured as well as the black community of Columbus in the paintings of the artist Aminah Robinson and in her related book, *A Street Called Home*.[9] The street is Mt. Vernon Avenue, the old commercial heart of the black community, and the time depicted, the 1930s and 1940s, is that of Robinson's childhood. Here are reminders of a way of life now largely lost and of a community more vibrant and dynamic, perhaps, and more comfortable with itself than it is now.

Robinson recalls the earlier migration of blacks into Columbus and their settlement in what was called "the Blackberry Patch," close to the finer homes of the white upper middle class on the city's East Side, where many of them worked. Change occurred when one of the earliest government housing undertakings in the country, Poindexter Village (named for the Reverend James Poindexter and dedicated by Eleanor Roosevelt), opened in 1940, and families moved out of the Blackberry Patch to raise their children in the new community.

Robinson's parents were among the early families to move into Poindexter Village. As she recalls, "They walked with everybody else up and down Mount Vernon Avenue. That was a self-sufficient street; it knew how to survive. People wove in and out with their horses and carts and trucks. You could hear the street cries; people bartered and bought and sold; people played and danced. Everything you could need you could find on Mount Vernon Avenue."

If her words ring true, her paintings and drawings do so even more. As we walk along Mt. Vernon Avenue with her, we meet a score of local characters, many of whom in those years had their counterparts in white neighborhoods as well. She recalls "The Vegetable Man," "The Umbrella Man," "The Chickenfoot Lady," "The Iceman," "The Ragman," and others. She remembers crowded Mt. Vernon Avenue, where the storefronts of Woolworth's 5&10, Mort's Menswear, Schiff's Shoe Shop, the Cameo Theater, Swan Cleaners, the Trolley Car Restaurant, Limelight Lounge, and others lined the street. As she says, it was "a self-sufficient street; it knew how to survive. . . . A street called home."[10]

But Mt. Vernon Avenue wasn't alone in providing the commercial and social life for the community. Long Street was also an early center for a variety of black and white businesses and places of entertainment. There were theaters, hotels, nightclubs, and bars catering to the cultural life of the community and beyond. The Lincoln Theater, still awaiting its revival, started out as the Ogden in 1929 and brought major black musicians to the community to entertain both black and white audiences that intermixed in the life of this street.

These remain the major commercial streets of the community today, although they are more subdued than in the past, for the community has changed over time. During the 1950s and 1960s, federal urban renewal activity and interstate highway construction helped to reshape the area and change the neighborhood. Throughout the United States, such efforts were seen by blacks as forces designed to bring about "black removal" from parts of the urban area rather than as positive actions that would enhance black neighborhoods. Certainly, the destruction of homes to clear the path for Interstate 71 through the East Side forced the movement of blacks eastward and isolated a remaining few west of I-71.

Just south of the railroads and north of Mt. Vernon Avenue, an area of over thirty acres was cleared, through urban renewal, of 250 dwelling units and commercial structures, all in dilapidated or deteriorating condition. Public housing was expanded in the area with the construction of 176 two-story apartments units and the two fifteen-story Bolivar Arms Towers with 558 units in the early 1960s. Later, in 1971, the Trevitt Heights development of 155 twin-singles was built in an attempt to encourage home ownership. With Poindexter Village a short distance to the southeast and Windsor Terrace to the north of the railroads, this area had the largest number of public housing facilities in the city.

In a sense, too, the concentration of public housing led to segregation by race, as the black population, which had accounted for 6.5 percent of the city's population in 1900, reached 11.6 percent by 1940. Today, blacks, who make up approximately one-fourth of the city's population, still live predominantly in this eastern section of the city, a reflection in part of the migration, primarily of whites, to the suburbs. One result has been the concentration of poverty in the city. Over time, these conditions have had a heavy impact upon the East Side neighborhoods that have traditionally housed the black population, and a disproportionate number there live in poverty. There is little doubt today that the public housing programs have been a key factor affecting these trends, despite their intent.

In the 1970s, revitalization of the community was underway, especially with the development of Mt. Vernon Plaza, the high-rise residential unit with commercial properties on the first floor. It remains the commercial core of the area. And in 1984, the rehabilitation of the historic Pythian Temple and Theater as the Martin Luther King Jr. Center for Performing and Cultural Arts was undertaken. More recently, the development of recreational park space and the related relocation and renovation of area homes have encouraged stability. The erection of the offices of the Columbus Urban League on Mt. Vernon Avenue has helped focus attention on the "street" once again.

SOUTH COLUMBUS AND GERMAN VILLAGE

"The Southside began as one of the city's early neighborhoods in the 1800s and reached maturity in the 1940s. Since the Second World War, the Southside changed relatively little." So states a Development Department review of the area in 1991.[11] In 1952 I undertook an assignment to research the relative growth or decline of the South Columbus community, since it was assumed by city leaders that this area lagged behind other parts of the city in several different ways. What was causing this lag, and why was it so pronounced?[12]

Part of the area had been platted within a few years of the city's creation in 1812, and it soon began to grow. Through the early years, immigrant settlement, especially that by German migrants in the mid-1800s, characterized this growth.[13] The pattern of in-migration would continue with industrial expansion even into the World War II period, when large numbers of Appalachian and southern black workers moved into the area seeking jobs.

In the late 1800s, with the coming of railroads and the development of southeastern Ohio resources, such as iron ore, coal, natural gas, and timber, the area began to expand as a major industrial site. By the 1900s, it was regarded as one of the three major industrial communities in the city.[14] In the immediate post–World War II years, the manufacturing plants, located principally along Marion Road, were major contributors to the local economy, and major firms like Buckeye Steel Castings, Federal Glass, Hercules Box, and J. W. Brown Manufacturing provided jobs and growth.

But as we looked at the area in the 1950s, it was clear that it was not keeping pace with changes taking place in other parts of the Columbus region. From 1930 to 1950, for example, the area accounted for only one-seventh of the city's population growth, and actual losses occurred in the census tracts on the southernmost fringe. Little new industry entered the area after the war, and by 1953 the area accounted for less than one-fifth of the city's manufacturing plants and a smaller percentage of industrial employment. Furthermore, the South Columbus community did not share in the areal expansion, especially through annexation, that was occurring elsewhere in the city.

Through interviews with community leaders and others, a number of issues emerged that explained, in part, some of the problems facing the area. For one thing, the area's age and related obsolescence contributed to both its residential and its industrial makeup. The area was densely settled with worker homes, usually small homes on small lots, typical of the German heritage. Likewise, much of the industry was old, with few new firms. Closely related were the perceived spatial limitations. Little vacant land was available for new construction, and no new developments were planned for the area. Old railroad lines still cut through the region, and highway access was restricted.

But the overriding set of conditions that were judged to have hindered growth were those related to various forms of pollution. Certainly, the area suffered from the by-products of its manufacturing plants and the railroads. Dirt, odors, smoke, and other forms of pollution spread over the residential areas, thanks to the working railroad yards and the "heavy" industries, such as basic steel furnaces, operating along the southern margin of the community. One suspects that these levels of pollution were accepted "norms" in the area in the heyday of industrialization.

More insidious were the airborne pollutants carried into the South Side community from the institutional and industrial facilities to the south and west adjacent to the Scioto River. As noted in chapter 2, the placement of such facilities in the direct path of the southwesterly winds that cross the region meant that fumes and odors from sewage treatment plants, rendering plants, and slaughterhouses would affect the environment of the South Columbus neighborhood, thereby limiting its growth. Thus, although this southernmost part of the city got an early start, the old maxim that "cities grow upstream" appeared to hold, and the neighborhood subsequently failed to change and grow with the rest of the city. Local consensus held that the dust, dirt, and odors so common to the area were factors contributing to its lack of growth.

More recently, the annexation of Marion Township and access to the interstate system and Outerbelt were important steps in calling attention to the potential for expansion to the south. The area is now well served by rail and major highways, such as I-270 and an improved Route 104 (Refugee Road), and the expansion of the Rickenbacker Air Base should increase its accessibility both within and beyond the region.

On the other hand, a renaissance of part of the South Columbus community was sparked in the late 1950s by a totally different set of actions. The threat of demolition of many blighted properties in the old German neighborhoods in the northern section of the community led to an effort by residents to save their community by rehabilitating some of the houses. Frank Fetch, a city employee, is generally given credit for organizing this activity and imaginatively creating the basis for German Village. The village was recognized in 1960 by the City Council, as were two related organizations. The German Village Society was formed as a private, nonprofit corporation to promote preservation and renovation in the area—an effort called by some, in a challenge to federal urban renewal efforts, "urban renewal through private enterprise."[15] The German Village Commission, on the other hand, was created by an ordinance passed by City Council to review proposed changes to buildings within the area to preserve the historic character of what became in 1963 the German Village Historic District and Commission. This was the first area commission created in Columbus. By 1975, the village was placed on the National Register of Historic Places.

German Village is a 233-acre area bounded by Livingston Avenue on the north, High Street on the west, Nursery Lane on the south, and Grant, Jaeger, and Lathrop Streets to the east. Within the area, the small brick worker cottages of the past, which might have brought a few thousand dollars in the market fifty years ago, share with the larger homes the increased prices that these much-sought-after properties now attract—the asking price for one property exceeding $1 million in 1999. This is in keeping with thesis research carried out in the neighborhood by Mary-Dixon Sayre Miller in 1981 that showed the beneficial effects of preservation on residential real estate values. Over time, the character of the German Village community changed as well, with new residents, many of them professionals, replacing the traditional blue-collar residents of 1955 and new activities displacing the old—for example, there were eighteen neighborhood groceries in 1955 and four in 1981, and the one law office present in 1955 had

Many of the German workers who came to Columbus in the mid-1800s would have lived in small brick homes such as these. With the evolution of the German Village Historic District, the area has seen the renovation and restoration of these dwellings, and an accompanying increase in demand for homes in the community.

become twenty-six in 1981. The long-term effect of preservation efforts "preserved an area with Old World charm . . . accompanied by less gentrification and resulting dislocations than might have been expected."[16] The village retains that "charm," with its red brick sidewalks and streets and well-kept homes and gardens. The result is a community that attracts tourists and others to its streets and homes and its restaurants and shops but has no real connection with the old South End and its industry.

Since the late 1980s, remains of the old breweries that once characterized South Columbus and especially the west side of High Street—at one time at least seven breweries lined the street—have been revitalized. All of the old brewery companies are gone—a number of them lost in the Prohibition period—and, unfortunately, many of the old buildings as well. But the area south of Livingston and west of High Street is now called the Brewery District and is an entertainment center attracting not only local crowds but visitors from outside the region with good restaurants and beer produced in local microbreweries. In a sense, South Columbus or the South End may have come full circle, with its long-term future still to be determined.

FLYTOWN

For many years, a historic marker dedicated by the Flytown Historical Association on June 18, 1961, stood on the south side of Goodale Boulevard. It read:

> Flytown was democracy's melting pot for the city of Columbus. But even more important it became known as a port-of-entry for the immigrant settlers of Central Ohio. New arrivals found friends and relatives who guided them through the initial steps of becoming naturalized Americans. Here was born a feeling of comradeship that led to patriotic loyalty that knew no division. Seventeen nationalities contributed of their knowledge and experience to the community of spirit and culture of Flytown. This is a section of Columbus that has become known and respected the width and breadth of the land.

Today, the marker and Flytown are both gone, victims of changes in the life of the community over time.

Flytown was an approximately twenty-five-block area roughly square in shape with about a half mile on each side. It lay just west of Neil Avenue and to the south of the more substantial middle-class homes of what is now Victorian Village. Its western boundary was the Olentangy River, and to the south were railroad yards and industrial plants. West Goodale was its principal artery, with numerous saloons, shops, rooming houses, and the like strung out along the road.

Its early inhabitants were Irish, German, and some Welsh laborers who lived in the tenements, three-storied brick and frame structures that were common to the area, and worked in nearby industry. In the late 1800s and early 1900s, the area along the Olentangy River was the location of a number of major industrial operations. The area's reputation for industrial pollution and the stream of in-migrants or "foreigners" who lived there helped identify Flytown as a slum neighborhood. In this period, Italian immigrants were attracted into the area, and before and after World War I southern blacks moved into the area in relatively small numbers. The St. Francis of Assisi Church was built in 1895 on Buttles Avenue to serve the largely

Italian congregation; it is one of the few buildings associated with Flytown that remains today.

In the late 1890s, Flytown experienced early efforts by charitable social services to bring their good works to the community to save "the sinners" and aid the children of the area. By 1898, the First Neighborhood Guild was organized, the first social settlement house in Columbus and one of the more than seventy such organizations in the country at that time. By 1899, Henry Godman, a major shoe manufacturer in Columbus, presented the Guild with a $10,000 matching gift to build a settlement house, which became the Godman Guild, whose works continue today from its offices just north of old Flytown on West Second Avenue.[17]

Along the Olentangy River and adjacent to it, in an area identified as one of the three major industrial groupings in the city at that time, was a cluster of important Columbus companies engaged in the manufacture of a wide range of products. Included among the firms were several foundries— Columbus Forge & Iron, Columbus Coop Foundry, and Simplex Foundry—and also the Columbus Coffin Company, Capital City Products (food products), and the Dresser-Ideco Company (structural steel products). Only the old Capital City Products firm continues to operate here, under new ownership and name. The old Dresser-Ideco Building houses an organ manufacturer, but virtually all other manufacturing has left the Flytown area.

Although the city liked to think that it was free of slums and tenements—and, in comparison to the large industrial cities, it was—the decision was made in the early 1950s to demolish the homes and buildings in Flytown and to clear the area. Considerable physical deterioration had occurred in Flytown during the Depression years of the 1930s and the war years of the 1940s and as a result of the constant turnover of the population. In 1953, the Columbus Redevelopment Authority declared the area blighted in accordance with the Federal Housing Act of 1949, and a bond issue was approved in 1956 to clear the area over the next few years. Then in 1957, the city began to build its Innerbelt, the northern leg of which cut through the southern part of Flytown as the Goodale Expressway. In this period of urban change with its focus on renewal, Flytown was one of the three major urban renewal projects undertaken in Columbus, along with the Market-Mohawk project in the Downtown area and the Bolivar Arms project to the east.

In the course of change, a total of 118 acres were cleared, with 547 families, 71 individuals, and 73 commercial businesses displaced. By this

St. Francis of Assisi Church is a reminder of Flytown's past as a point of entry for many migrants into Columbus. The church continues to serve the community and the Victorian Village area.

time, the black population in the area had increased considerably. With displacement, the white population largely moved northward out of the area, and the black population to neighborhoods largely east and southeast of I-71.

Redevelopment plans for the area, renamed Thurber Village, initially amounted to $6 million and called for a mix of apartments, both high-rise, such as the 10-story Thurber Towers, and two-story apartment clusters. A small commercial area, the Thurber Village Shopping Center at the southwest corner of Neil and Buttles Avenues, was constructed early in the redevelopment process and remains an active center today. The two-story apartment units were slow to develop, but ultimately investments by the Galbreath Company and major national insurance companies created a pleasant setting for apartment living. By 1965, a second high-rise was built by the Ohio Presbyterian Retirement Services, the seven-story Westminster Terrace, a senior apartment complex. In 1975, this group acquired Thurber Towers and now operates both facilities as retirement units.

There were also planned industrial areas in the community to the south

The old Flytown neighborhood gave way to urban renewal in the 1950s and the development of new housing. The high-rise Thurber Towers was an early response, along with adjacent apartments, such as the Tivoli unit, that attracted a new group of residents to the area.

along the Innerbelt and to the west along Michigan Avenue. They attracted a variety of commercial establishments and offices, such as the U.S. Trotting Association's headquarters, but little new manufacturing. Initially, this area served as a bit of a buffer between the residential areas and the older industrial section that is now largely gone.

Thurber Village—the old Flytown—has contributed to and shared in the long-term revitalization of the Goodale area and Victorian Village and in the dynamic changes associated with the commercial Short North strip. It serves as a positive example of the urban renewal efforts that marked Columbus and the nation in the early 1950s.

THE LIFE AND DEATH OF AN
INDUSTRIAL NEIGHBORHOOD

In the postwar 1950s, one of the major industrial neighborhoods in Columbus was still located along the New York Central/Big Four railroad tracks north out of Union Station. Within roughly one mile between First Avenue and Eighth Avenue, and lying between Fourth Street and Cleveland Avenue, were more than ten well-established and reasonably large manufacturing plants linked to the railroads and local highways (primarily Routes 23 and 3) well before the development of the interstate system.

Included in this industrial mix were several of the city's largest employers and several of its old home-based industries, the latter a litany of the major firms in the Columbus area at that time: Kilbourne & Jacobs (1865), Jeffrey Manufacturing Company (1877), Berry Brothers Iron Works (1881), Columbus Coated Fabrics (1900), and Clark Grave Vault (1900). By 1912, the Columbus Auto Parts factory had located along the NYC tracks near Hudson Street as an outlier of this group, and by 1919, Timken Roller Bearing had located its large plant at Cleveland and Fifth, adjacent to the railroads. It was the largest employer in the area in the early 1950s, with about 4,400 employees.

When established, these plants were located at the northern edge of the city to take advantage of favorable access to transportation by rail and highway, especially to northern markets, and to have room for possible expansion, much of which had been used up by the 1950s. They also sought to minimize contact with residential communities and highly urbanized areas. Over time, of course, the growing city encroached upon the industrial area and neighborhoods.

In general, the firms' major markets were to the north, to the industrial cities of northern Ohio and southern Michigan and to the auto industry. The companies saw the industrial market of the midwestern United States to be their principal target, with only Jeffrey, at one time the largest producer of mining machinery in the world, having a major market overseas. There was little market integration among the firms, although Jeffrey Manufacturing owned Kilbourne & Jacobs at this time and Ohio Malleable Iron was a Jeffrey subsidiary. In addition, the Berry Brothers Iron Works, which located adjacent to Jeffrey in 1881, was selling half of its output to Jeffrey in the 1950s.

For many of the companies, the Columbus labor market was seen to be a positive factor in attracting industry. Labor was judged to be available in adequate supply with lower wages prevailing in Columbus than in larger industrial centers and with minimum labor problems over the years and little union activity. The historic presence of the industries when they were at their peak of operations perhaps stimulated community growth as the labor forces expanded. Residential growth in the surrounding areas—such as Milo-Grogan and north into the Linden area, often defined as "a work-ingman's neighborhood"—was spurred by industrial jobs and a public transit system serving the residential and industrial areas.[18]

Of the eleven plants located in the defined "neighborhood," only four remain today, and two of these, Timken Roller Bearing and Columbus Coated Fabrics, are essentially shells of their former selves. Timken's huge plant site is now largely vacant. The plant was closed in 1989, after foreign competitors had taken over a larger share of its market for automobile bearings, and it was razed in 1996. Only a small operation continues to function at the south end of the lot. The future of a much smaller Columbus Coated Fabrics hinges on management decisions within Borden's corporate structure. One "survivor" is the Berry Brothers Iron Works (or Bolt Works, as it is now called), which continues to produce nuts, bolts, and rivets in its historically interesting old plant. The firm celebrated the hundredth anniversary of its building on East First Avenue in 1988. The other survivor is Clark Grave Vault Company, which expanded its production facilities during World War II but has since returned to its original product line, grave vaults.

For the most part, the remaining seven firms, including those representing long-established Columbus-based firms and families, have either closed up shop or been acquired by outside business interests who have largely removed production from Columbus or assumed the assets of the firm and closed operations completely. These losses have redefined the nature of this industrial sector in Columbus. A vivid visual example of the effects can be seen in the drive north along Fourth Street, out of the Downtown and past the vast wasteland of the old Jeffrey plant, through the deteriorated neighborhoods that were once home to the industry's workers. These losses and voids are symbolic of the decline in the historic role of manufacturing in the Columbus area and the loss of familiar industrial names from the roster of local businesses.

OLD BEECHWOLD

The Old Beechwold community is part of the larger Beechwold neighborhood within the Clintonville area. It was developed on wooded lands two miles north of the city boundary and approximately ten miles north of Broad and High as a planned, suburban community, but with easy access to the city—so much so that it has been identified as "a country setting on the bus line."[19]

The Old Beechwold area is a well-defined segment of the Rathbone Tract of the U.S. Military District, an area set aside by the young government in 1796 east of the Scioto River and north of the Congress Lands and Refugee Tract to the south with the purpose of providing land grants to soldiers of the Revolution (see map 2). John Rathbone was awarded a tract of 4,000 acres for military service; by early 1900, only 75.45 acres remained of Rathbone's original tract.

The northern part of the land was deeded to the Columbus Zoological Society on December 30, 1902, and named "Zooland," reflecting the intended purpose of establishing a zoo on the site. Neighborhood folklore suggests that bear pits were established in one of the ravines, but this may be only folklore; the area was, however, a site for family picnics. By 1906, the Zoological Society was prepared to sell the land and whatever buildings existed. A buyer was found in Joseph A. Jeffrey, founder of Jeffrey Manufacturing Company, and a home, variously described as a suburban estate or a summer house and named "Beechwalde" ("the beech forest") by Mrs. Jeffrey, was built and still stands in the area, as does a residence built for one of Jeffrey's associates at the southeast entry to the neighborhood.[20] By 1914, Jeffrey had sold his land to Charles H. Johnson, a local developer who changed the name slightly to "Beechwold." Johnson began to develop the forested acreage with its ravines in a way that residents might "enjoy all the charms of suburban life, and yet have the comforts and advantages of the city right at hand."[21] Winding streets and architect-designed homes and unfenced landscapes on irregular lots were planned to take advantage of the setting. In the brochure *Beechwold the Beautiful,* produced by Johnson's company, the plat of the community is described, focusing on these features. The design of any home and property was limited by a set of guidelines and "restrictions" intended to maintain the community's character.

Beechwold was planned by Johnson to be an upper-middle-class community that would appeal to businessmen and others. Johnson argued that the area could be readily reached from Downtown by streetcar or interurban transport and by private car. As time passed, the homes became attractive to professionals and academicians. Today, the neighborhood remains highly accessible to the larger community without many of the problems confronting the newer and more suburban communities.

Currently, there are 135 homes in Old Beechwold, representing a range of architectural styles and bounded by High Street on the east, the Olentangy River on the west, Jeffrey Place on the north, and Rustic Place on the south. Old Beechwold is heavily treed with beech, oak, maple, walnut, tulip poplar, and osage orange. One prospective buyer of a home, who discovered that he could not take down a large protected walnut, decided he did not want to live in Old Beechwold. "If you don't like lots of trees, you can't be happy here," residents said, and he left.

The homes in Old Beechwold, once "large," are in today's market comfortable midsize family homes. The neighborhood is an easy mix of the retired, the middle aged, and the young, as well as dogs, cats, squirrels, and, regrettably, raccoons.

We moved into Old Beechwold more than thirty years ago as our family grew and after living for ten years in our first and smaller home in the first block east of High Street across from Old Beechwold, an area once known as the "Zooland Addition," with streets named for various animals, an idea that apparently did not sell well in the market. The east side of High Street is populated by smaller, well-kept and tended homes along pleasant tree-lined streets that stretch one mile from High Street to Indianola Avenue. The majority of the houses were built in the immediate postwar period to accommodate the demand for homes for returning veterans.

In 1983, I initiated an effort, working with neighborhood women, to have the Old Beechwold area placed on the National Register of Historic Places and the Columbus Register of Historic Properties. Our concern was to identify and maintain the historic integrity of the community.[22]

Through its Association, the Old Beechwold community has been an active and responsible force in challenging various threats not only to the immediate neighborhood but to the larger Clintonville community as well. Leadership from Old Beechwold has joined forces with others to attack such varied issues as the proposed Ford plant at the old juncture of Morse Road and the railroads in the late 1950s, and, almost continuously—with Delawanda neighbors to the north—the proposed Bethel-Morse Road connector. Along the way, the community has challenged the City Council's support for rezoning the northwest corner of Morse and High for an ill-fated banking establishment, and joined in support of those seeking to protect the Olentangy Valley from being converted from a natural preserve to an expanded highway system with related development.

In 1991, in a study of community lifestyles supported by the Department of Development, Frank Elmer, architect and planner, identified Old Beechwold residents as possessing lifestyles of "God's Country."[23] While one might not agree with his description of that lifestyle, most residents would probably agree that living within this pleasant and readily accessible natural environment is about as close to living in God's Country as most of us will ever come.

THE DOWNTOWN AS NEIGHBORHOOD

We don't usually think of the Downtown in the same way that we view community neighborhoods. One reason is the absence of residential units and their closely linked shopping areas and cultural ambience. Although there are indeed relatively few residential units in the Downtown, a few upscale residential facilities, such as the Waterford condominium, have been built, and more are underway, such as Miranova Corporate Towers along the Scioto. Historically, the Downtown was home to the many who worked in the businesses and industries located there. But over time, the typical worker housing gave way to new offices and high-rise buildings, so that today most of the 90,000 or so Downtown employees are commuters. This is reflected in the fact that Downtown Columbus has almost 66,000 parking spaces, a ratio of only 1.4 persons per space. This is higher than comparative figures for cities such as Cincinnati (2.2), Cleveland (1.8), Indianapolis (1.8), and Portland, Oregon (2.4). The latter is a city that seems to have its core area transit under control.

Perhaps we need to consider an observation that Mayor Tom Moody made in 1983: "Downtown is everybody's neighborhood, and Downtown is the only neighborhood that takes care of itself and subsidizes all the other neighborhoods and makes possible all the other neighborhoods."[24] He was referring to how money was divided between Downtown and the other neighborhoods, an issue that may be even more vital today as the Downtown of the Central City competes with the many neighborhoods that make up our region.

10

Historic Preservation

I CAN'T BELIEVE THIS HAS HAPPENED." IT WAS the early 1980s, and I was calling New York to purchase tickets to a Broadway play. The operator had taken my order, my Visa number, and other relevant information that she required.

Then—"You from Columbus? Say, someone told me that the Chittenden is gone?" I started to assure the questioner that the hotel was, indeed, gone—and for quite a few years now. "My husband and I stayed in Columbus at the Chittenden twenty years ago. It was a nice hotel; we had a good time. But we'd have liked to have stayed at the Neil House."

"Well," I interrupted, "the Neil House is gone too."

"I can't believe that this has happened—the Chittenden gone—and the Neil House—oh . . ."

I was taken aback by two things: first, the friendliness of the New York native—after all, aren't they supposed to be different from the rest of us?— and second, her recollection of pleasant times spent in Columbus, Ohio— of all places!—and the fact that it was the hotels she remembered. I suspect that had I encouraged the conversation further (and I wish now that I had), we might have discussed restaurants, maybe a theater or two, and who knows what else?

Here in Columbus we have had a penchant for removing our old hotels and other buildings with which people both near and far identify the city and their own history—the Deshler Hotel, Central Market, the Union Station, and the Peruna Building, to name a few. It occurred to me then—I was at that time president of the Columbus Landmarks Foundation—that we were busy creating a community without identity, and it seems, almost twenty years later, that the search for an identity goes on in the mad desire to have some event or some team, first rate or second rate, it doesn't seem to matter, that can somehow broadcast the news of Columbus across the nation. The truth is that by the 1980s, the city's history as reflected in its built environment and in preservation-related activities was, perhaps, better appreciated than at any previous time, despite the losses that had occurred. This chapter focuses on the formative years in the development of an appreciation for historic preservation and its impact upon the city.

Interest in individual buildings and in distinctive neighborhoods in the city goes back to even earlier days, and, in fairness, many homes and buildings were restored or renovated. Just as surely, losses were occurring in the post–World War II era as the old Franklin County Courthouse on South High was torn down; the Greek Revival Kelley Mansion (1832–35) was lost, its only trace a pile of marked stones in Wolfe Park that were later shipped off to Cleveland; the Deshler Hotel was torn down by outside interests to become one of Columbus's trademark parking lots; and the old Central Market was demolished as part of a widespread urban renewal program. Some have argued that the genesis for any major preservation effort in the city was the effort of Dixie Miller, and friends, to save the Kelley Mansion in 1961.[1]

By the early 1960s, what was to become the renaissance of the blighted German Village neighborhood was underway, not only marking a critical period in that community's history but serving as a landmark event for the larger community. Even so, no other effective preservation movement was active here, nor was there any organization ready to coordinate efforts to raise the community's conscience with respect to its past, as represented by its historical buildings, and its future, in plans for meaningful and efficient development.

In 1976, several events brought the question of historic preservation to the fore. A comprehensive review of Columbus's history and its architecture, *Architecture Columbus,* published by the Columbus Chapter of the American Institute of Architects (AIA), captured the city's attention.[2] Then, led by the City Action Task Force of the Junior League of Columbus, several local organizations—the OSU School of Architecture, the AIA, the Preservation Office of the Mid-Ohio Regional Planning Commission (MORPC), and the Ohio Historical Society—joined that fall to consider the need for preservation and urban planning in the city.[3] In so doing, they noted the loss of architecturally significant buildings in the city that, once destroyed, could never be replaced. They also made tentative plans for what was to become the Columbus Landmarks Foundation.[4]

Perhaps the trigger event, however, the event that rallied the various interests to action, was the demolition of the Daniel C. Burnham Beaux Arts Union Station in 1976. My wife and I happened to be driving north on High Street after midnight on October 23 as the first swing of the wrecking ball struck the building; demolition continued through the night and the following days. Like others, we bemoaned the action and the loss but were ill equipped to respond. But as the process went on, a number of concerned citizens gathered to form a group—Citizens for the Union Station Arch (sometimes called the "Save the Arch" committee)—committed to saving at least one of the station arches. They were successful in that effort, and the arch was moved to a site on Marconi Boulevard—Arch Park—where it was rebuilt and erected in summer 1979 on land donated by the Columbus and Southern Ohio Electric Company. As part of the redevelopment of the old penitentiary site, the arch was moved in early 1999 to serve as an entryway to a park near the new Nationwide Arena.

It was a similar event in New York City in the 1960s—the demolition of the great McKim, Mead, and White Pennsylvania Station—that spurred the creation of the landmarks law in New York City, which was a significant force in focusing national attention on historic preservation. This law, upheld by a 6-to-3 vote of the Supreme Court in 1978, would later be a critical factor in the preservation of the Grand Central Terminal. A *Citizen-Journal* editorial noted at the time that "the immediate beneficiaries . . . are the growing number of cities—which should include Columbus—which have become alarmed at the way bulldozers are destroying the local heritage but have been reluctant to order a stop to it for fear of lawsuits. . . . The ultimate beneficiaries are the future generation of Americans who will be able to see for themselves the way it was decades, even centuries ago. That benefit is priceless."[5]

In 1977, the Junior League task force and others sponsored a preservation seminar at which nationally recognized preservationists Arthur Ziegler, president of Landmarks, Inc., in Pittsburgh, and Lee Adler, from Savannah, discussed preservation issues and considered the situation in Columbus. Ziegler noted that "in spite of the tragic architectural losses in Columbus, you still have an unusually promising situation in which to develop preservation."[6] One result was the joining of participants in the "Arch" effort with

One of the old Union Station arches, photographed in Arch Park. The arch has since been relocated as a portal to Arena Park, across from Nationwide Arena.

other concerned citizens to create the Columbus Landmarks Foundation. The foundation was incorporated in July 1977 as a nonprofit organization whose basic purpose was to "preserve, protect and perpetuate . . . the growing architectural heritage of the Greater Columbus community."[7]

With the formation of the Columbus Landmarks Foundation ("Landmarks"), Columbus had its first organized group committed to historic preservation. Leadership came primarily from those who had been active in previous efforts to save local landmarks, including the traditional "little old ladies in tennis shoes," who not only helped to fund the organization but also volunteered their time, along with others, to establish Landmarks as a force in the community. James Keyes, who brought his enthusiasm for good architecture and preservation with him from Columbus, Indiana, and had been active in the Arch group, was elected first president in 1977. Larrilyn Edwards, active in the Junior League and the Arch group, was appointed director of the foundation.

A grant of $15,000 in November 1977 from the Columbus Foundation was made to Landmarks to "complete the survey of historic buildings in the city and the development of a preservation plan for the city based on the survey."[8] Earlier, Paul Young, a professor of architecture at Ohio State and a vice president of Landmarks, presciently identified "11 critical issues" needing attention in the community: the old Deaf School building, Capitol South, the Old Post Office, the Atlas Building, Nationwide Plaza, the Crane Building (City Hall Annex), North Market, the Wyandotte Building, a private residence at 1349 East Broad Street (rezoning was the issue), the High Street corridor, and Sawmill Road.[9] It was felt that most of the buildings, or buildings that might be affected by them, were at risk. In referring to Sawmill Road, Young expressed concern that mistakes associated with Morse Road might be repeated.

By late 1977, then, historic preservation was alive and active in the community, with Landmarks focusing attention on saving several historic properties, such as Burnham's 1897 Wyandotte Building on West Broad Street, the first steel frame building in the city and, as such, a fine example of the seminal "Chicago School" of design, and the Harrison House in Franklinton. It was recognized that not only buildings should be preserved but neighborhoods as well, and a revolving fund was initiated to provide funds to rehab housing in defined neighborhoods, initially the Near East Side. I suspect that many of us felt that "preservation was in the air" at that time and that the mood of the city was receptive to the idea that there was value—historic and economic—in preserving and reusing historic structures.

Efforts to produce landmark legislation for the city was also underway by 1976, and in 1977 Councilman Daniel Schoedinger introduced legislation before the City Council to create a Historic Structures Preservation Commission. Later, such legislation became an issue for discussion using the Negotiated Investment Strategy (NIS), a technique developed to encourage local groups to reach agreement on urban issues, with federal, state, city, and community participants engaged in the process. The NIS was a product of the Charles F. Kettering Foundation's work early in 1977 to help formulate a national urban policy. It proposed to help set urban policy within an area by bringing the participants to the table to discuss urban issues of importance to the community. Columbus was one of three cities, along with St. Paul, Minnesota, and Gary, Indiana, to have "teams" prepared to represent the different levels of government as well as key groups in the private sector. One of the critical issues under discussion in Columbus was historic preservation. From the private sector, key "players" included representatives from Landmarks and from the real estate and development interests in the city, both of which had an interest in the process and its outcome but were usually at odds with one another.[10] The NIS process was to continue until April 30, 1980, the "sign-off" date for the final set of agreements for several important local projects.

Meanwhile, other issues were before the community. Landmarks became involved in planning for the future of the old Deaf School on Town Street. Threatened with demolition in 1978, it was being considered as a potential home for the elderly, presenting a challenge to preservationists. So did the monitoring of the Capitol South project and the demolition of the Hartman Building—the Hartman Theater had been torn down in 1970—and several other buildings listed on the National Register. The project had to justify the removal of the buildings and complete a federal review of artifacts or risk losing federal funding. The Junior League dedicated its restored Kelton House in September 1979, and early plans for the North Market area opposite the new Ohio Center were being considered, as well as ongoing initiatives for redevelopment and restoration in both the Victorian Village and Italian Village areas.

Then there was the confrontation between City Hall and preservationists and other interests when the city decided to demolish the City Hall Annex just to the north of City Hall as part of a plan undertaken in 1977 to redesign the Civic Center Complex. The Annex was built in 1905 as the Higgins Grocery warehouse (and later known as the Crane Building) in an area that was then occupied by wholesale warehouses and small industrial shops. The area was the focal point for the city's Civic Center Plan of 1908. The Annex Building survived an earlier effort to clear the area, only to face the threat of demolition with the new Civic Center Complex plan.

Key parts of the new complex, an underground parking garage and a multistory city office building, were to be built on the site occupied by the Annex, with park space along the river and a plaza between the buildings. It was clear that the Civic Center project had the backing of the city's most powerful family, the Wolfes. Their strong role in shaping local politics certainly influenced support for the project and the demolition of the Annex. Preservationists were concerned about the loss of a potentially viable building and its replacement by yet another parking lot.

Landmarks had challenged the concept of the proposed civic center since the plan's inception, raising questions about the costs of new construction given energy and resource conservation issues, and about the efficacy of plans for further low-density use in the city's core. By late 1979, the City Council remained committed to the plan and to the demolition of the Annex Building. Councilman M. D. Portman was quoted as saying that he had "waited 23 years to see that thing bite the dust," in a sense supporting the observation of Michael Gable, the city's finance director, that "it's the wrong building in the wrong place at the wrong time." Even Landmark's director, Larrilyn Edwards, admitted that Landmarks "couldn't have picked a more unpopular building in town to try to save."[11] Nonetheless, the Landmarks board voted to challenge the city's plan and hired the Chicago-based firm of Harry Weese & Associates, a well-known and highly respected national planning and architectural services firm, to develop conceptual alternatives, which represented as well sound economic considerations, to the city's proposal for a Civic Center Complex and the Annex Building. These were presented to the city on January 17, 1980. Criticism of the alternative plan noted its failure to address the parking issue, although it was generally agreed that Landmarks and the Weese firm had not had sufficient time to redesign the complex in a manner that would win local approval.[12]

It goes without saying that Mayor Moody was committed to the Civic Center Complex and the consequent demolition of the Annex Building. Nonetheless, in early January several Landmarks officers—its first president, James Keyes, Larrilyn Edwards, and I, as the second president—tried to "sell" our efforts to preserve and reuse the building. I also forwarded an abbreviated version of a paper I had prepared, entitled "Preservation and Economic Development," to the mayor on January 11, and Paul Young, a Landmarks board member, sent an incisive discussion of the issues to council members the same day.[13]

On the afternoon of January 21, I met with the mayor to plead our case, as I would also do in the council meeting that evening. Landmarks was requesting a further stay of demolition and three months' more time to provide a more thorough development and study of alternatives. The mayor and I had a good working relationship and shared a mutual respect, but he warned me that his remarks at the council meeting would not be at all sympathetic to Landmarks or to me—and they were not!

I learned a bit about local politics when at one point in our discussion the mayor stated that he "couldn't let Maury down," a reference to the senior Democratic councilman, M. D. Portman, who had waged the campaign to demolish the building despite Landmarks' rationale showing the favorable costs associated with saving and rehabbing a structurally sound building. It was clear that over the years the Republican mayor and the Democratic councilman had developed a cooperative working relationship.

At the meeting that evening, the City Council voted 6 to 1 to approve demolition of the Annex Building and, presumably, to get the Civic Center Complex underway. One wag asked, in an editorial, "Is the razing of the old

Annex to be the first step in a grandiose governmental office complex? Or is it just to be another parking lot?"[14] Nearly two decades later, the parking lot still awaits the office complex.

With the demolition of the Annex, that confrontation between the city and Landmarks came to a close. But it was clear that the debate that was generated had been "good for the whole city" in the sense that it created greater community interest in historic preservation and its potential role in Columbus.[15] It was also clear, however, that with the demolition of the Annex—and with the later demolition in June 1980 of the Monypeny-Hammond Building, a key piece in the development of the North Market area plans—Columbus's reputation suffered nationally. It was the rare large city at this time that did *not* have a preservation plan in effect. Locally, development and real estate interests opposed such efforts even as landmark legislation was under discussion. It was reported that following the demolition of the Monypeny-Hammond Building, Mayor Moody signed a pledge to federal officials that the city would create a method to review and preserve historic sites and that legislation would be drafted to create a historic preservation commission.[16] The mayor knew that federal funding for many projects could be withheld (after all, Capitol South was underway, and it had been estimated that the city had lost millions of federal dollars with the demolition of Union Station) if city leadership did not become more enlightened and responsive in this regard. Thus, the confrontation had long-term positive effects, but construction of a civic center complex has not been one of them.

The fact that the Annex Building was demolished and replaced by one more *surface* parking lot in the Downtown core—as predicted by opponents of the demolition—also added to the city's negative image. Visitors to Columbus at that time frequently expressed amazement that the city's appearance from the air was somewhat akin to the bombed-out cities of Europe following World War II. The prominent local architect Friedl Bohm, whose firm had drawn up the plans for the Civic Center Complex, was quoted by *Business First* as saying, "Initially, when I came here [in 1968] I was shocked. Because I thought Columbus looked worse than Vienna after the Second World War. Vienna was bombed out: Columbus was full of parking lots."[17]

By early 1980, then, the Annex battle was over, but numerous other preservation and development issues needed to be faced. The city's commitment to the Capitol South project was a major issue, involving as it did the loss of many buildings in the three blocks south of Capitol Square and,

especially, the retail stores that fronted South High Street. The funding of
a project to develop retail space linked to the Lazarus main store was a major concern, with a $12-million federal Urban Development Action Grant
(UDAG) essential to its realization. An earlier grant of $4.6 million had al-
lowed construction of the short-lived Centrum—a skating rink, café, and
special events site—at Town and High Streets as a short-term gateway to
the Capitol South area.

Another challenge was the ongoing proposed conversion of the old
Deaf School building on East Town Street to housing for the elderly. Once
again, Landmarks was an active participant in the early planning process,
sponsoring a detailed feasibility study of the building in March 1979.[18]
There was opposition to the project even though restoration experts—Lee
Adler of Savannah, Arthur Ziegler of Pittsburgh, and local experts, who
made an on-site visit in the spring of 1980—praised the concept as "one of
the most creative ideas [for the elderly] in the country." Otto Beatty presented legislation in the General Assembly supporting the conversion in
November 1980. The school's favorable site and location with respect to
other amenities and services related to the needs of the elderly were particularly attractive features, as was as the fact that the building was judged to
be an economically viable project.

While these projects were underway, landmarks legislation was still being discussed. As noted earlier, such legislation had been introduced for
council action in 1977 but was tabled because of opposition, and it was a
topic for discussion at the NIS meetings. By February 1980, the future of
the Deaf School became another topic for NIS consideration.

In November 1980, after at least three years of discussion, the City
Council passed a historic preservation ordinance to establish the Historic
Resources Commission, which would compile and keep a list of the city's
historic buildings and districts. In addition, the ordinance provided guidelines affecting the alteration or demolition of properties and the property
owners' responsibilities. A major issue that had been debated through the
years had to do with the length of a so-called cooling-off period prior to
demolition or alterations on the part of the property owner. The council
had defeated proposed legislation in 1977 that would have established a
180-day waiting period, a length of time consistent with that mandated in
other major U.S. cities; it was strongly supported by Landmarks but just
as strongly opposed by real estate and development interests. The 1980
ordinance established, instead, a 105-day waiting period.

Another matter of controversy related to the size of the commission and its composition. The commission was finally established with fourteen members to be appointed by the mayor and confirmed by the City Council. Membership was to include one appointee each from the Board of Realtors, the Columbus Landmarks Foundation, the Columbus Chapter of AIA, the Columbus Chapter of Professional Engineers, a professional architectural historian, the Columbus Chamber of Commerce, the Buckeye Section of the Ohio Chapter of AIA, a financial institution (in rehabilitation and construction), a developer (in development and rehabilitation), and five representatives of neighborhood groups or organizations. Mayor Moody praised the passage of the ordinance but refused to sign it because he had some questions concerning its penalty section. It became law without his signature on December 3, 1980.

While the legislation was being debated and finalized, it was announced that the venerable Neil House would close on December 19, 1980. The original Neil House was built in 1838 and replaced by a second, five stories high, in the 1860s. The present building had been erected in 1925. Through the years, several presidents and a number of other distinguished guests had stayed in the hotel. It was also home to many state legislators. Landmarks endorsed the plans to replace the hotel with a new highrise, the Huntington Bank Center, observing that "the present Neil House is neither architecturally outstanding nor apparently is it an economic success."[19]

Landmarks has never been a large organization in terms of membership or financial resources and is not today. Shortly after its incorporation, as noted earlier, it applied for and received a $15,000 grant from the Columbus Foundation to carry out an architectural survey and evaluation of the buildings in the Columbus Central Business District and to complete a preservation plan. Although other funding was applied for, Landmarks used up many of its resources in the controversial battle over the Annex but had established itself as a force to be dealt with not only in terms of historic preservation but with respect to sound new development in the city as well. Still, funding remained a problem.

In a meeting with Mayor Moody in his office on June 2, 1980, at which Bill Habig of MORPC was also present, we discussed ways in which Landmarks and the city might cooperate in our mutual interest to preserve and restore certain buildings in Columbus. Knowing something of our financial situation, the mayor suggested the possibility of tapping a funding source to help Landmarks finance a director's position. Over the next several months, the mayor provided "anonymous" assistance to me in applying for a grant from the Jeffrey Endowment Fund of the Columbus Foundation. This fund of $249,000 had been given to the city in 1930 to be used for benevolent and charitable purposes. In August 1980, Landmarks requested a grant of $20,000 a year for a three-year period to fund the office of executive director. By October 1, 1980, Landmarks submitted the completed *An Inventory and Evaluation of Historic Buildings in the Columbus, Ohio, CBD, September 1980,* fulfilling the obligations established in the original grant of November 1977. Despite this, the Columbus Foundation declined to provide the grant.

Later, in further conversation with the mayor and Joseph Imberman, director of the Columbus Foundation, Landmarks was encouraged to resubmit a modified version of its earlier request. This request was approved on May 8, 1981, by the Columbus Foundation board. With receipt of the grant, I felt that my relationship with Tom Moody, despite his stand on the Annex, had been proven. He was not in any way an ardent preservationist; indeed, he was perhaps just the opposite. As mayor, he may have been much more concerned with encouraging economic development in the community than with the risk of losing historic properties in the process. But Landmarks' proactive position, especially with respect to federal funding and legislation, led him and a number of city officials to realize that historic preservation legislation was a must in this city in this day and age (1980s). The passage of the Historic Resources Ordinance in December 1980 and the creation of the Historic Resources Commission were positive steps in the process. And with the Columbus Foundation grant in place, the Landmarks appeared to be here to stay.

The completed survey of historic buildings was to be *the* inventory used by Landmarks in its monitoring and concern for building preservation. Landmarks noted that "as a result of the Negotiated Investment Strategy [NIS] process carried out in Columbus during the last year, an ordinance has been drafted and reviewed by the Columbus City Council with respect to establishing an Historic Resources Commission. One task of such a commission . . . has been viewed as providing an inventory of community structures and an evaluation process. It may be argued, properly, that this task has been completed" with the Landmarks inventory.[20]

The initial area for the inventory was defined as the Central Business District, or that area lying within the so-called Columbus Innerbelt. Only buildings forty years of age or older (as of 1977) were to be surveyed. A standard "Ohio Historic Inventory" form was completed for each building or site that met this criterion. Approximately 590 buildings were reviewed, and inventory forms were completed for each. A team of four professionals evaluated and classified the buildings, sites, public sculptures, and other features, assigning each to one of five categories based upon their appraised *significance* (number of properties are as of October 1980):

> *Category A, Primary Significance.* These include already identified Landmark buildings, such as the Ohio State Capitol and the Ohio Theatre; buildings already on the National Register of Historic Buildings, such as the Wyandotte Building; or those having the potential to be on the Register. (41 properties)

> *Category B, Secondary Significance.* These are properties whose unique historical, architectural, or community significance gives them importance—that is, buildings that stand out in at least one of these attributes. (37 properties)

> *Category C, Tertiary Significance.* These are properties whose historical, architectural, *and* community significance gives them importance—that is, the property is important when two or more measures are considered. (93 properties)

> *Category D, Distinctive Reuse Potential.* These properties may have no particular significance but are useful buildings with reuse potential. (187 properties)

> *Category E, Questionable Reuse Potential.* These properties have less redeeming significance or potential. (157 properties)

> *Category X, Demolished.* (75 properties)

The inventory became a key guide to the historic structures and properties in Columbus not only for Landmarks but for the city and the citizenry. In addition, the inventory identified existing and potential National Register properties and provided a basis for the development of the Columbus Register of Historic Properties by the Historic Resources Commission.[21]

So, by early 1981, there were two principal preservation-oriented groups in the city: Landmarks, a volunteer nonprofit organization in the private sector; and the city's Historic Resources Ordinance and Commission, a product of the NIS project, in the public sector.

The Columbus Landmarks Foundation continued its role in the community, providing educational programs and field trips for a variety of audiences and maintaining its monitoring of historic structures in a developing city. A Neighborhood Advocacy Project was undertaken in early 1981 as a positive effort to assist neighborhood groups in renovation activities. A crushing blow was the destruction of the Deaf School, long a serious Landmarks project for development, in October 1981 by a mysterious fire attributed to homeless persons who used the building for shelter. The fire effectively discouraged any further plans for the building and site at that time.

Another undertaking, funded by the Ohio Historic Preservation Office and the Ohio Arts Council, resulted in the publication of a study related to possible new and adaptive uses for surplus public school buildings then being closed by the school system.[22] At least fifty Columbus public schools had been closed since 1972 and were either retained for possible future use or leased or sold in the private sector.

Meanwhile, the Historic Resources Commission was just getting organized. Appointments were made to the commission, and on September 17, 1981, the first meeting was held under the guidance of Kay Benton, the city's first historic preservation officer. Mayor Moody had appointed me as the representative from Landmarks; I was elected first chair of the commission, and another preservationist, Judy Kitchen of the Ohio Historical Society, was elected vice-chair. In the following meetings, information was reviewed relating to such matters as the City Code, preservation philosophies and policies, and terminology. The inventory of buildings compiled by Landmarks was introduced, and discussion began concerning the city's Register of Historic Properties. Landmarks' inventory dealt only with buildings within the Central Business District, whereas the intent of the city Register was to identify any property within any part of the city that was deemed worthy of being a listed property on the Register. A worthy building, district, site, structure, or object could qualify if it was over forty years old and met at least one of four criteria: it was a design or architectural style of significance to the city's historical, architectural, or cultural development; it was closely and publicly identified with a person who had significantly contributed to the development of the city, state, or nation; it was identified as a significant work of an architect or builder whose work had influenced development of the city, state, or nation; or it demonstrated significant craftsmanship in architectural design, detail, or use of materials. Once placed on the city Register, any change to the exterior of a structure, including demolition, required that a Certificate of Appropriateness be obtained from the commission.

Members were asked to compile personal lists of prospective buildings for the Register, but a decision was made early on to focus first on what might be called "noncontroversial buildings," the idea being to get the commission started on its work on a harmonious basis—and this aim was in fact accomplished.

On January 21, 1982, at its fifth meeting, the commission recognized its first two properties for review: a public property, the Cultural Arts Center (the Old State Arsenal) on West Main, and a private residence, the 1880s Italianate Krumm house on South High Street. In the next six months, eight more buildings, including the U.S. Post Office (the so-called "old, old Post Office" at State and Third Streets), four Downtown churches (First Congregational, Central Presbyterian, Trinity Episcopal, and St. Joseph's Cathedral), the Weisheimer (Teater) residence in Clintonville, the Southern Hotel and Theatre, and the LeVeque Tower were reviewed and added to the Register. Any property could be nominated for consideration, but the owners had to be informed of the nomination and approve of it.

By November 1982, fifteen structures had been nominated to the Register from all sectors of the community; thirteen of these nominations had been approved by the City Council. As I wrote in a letter to Mayor Moody, the commission "moved somewhat slowly and judiciously . . . while . . . achieving a remarkable degree of harmony." This was important given that the commission represented "diverse groups in the community with widely disparate views concerning preservation . . . [who] have been unusually cooperative and supportive in carrying on the work of the Commission. It is apparent that there is real concern about the effective future development of the community and, also, about the proper retention of its historic heritage."[23]

Early in 1982, the decision by the Columbus Board of Education to close Central High School and perhaps dispose of both the site and the building was an issue to which both the Historic Resources Commission and Landmarks responded. Clearly, the building was a candidate for the Register, and there was immediate concern as to future use of the site, but the building's architectural and cultural significance were the concern of the commission. Landmarks was asked to comment about the issue and in a position paper noted the architectural and historical qualities of the Neo-Classical Revival building, with its great site and location on the Scioto. Central High School was the first building constructed after the 1908 Columbus Plan, and it reflected innovative concepts in the design of the education facilities.[24] At the request of the Board of Education, immediate action was delayed to allow further consideration of the issues involved.

Landmarks continued to work cooperatively with city leaders to the extent that National Historic Preservation Week in May was recognized in a joint effort between Lazarus, the Chamber of Commerce, and Landmarks and was identified as "Look Up Columbus: Lazarus Salutes the Columbus Landmarks Foundation." Mayor Moody prepared the proclamation announcing the week.

Almost a year after the Deaf School fire, Landmarks undertook initiatives to attempt to save the remaining structure on the site, the large Art and Gymnasium Building located on the west end of the site. The site and building are important as a reminder of the state of Ohio's commitments to the care and welfare of its less fortunate citizens. In this building, care was provided for handicapped individuals, part of the network of social services available then in state facilities. The building was designed by the architectural firm of Richards, McCarty & Bulford and was built in 1898. Landmarks undertook steps to alert the community to it and to its rehabilitation and further useful life. In this effort, Landmarks recognized the state's cooperation in seeking developers for the building.

On another front, Landmarks was again involved with Capitol South and its plans to demolish the half-block of storefronts on South High from Rich Street to Cherry Street, including the old Knickerbocker Theater, with its unique multicolored terra-cotta facade. William Bonner, owner and restorer of the Great Southern Hotel, proposed alternative uses for the buildings, but to no avail. Interestingly enough, this High Street frontage has never been built upon after the small shops that were once there were displaced. The intimate shopping opportunities that these shops provided are precisely the kind of retail activity missing today from South High Street, and they are replicated, in a sense, in the newly built Easton Marketplace.

Obviously, Landmarks and the Historic Resources Commission are usually interested in some of the same issues, but how each approaches an issue and the roles that each can play in communicating a position to the public vary. This is illustrated in the continuing concern both had in 1983 with developments in Capitol South, notably with the future of the Beggs Building and with the acquisition and planned demolition of buildings in the North Market area near the Greek Orthodox Church. For one thing, Capitol South was excluded from the purview of the commission, but Landmarks was not bound by ordinance from continuing to monitor its activity. When the future of the Beggs Building was being discussed—rumor had it that the plan was either for wrapping a new building around it and integrating it into Capitol South or for slating it for demolition—Department of Development Director Ralph Smithers met with the commission to explain that at that time the department had no role to play in Capitol South.

On the other hand, Landmarks had been involved with Capitol South since its beginning, often as a constructive and positive force. It noted that the 1927 art deco–style Beggs Building, with its terra-cotta finish, was one of the more decorative buildings on Capitol Square and worthy of National Register status. Landmarks urged that it be retained to be part of "a revitalized and productive downtown."[25]

The Greek Orthodox Church issue was a different matter. The Historic Resources Commission and Landmarks were alerted in early 1983 to possible plans by the church to purchase existing buildings in the neighborhood and demolish them in order to make room for a new church. The North Market District, which had been nurtured by Landmarks for quite some time, was placed on the National Register in January and was approved as a Historic District by the Columbus City Council on September 19, 1983. The church informed the commission that it had acquired most of the properties adjacent to it, several of which it had owned since the 1970s, and that it planned to go ahead with demolition of the structures, many of which were expensive to maintain, by late 1984. The plans were presented to the commission on December 15 and were discussed in detail; the commission refused to grant a Certificate of Appropriateness to permit demolition.

At its first meeting in 1984, the commission was faced with the continued threat of demolition. Most neighborhood associations, such as the Victorian and Italian Village Commissions and Citizens for a Better Skyline, opposed the demolition, supporting instead the idea of a redeveloped North Market District. Landmarks had worked with residents, merchants, and the church, sponsoring architectural and planning studies aimed at bringing about revitalization of the area, but apparently to no avail. The church indicated that it would begin demolition of the structures once the required 105-day waiting period had expired.

While these issues were being considered and brought to resolution, both organizations were engaged in other activities as well. The Historic Resources Commission continued its review of properties for the Register, with some attention focused on one or two controversial structures. For example, questions were raised concerning the possible historic status of the old-style White Castles. Two were left in Columbus: the oldest at Fifth and Cleveland was built in 1948, and a second on North High at Arcadia was built in 1951; there were six others in the nation. In a similar vein, the

Lustron house was suggested as a potential listed property. Interestingly, both types of structures were particularly relevant in the Columbus setting. The White Castle organization, with its porcelain steel-clad buildings, was headquartered in Columbus; the Lustron house, the postwar porcelain steel-clad home, was created and produced in Columbus at the Curtis-Wright aircraft plant. The White Castle building on Cleveland Avenue was approved for the Register but was removed from that site and moved to the Columbus Zoo. A Lustron house has yet to be recognized for its historic significance in the Columbus community.

After the death in early 1983 of James Recchie, an officer and founding member of the Landmarks organization, the Recchie family established an award program in Jim's memory. Memorial gifts and several grants provided funding for the first James B. Recchie Design Award in May 1984. The awards program sought nominations from the public for excellence in architectural design, whether in new construction or historic rehabilitation. In the first program, held in the art deco Ohio Departments Building on Front Street, jurors reviewed the nominations for the award and selected the rehabilitated warehouse housing the firm of Trott and Bean, Architects, on Nationwide Boulevard. Honorable Mention went to the Battelle Sculpture Park of the Columbus Museum of Art. Wolf Von Eckardt, architecture critic of *Time* magazine, was the speaker, the first in a series of nationally recognized critics to address the awards ceremonies. A reception following the award ceremony was held in the Huntington Center Building, then under construction. The Recchie Award became a major event for Landmarks in coming years, achieving community recognition for what it sought to do in advocating and rewarding outstanding design.

By this time, both Landmarks and the Historic Resources Commission were well established, each having its own agenda but both continuing their individual roles in broadening community interest in preservation. The role of the commission would expand as the number of Register properties and districts increased and as it continued to grant Certificates of Appropriateness to worthy owners of historic properties. In addition, the city became more active in its promotion of historic preservation. In 1985, it published a brief report, *Preservation Means Economic Development,* that noted the availability of federal tax incentives to encourage the reuse of certified historic structures. And in 1986, the city's Development Department published *Historic Preservation: The Investment Alternative,* in which it argued the importance of historic preservation in development. Examples of successful rehabilitation projects were discussed, and the city's role was explained. Landmarks was one of several groups contributing to the publications.[26]

Landmarks continued its activities as it dealt with historic buildings and neighborhoods and prepared a series of position papers relating to preservation issues that provided information about the structures involved and expressed the organization's interest in them as community resources. It also published several studies. *Goals for a Better Built Environment in Columbus,* published in 1988, identified sets of goals intended "to provide a positive framework for making and evaluating the decisions which affect the quality of our urban environment."[27] *Landmark Decisions: Visions of Our City,* published in 1989, identified seven projects for which the time had come "for the city to develop its vision and to put in place a decision-making framework that is both deliberate and consensus building."[28] The publication was a product of a Landmarks initiative in 1987 to recognize its tenth anniversary by displays and discussions of the "decisions" in the community. It seems correct to say that Landmarks saw itself at this time as the conscience of the community, seeking to invigorate the planning process to help forestall the loss of the city's historic heritage.

In the 1990s, Landmarks continued its efforts to alert the community to the continuing loss of historic properties and to encourage preservation of worthy buildings. As part of its mission, it has developed an extensive number of educational programs and field trips for use in the schools and the community generally. Recently, it has reviewed its original inventory of buildings and produced a revised—"gone but not forgotten"—list showing the loss of buildings since 1988. Approximately 117 buildings were lost to demolition in this period—33 of them, or 28 percent, to provide surface parking lots!

During this time, two studies were completed for city departments to help identify and evaluate both historic properties and districts as potential candidates for the city Register.[29] And in 1992, a project team completed a document, *Reinvest-Reuse-Renew,* intended to "provide an action-oriented framework for a comprehensive city preservation program" and to "integrate preservation with, rather than separate it from, other planning and development activities such as zoning, regulations, code enforcement, housing, and economic development."[30] These studies are evidence of increasing city initiatives in support of community preservation efforts.

The Historic Resources Commission continues to develop and monitor the city's Register of Historic Properties. In 1989, the Board of Commission Appeals was organized to provide for a nonjudicial process of appeal of commission decisions. Meanwhile, the number of Historic Districts increased to fifteen and the number of Historic Properties to thirty-eight by 1999, and the number of neighborhood Historic Commissions has grown

The Ohio Penitentiary was demolished in late 1997 to make way for the new Nationwide Arena and development of the adjacent area as steps in revitalizing the Downtown.

from the initial three—German Village (1963), Victorian Village (1973), and Italian Village (1974)—to include the Brewery District. The North Market Commission was established in 1987 but is now within the Historic Resources Commission. The Historic Resources Commission continues its important role of reviewing and passing on planned redevelopment efforts for historic homes and neighborhoods on the Columbus Register through the issuance or denial of a Certificate of Appropriateness.

In response to the demolition of a historic Town Street house in 1993, the city prepared legislative changes, with community input, for the preservation chapters of the City Code. With respect to the Historic Resources Commission (Chapter 3117), there were several major changes in the appeals process: the 105-day waiting period was eliminated, the fourteen-member commission was reduced to nine, and the appeals process was clarified. Changes were also made with respect to architectural review (Chapter 3116), in an attempt to speed up the appeals process and reduce the financial burden on a property owner, and with respect to the operation of the Board of Commission Appeals (Chapter 3118), also in an attempt to streamline the appeals process.

The point is that interest and concern in historic preservation has come a long way in Columbus over the last fifty years. Certainly, there have been successes, including the work of the two organizations, the Columbus Landmarks Foundation and the Columbus Historic Resources Commission. Buildings and neighborhoods have been preserved, usually reflecting the roles of the various historic commissions and districts at the local neighborhood level. And despite the dwindling number of historic commercial and institutional buildings in the city, there have been important "saves," including the Masonic Temple, the renovation of a number of aging buildings such as the Carlile and Worly buildings into desirable quarters, and the current ongoing renovation of the Smith Brothers Hardware Building.

But too many buildings have been lost to demolition in the name of economic development, especially in the Downtown. Major losses in the 1990s include the Columbus Auditorium, or, as it was known to most of us, the Lazarus Annex, the Born Brewery building in the Brewery District, and, of course, the most recent major loss, the Ohio Penitentiary. It is clear that there has been a failure to recognize how history and historical artifacts may play a dynamic role in the promotion of a more successful tourist industry. So although it is proper to acknowledge that the preservation concept has been pursued and studied through the years, it is unfortunate that so little of the historic fabric of the community remains.

11

Quality of Life

I F WE HAD THOUGHT ABOUT "QUALITY OF LIFE"
fifty or so years ago, we probably would have considered that even with
our modest income and modest living environments, we were better off
than we were during the war years of the 1940s or the Depression years of
the 1930s. If there weren't many of the "arts" available in Columbus then,
that was okay too because we couldn't have afforded the luxury of the theater or the symphony. We were able to relax and enjoy the football season
only because, as students at Ohio State, tickets were available at reasonable
cost. But we found our pleasures elsewhere, and it didn't occur to us to
claim that our lives were wanting.

For one thing, we can still recall the fun it was to shop High Street
from the Union Store at Long and High south to Lazarus's big store at
Town and High, strolling in and out of the myriad specialty shops that
lined what some called "the great wide way." There was no Muirfield, no
"Wexley," and only a vintage Dublin then, and there was certainly no City
Center mall or Tuttle mall. Upper Arlington was the place to take out-of-
town visitors to see the new homes and the big cars parked in the neat
driveways. We could get a wonderful minestrone soup lunch at Marzetti's
on Saturdays along with dessert and all the coffee we could drink for about
$1.25. And on special occasions, there was Wilson's on North Fourth Street
in the campus area, with classical music (from a jukebox), Emerson Burk-
hart paintings on the wall for sale, and a wonderful chicken vatel. Then, if
we still had a few cents in our pockets, we could take in a foreign film at

the World Theater on North High or, further up the street, at the Little Theater. Chet Long (corny) and Jimmy Crum (canny even then) were on the radio along with the Early Worm (Erwin Johnson), who had fallen in love with "Lida Rose." Columbus was still small-town America, fairly comfortable, easy to get around in, and, as it liked to think, with only one murder a year.

So, while unaware of "quality of life" as such, we were aware of some of the "qualities" that seemed to satisfy Columbus natives and, almost reluctantly, even us. After life in Pittsburgh, it was indeed small-town Columbus, but it was easy to find one's way here, the wave of new home construction was encouraging, and the schools were good. And it was clear—or so the press and the Chamber of Commerce told us—that the well-balanced economy was a plus, and it had stood the test of time during the Depression years, reflecting a reasonably stable and honest local government. In retrospect, these aren't such bad "qualities" after all!

Almost fifty years have passed, and the city and region have undergone tremendous change—not surprising given the events of this period. We are likely to assume that the change has been for the better, that is, that the society, collectively, is a better place in which to live and that, specifically, our own community is as well.

One thing is certain: Columbus is a much larger community, offering a wider range of goods and services than in the postwar years, and it is likely that it is much more sophisticated—whatever that may suggest—than its earlier "cow town" image would lead one to believe. Its economy is more complex and integral to the high-tech age confronting the nation and the world, and its cultural resources are more diverse and exciting.

On the other hand, many of those features of the city fifty years ago that made us feel comfortable and perhaps relatively unburdened are gone, often replaced by increasing instability resulting from change and necessary adjustments to the new. If, in the early 1950s, we sought to reduce traffic congestion and parking problems in the Downtown retail sector, we now face what appear to be almost insurmountable congestion and traffic tie-ups on our highways that often lead to "road rage" and all that that implies relative to our quality of life.

Over time all good things change, and with luck and a modicum of good planning they change for the better. Many of those things that satisfied us fifty years ago are gone, along with the values they represented, and a new generation has responded to the challenges of change in the present even as it anticipates with some anxiety what the future will bring.

Recently, headlines from the *Columbus Dispatch* and the *New York*

Times suggest what is, perhaps, a different sense of life's qualities. "Central Ohio Still Growing" and "Columbus among Nation's Most Generous Cities" may give us a sense of satisfaction, but we're reminded, as well, that "Schools Rank Poorly." The latter may be reflected in the fact that these are "Prosperous Times, Except for the Young" and "Workers Spending More Time on the Job."

These headlines, like many others, reveal something about the quality of life that we experience here in Columbus and, for that matter, at the national level. Certainly, the rise and fall of the stock market affects individual budgets as well as national economies and thus our quality of life. At the same time, problems in our schools and neighborhood vandalism and crime may negatively affect the quality of our lives at the local level even though we may be satisfied at the dramatic advances made in the arts that enhance our lives. So just what does this term *quality of life* mean, and what does it tell us about life in central Ohio today?

DEFINING *QUALITY OF LIFE*

The term *quality of life* has been around for some time, but it became part of our daily vocabulary in the 1960s and more common in the 1970s when society became concerned about broad environmental issues such as the depletion of our natural resources, air and water pollution, wildlife and wilderness preservation, and other problems associated with the physical environment. We reacted as a society to our perceptions of the physical world and to our expectations regarding it. The term then in vogue was *environmental quality,* with the focus on maintaining the physical well-being of our communities and our planet.

A series of studies was undertaken in the mid-1960s by a group of geographers interested in the public's response to environmental quality within urban areas. One such study focused on Columbus and sought to understand four related issues: how people conceived of their outdoor milieu or environment, what connections they made between various environmental attributes, what kinds of environments they preferred, and the measurement of the extent "to which differences in personal background and environmental setting affect these judgments, choices, and relationships."[1]

The research laid out ten routes in the city, "all more or less residential" and all north of Fifth Avenue to approximately Dunedin Road, east and west a short distance from High Street. The routes were to be walked, observed, and then used as the basis for assessment. A brief introduction that summarized the findings provided three "composite impressions of Columbus as seen by students and residents" who participated in the study. The impressions are worth noting, keeping in mind that the research was carried on in the 1960s and in only a limited part of the city. One set identified Columbus as "the All-American city. . . . A nice town for families, a great city to rear children, a friendly place." A second set was a bit more critical, noting that the city was "flat, old, cold, and windy. Very dull . . . an overgrown farm town, the best location for the state fair." And the third set "watched it grow from a small crossroads to a large metropolis" and wondered "if city planning has kept abreast with the growth," noting that it was "an expanding city with non-expanding people; possibly this lackadaisical attitude is due to the summer weather, static, calm, and peaceful." We might not necessarily agree with the composite impressions, but we continue to hear some of the same observations today as we reflect on environmental quality in the central Ohio region.

A number of other studies were done by geographers in the 1970s to gauge the "environmental perception" of students and others with respect to many environmental quality issues, including their perceptions of desirable cities or states in which to work and live. One result among the students in my "Geography of Ohio" classes was a clearly marked negative perception of southern and northeastern states. On the other hand, at a time when society was giving considerable attention to the country's physical well-being, students showed a clear preference for states such as Colorado, Washington, and Oregon in which the perception of the physical environment was highly favorable. When their perceptions were confronted by reality—that is, with factual information about the choices they had made—they usually recognized that their lack of knowledge had biased those choices.

By the 1970s, the term *quality of life* had broadened to include issues related to the social and economic status of a population. It became a way of assessing and explaining the relative social and economic well-being of our community and of ourselves, for that matter. The term came into popular usage, replacing, in a sense, other terms, such as *general welfare,* used in government; *social indicators,* used by sociologists to reflect human progress; and even *social accounting,* used in the business world. The issue of quality of life was "in the air," so to speak, and attempts to define and explain it were underway.

In 1969 and 1970, hearings on "The Quality of Urban Life" were

Private neighborhood renovation and restoration of historic properties characterizes the success of several Columbus neighborhoods. North of the university campus on High Street is the Pavey block of late nineteenth-century townhouses,
which have been an important factor in maintaining a sense of neighborhood in
that community.

underway in the U.S. Congress, with expert testimony forthcoming from
a range of well-known academics, architects, planners, and business leaders.[2] At the Ohio State University, Byron Munson, sociologist and director
of the OSU Center for Community and Regional Analysis, conducted research to determine the social structure and functions implied by the concept of "community" in the eighty-eight Ohio counties. The research, based
upon the measurement and evaluation of 113 community variables for each
county, did not seek specifically to determine quality-of-life standards, but
it did provide generalizations about the concept and structure of "community," with the goal of gaining "a better understanding of community
dimensions and interrelationships." Munson observed that "social institutions . . . are all modified substantially in the transition from a rural to
urban way of life," a point of relevance today as suburbanization continues
to sprawl into our rural areas.[3]

Despite all the research that's been done, there may be no universal
agreement on what constitutes a desirable quality of life, but in general, a

satisfactory quality of life assumes that incomes are adequate to support basic needs along with a reasonable standard of living, with sound housing and good neighborhoods. The term *standard of living* may be defined as the average level of goods and services that a nation can provide its citizens. It is often thought of as the level of subsistence in a society, referring to the adequacy of the necessities and comforts of life. A reasonable standard would presumably include the availability to all of quality health and educational facilities, as well as adequate cultural and recreational opportunities. Thus, the socioeconomic and the physical environment of the society would be healthy, and negative features, such as crime, social disorganization, and family instability, would be minimized.

In 1988, Paul Minus, then director of the Council for Ethics in Economics here in Columbus, offered a useful definition of the quality of life as "a community's . . . totality of opportunities and resources available for all of its citizens to move toward the realization of their personal and collective well-being."[4] This definition may be overly optimistic, especially if we consider more carefully the implications of the word *available*. It suggests that a common mix of opportunities and resources should be available to all. Does the term imply that the mix, even if available, is then *accessible* to all? The question is raised because, clearly, what is *available* and what is *accessible* may differ in a society and between individuals. In turn, so then does the quality of life that we may each seek and enjoy, for there are constraints placed upon us by our ethnic and racial status, by our social and economic class, and by the access that each of us has to the market and to power. Simply put, we recognize that there is inequality in what might be termed the "life chances" that affect the quality of individual lives as well as the collective life of the community. It is also important to recognize that the attitudes or perceptions that a group might have with regard to desirable features in their community will vary between groups and areas. For example, to suburbanites, the home and neighborhood setting may be a key factor reflecting their aspirations and goals. On the other hand, a low-income urban family living in the inner city may regard its location in relation to jobs and city services as the principal consideration in making whatever choice they have made.[5]

QUALITY OF LIFE IN CENTRAL OHIO

What do we mean, then, when we talk about the quality of life in Columbus? Surely, we have a sense of it as individuals in terms of our own lives and, perhaps, collectively as we consider the term with respect to the city or region. It is a highly subjective term not easily given to scientific measurement, although we do use any number of statistical methods in an attempt to evaluate and proclaim it. Because evaluation is highly subjective, it is difficult to identify trends and changes in quality of life over time and between individuals or groups. Furthermore, quality-of-life studies try to identify the collective measures that set the standards; few seek to identify individual responses. On the other hand, data are readily available that provide clues to the quality of life in a region, such as population growth and change; specific demographic characteristics of the population, such as age, ethnicity, and educational attainment; and information regarding per capita income, housing and household size, and employment opportunities.

An early study by Ben Chieh Liu sought to identify Quality-of-Life (QOL) indicators for metropolitan areas in the United States and to evaluate and rate the findings. Using 1970 data, the study developed 123 indicators or measures in five component groups—economic, political, environmental, health and education, and social groups—and rated the findings for the then 243 Standard Metropolitan Statistical Areas (SMSAs) in the United States. Examples of QOL indicators used in the survey included per capita income, employment, percentage of low-income households, local government professionalism and performance, crime rates, pollution, medical services, infant mortality, educational attainment, living conditions, and recreation. Each component group was evaluated and rated by SMSA, with scores assigned for each and a ranking established. In any such ranking of QOL measures, large cities tend to reveal considerable variation from one measure to another: that is, they have their strengths and weaknesses, as the data revealed.[6]

In the Columbus area, I suspect that most of us would admit to enjoying a satisfactory quality of life as we live here and go about our daily work. Individually, we may have our own personal problems that fluctuate from day to day, but our perception of the quality of life in the community, and in our lives as participants, is surely quite high. We are reasonably comfortable with the good life that is available here; it *is* a good place to live and to raise a family, and it seems to be getting better and more interesting all the time. After all, ours is a dynamic and progressive economy, one of the fastest growing in the northeastern quadrant of the nation. Within the Columbus Metropolitan Statistical Area in late 1998, six counties had unemployment rates among the ten lowest in Ohio, and both population and new employment opportunities are increasing at a higher rate here than in any other Ohio metropolitan area. Furthermore, employment growth is in the expanding service and high-tech information and communication economy, which promises much for the future. And fortunately we have a higher percentage of high school and college graduates in our population than does Ohio as a whole. Our people are living longer in better health and in better housing, and our cultural environment has been improved dramatically, with growing support for the symphony, ballet, theater, the arts, and the various sporting events that are so much a part of our culture. Our perceptions of our good fortune are supported by the data, and the Chamber of Commerce and the Columbus Visitors Bureau are not hesitant in telling the world about it.

As early as 1974, results of a study of quality of life in metropolitan Columbus based on survey research involving 2,401 residents showed "Columbus area residents expressing a generally high level of satisfaction with most aspects of their everyday lives." The study also identified "urgent social problems," noting "crime and general 'public safety' issues [such as police protection and juvenile delinquency] to be the highest ranking concerns of Columbus area residents." A second layer of problems included concern about urban growth and expansion, drugs, lack of sufficient income, housing, and intracity transportation—an interesting mix of issues. This report is cited here as an early example of local research related to the concept of quality of life and to indicate the range of issues examined in one local study as potentially affecting the perceived quality of life in the community.[7]

In a healthy society, the positive quality of life that is enjoyed should be catching—that is, ideally it should be extended to others and made available to the less fortunate. We know, however, that for a subset of our population the quality of life is less than satisfactory. The causes may be many, but in general poor life quality is usually spatially, socially, and economically concentrated and, at the same time, usually isolated. And it is characteristic of the experience that those facing these problems are among the least able to resolve them.

One of the unintended consequences of a growing society, one intent on achieving a highly satisfying quality of life, is that we who have choice often separate ourselves from those who are less fortunate or somehow different from us. This leads to isolation that may be geographic, as with the suburbanization of residential housing and the relocation of employment opportunities from the city core to the suburbs, which leave behind an increasingly disadvantaged population, often in older deteriorating neighborhoods. Isolation may also be socioeconomic, as we tend to separate ourselves from others by income, education, and social experiences. These conditions reflect our individual ability to make choices, and it is obvious that those who are richer—a relative term—have greater choice in our society than the poor, who have little or virtually no choice. Thus, whereas certain experiences or conditions are available in the community, they may be increasingly inaccessible to a subset of the larger community. For example, despite the expanding economy and low rate of unemployment, many workers lack the skills to find employment in the new industries, and sound retraining programs for them may be lacking. In the minority population, median family incomes lag, and there is a higher percentage living in poverty. Without adequate income, there is no possibility to share in the good housing available in the region, and the expansion and upgrading of the cultural life of the community may truly be inaccessible to many.

Of concern to many urban specialists, then, is the potential for the polarization of certain groups within a community by race or ethnicity. The notion that blacks are more urban and whites more suburban in their orientation arose from patterns of social mobility, or the lack thereof. History shows us that when blacks were moving into the cities, jobs were available in the core area of the city, where housing and public transportation were most readily available as well. When well-intentioned public housing evolved nationally and in Columbus, low-income families found homes in the housing projects. Over time, public housing became predominantly black housing, leading to polarization and poverty. The inequality in life chances and choices that we noted earlier was then made manifest. In an almost perverse way, and for totally different reasons, the rich may also be isolated in their high-rent suburbs and gated communities, as income has been the most egregious form of segregation. Of course, such isolation is usually deliberate, even though it may further the lack of understanding between social groups within our city.

Our quality of life can also be altered not only as a result of national disaster, such as a physical catastrophe or a depressed economy, but as the result of local changes over which we may have little control, and also as a result of personal changes, such as aging, feelings of depression, or declining health. For many of us, there is a sense that we are working longer and harder, with a resultant increase in stress in our lives. The historic worker ideal of increased leisure time has been replaced by intense job pressures, increased time on the job, and shortened time for vacations. Even something as familiar as traffic congestion that responds to the geographic spread of the area and the changing social mores in vogue may affect our quality of life. Suburbanization has contributed to a separation of the worker's residence from his or her place of work and a consequent increase in travel time required in the workday. And the increase in the number of women in the workplace results in more trips being made—not only by commuters to work but by "soccer moms" transporting their children to school, day care centers, and recreation sites. "Phone Friends," an after-school telephone response service for latchkey children in its thirteenth year in Columbus, is one example of how dramatically the quality of family life has been altered. In other words, quality of life may reflect what is happening *within* a community as much as it reflects the impact of the larger society on the individual and the community.

THE RATINGS GAME

The ratings game, in which a singular quality or a collection of qualities relating especially to individual cities or states are evaluated and rated, has become a popular activity spurred on by magazines and the news media, chambers of commerce, city and state economic development departments, and the like. Any of a number of "qualities" may lead to such ratings, including, of course, the quality of life. But what do the ratings actually tell us about quality of life?

Susan Cutter, in her book *Rating Places,* suggested that there is a "goal state" relative to place that is essentially subjective and culturally biased. It involves the collective impression of a place that we aspire to or what we think the place ought to be—in other words, our "perception" of the place. A second state, the "appraisal state," attempts to measure the actual environment to identify what is present there as opposed to one's perception.[8]

Obviously, almost any survey and study of the quality of life in American cities is fuel for the "ratings game." Many such studies have developed through the years as a by-product of serious research aimed at understanding the concept and its importance. The ratings result from the analysis of a specific set of measures used in an evaluative survey for individual places that are then compared. Basic to the results of such ratings is an understanding of the indicators or measures that have been used in the survey. In other words, if quality of life is the issue, what measures have been considered and evaluated in coming up with meaningful results? To some extent, the idea of ratings may have gotten a start with Liu's 1976 study, discussed above. That research ranked Columbus twenty-second overall among the sixty-five largest SMSAs in the nation. The city scored well on the political and social components. Cleveland and Cincinnati were close behind, ranking twenty-third and twenty-fifth, respectively.[9]

The media are absorbed with the rating game. In 1998 *Time* magazine carried a brief report from a major accounting-consulting firm for "the best prospects for investing" in prime real estate. The report suggested that older metro centers offered the best prospects at the time in comparison to "overbuilt suburban cities."[10] But the article could just as well have been a report in *Psychology Today* on how various cities respond to stress, or on the best cities for business by *Fortune* or *Newsweek,* and so on, with the crucial ranking of comparative cities being the ultimate purpose. The *Places Rated Almanac* began publishing a ranking of the nation's Standard Metropolitan Areas (SMAs) in 1981 and has continued to the present. Columbus was not ranked in the top twenty-five in 1981, nor does it appear in the top thirty of the 351 U.S. and Canadian metropolitan areas in the latest publication. What is ranked, when it is ranked, and the measures that are used to make the rankings all affect how a community or state or region is perceived over time. As the measures change, so may the rankings.[11]

The results of any such survey are at best a mixed bag. Chambers of commerce, convention bureaus, location specialists, business firms, and others are all interested in the findings and what they may reveal. Communities that are highly ranked may use the survey to publicize their standing; communities that do not fare so well in the ratings would, one assumes, just as gladly forget them and ignore the implications. But, once again, the ratings are not a science, no matter what statistical base they have; rather, they are perception-laden assessments of carefully selected factors.

In any case, it's often difficult to ignore the ratings, and if they are favorable, it's hard not to want to crow about your community's good fortune. But we can't be carried away by national ratings alone. If we are prepared to compare our community with others, isn't it important also to look at how quality of life varies within our own geographic area—that is, within Columbus, between political Columbus and the suburbs, between differing suburbs, and between differences in ethnic, racial, and class status?

12

The Cultures of the Community

I N A VERY REAL SENSE, THE CULTURE OF THE community is a measure of the quality of life in the community. My old dictionary defines *culture* as "enlightenment and excellence of taste acquired by intellectual and aesthetic training," but it also indicates that the term may apply to "behavior typical of a group or class." It is the latter definition that I am using here, as we consider not only the "finer arts" but also those physical activities, participatory and spectator alike, that are an inherent part of our broadly conceived culture.

We may share daily in a variety of forms of culture at many different levels of sophistication. The diverse and complex cultural offerings of the national press, radio, and, particularly, television are a case in point, but there is also a considerable assortment of cultural events in our community that we may share in more intimately. In general, the larger the community in terms of population, wealth, and educational opportunities, the greater the cultural smorgasbord from which its citizens may choose. That is, there must be a "critical mass" of people to provide the means of support to achieve the kind of cultural environment we may seek.

It almost goes without saying that the culture of Columbus, no matter how defined, is remarkably different today from that encountered fifty years ago, if for no other reason than that there are far more cultural opportunities available today. That is, there is a now wide-ranging set of activities that appeal to the broad spectrum of interests in the community and allow considerable flexibility in the choices one can make. It wasn't always so.

Growing up in Pittsburgh in the 1930s, I had the good fortune to experience certain activities not typically available to a child living in poor and middle-class societies—it was the Depression after all—primarily because the public school system, then one of the finest in the nation, attempted to broaden our cultural experiences. From junior high school on, we were privileged once a year to hear, in our school auditoriums, the Pittsburgh Symphony Orchestra, with the renowned Fritz Reiner conducting, and Walter Damrosch, the well-known conductor, brought a small orchestra to the elementary school where I was a student to play for the assembled children.

It wasn't music alone that we were treated to. Annually, we were taken to the Carnegie Museum to encourage any latent interests in the arts. I remember especially on those school tours seeing the Carnegie International Art Show, then a major art event in this country, and puzzling on one occasion over the winning entry, Braque's *The Yellow Cloth,* perhaps my first contact with cubism. In high school, we were given the opportunity on occasion to see a Broadway play at the Nixon Theater or to attend a lecture at Carnegie Museum, where I once sat in awe listening to Eleanor Roosevelt. Obviously, the support for these activities came from the wealth generated by the economic activities that were then so vital to the city.

The experiences weren't all so cultural. Pittsburgh had major league baseball with the Pirates and a not too successful pro football team in the earlier years of that sport. But no charitable group supported my interests in sports, and a pro game was not on my youthful agenda. College football was more important to us, with strong teams at Pitt, Carnegie Tech (now Carnegie Mellon), and Duquesne.

The point is that Pittsburgh had the necessary critical mass to support a broad range of activities. It was at that time one of the ten largest cities in population and the center of the nation's steel industry, if not the world's. I'm reminded that my mother would explain to me, as we took the streetcar from our home into the downtown, that as long as the smokestacks along the Monongahela River were smoking, everything would be all right. Not only was there the population to support varied activities, there was corporate wealth reflected in the steel mills and in other industrial and commercial enterprises, and in the names associated with them—Mellon, Heinz, Frick, Westinghouse—that helped to make available many of the opportunities we had then.

Coming to Columbus in late 1949, we came to a smaller city, one perhaps worthy of being described as "small-town America." It took some getting used to, as the saying goes. Leaving a city noted for the dominance of its many fine department stores within the Golden Triangle and its symphony orchestra, it was surprising to find only one true department store in Columbus. What was noticeably missing was a set of cultural activities that represented the spectrum of the arts. To a considerable extent, the university offered a kind of refuge where lectures, concerts, and plays were available to students and, on occasion, to the public. As for sports culture, it was obvious that intercollegiate football and basketball at Ohio State could satisfy the community's demand for spectator sports at that time.

Our Columbus story really begins in the postwar years, when the city embarked on a growth curve fueled in part by new industry and related commerce and by steady population growth. It slowly became alive to the many possibilities open to it. There was no symphony, ballet, opera, dance company, or COSI at the time. But there was the old Hartman Theater for Broadway plays, where we sat in the upper balcony in our $1.00 seats with my wife's English class from East High School to enjoy *The King and I* with Yul Brynner and Gertrude Lawrence. There was also the Players Theatre, dating back to 1923 as a club and then community theater; the relatively small but impressive Gallery of Fine Arts; a struggling zoo; and a fairly good minor league baseball team (still here and rather underappreciated).

In the section "Reasons for Dynamic Growth" in the *Blue Plan: The Comprehensive Regional Plan for the Columbus Area,* a short paragraph summarized the general observations about "Cultural Facilities" as they appeared in Columbus in 1966. It noted that

> Columbus is emerging as a cultural center, to some extent. The enthusiasm for the "arts" may not yet match the enthusiasm this city has for its various "sports" programs, but a change is in the wind. Active support is now available for the city's art gallery, symphony orchestra, museum, and zoo, and for a host of smaller and less readily identifiable cultural media. In this respect, the community offers to the new resident a varied and exciting series of opportunities to participate, especially when contrasted with the community as it existed 20 years ago.[1]

Clearly, change *was* in the wind. And, there was the recognition that the city's cultural resources included both the arts and sports.

The Ohio State Fairgrounds is another example of the state of Ohio's presence in Columbus. The fair in August attracts many thousands of visitors to the city and is a cultural function in its own right.

In the rest of this chapter, we will consider first the emergence of the arts to their place of prominence in Columbus and then the role of the sports culture in helping to shape the city and region.

DEVELOPMENT OF THE ARTS

I can't remember just when we attended our first symphony program in Columbus, but I do recall that it was in Veterans Memorial and that Evan Whallon was the conductor. The forerunner of a symphony orchestra was the Columbus Philharmonic, founded and governed by local women. By 1951, their efforts to found a fledgling symphony orchestra were successful, and by 1952 the Columbus Little Symphony was incorporated, with George Hardesty as conductor. The name of the orchestra was changed in 1955 to the Columbus Symphony Orchestra, in recognition of the increasing stature of the group. Evan Whallon was hired as conductor in 1956, and by 1961 men were brought onto the Symphony Board. In 1966, the symphony was selected as one of fifty orchestras in the nation to receive a $500,000 challenge grant from the Ford Foundation to establish an endowment for the symphony. At this time, concerts were held in Veterans Memorial, although a change in venue was desirable. The success of the symphony was an important step for the city, and it helped pave the way for initiatives to widen the scope of cultural offerings to include opera, ballet, and dance.

The experiences related to the development and success of the Columbus Symphony Orchestra seem to have set the stage for the city's emergence as a cultural center. That, along with the founding of the Columbus Association for the Performing Arts (CAPA) in 1969 and the eventual saving of the ornate Ohio Theatre, built by the Loews Corporation in 1928, altered dramatically how one considered this city. For one thing, the commitment to these efforts by community leaders established that the city had the momentum and the wherewithal to undertake to improve its cultural base. Funding groups such as the National Endowment for the Arts (NEA) and the Ohio Arts Council (OAC) were established in the late 1960s, and locally Battelle Memorial Institute was prepared to support the effort to save the Ohio Theatre with a $750,000 matching grant in 1969. The community rallied to the challenge, with additional contributions from over 3,500 individuals and businesses.[2]

Perhaps not part of the arts scene as such, but surely a part of the city's culture, COSI, the Center of Science and Industry, was launched in 1964 with support of the Franklin County Historical Society. Located in Old Memorial Hall, its focus was on local history as well as on science and industry. By the early 1970s, the Gallery of Fine Arts was adding a new wing, and the Columbus College of Art and Design (CCAD) a new building. The Columbus Arts Council was revived, sponsoring the annual art festival as well as its "Artists in Schools" program. And by 1972, the symphony had its first full-time musicians and now presented its programs in the renovated Ohio Theatre. The staging of the first opera in the theater, *Die Fledermaus,* took place at this time.

In 1975, the Battelle Memorial Institute Foundation (BMIF) was established, and, in the following year the symphony sought a grant from the foundation.[3] BMIF joined with the Junior League of Columbus to recommend, first, that a "Cultural Explorations" study be undertaken to document the cultural activities in Franklin County and to determine future needs and goals for further development. "The primary recommendation of the Cultural Explorations report . . . was that the community establish a 'strong coordinative body for the arts.'"[4] One result was that BMIF encouraged

The Festival of the Arts was a modest affair in 1972 when this picture was taken, but it has since blossomed into a major event. In this photo, the newly restored Ohio Theatre offers a "Free Pops Concert" as part of the festival.

and helped to restructure the Greater Columbus Arts Council (GCAC) to take on a larger role in the community. The study also provided funding to endow five chairs and program development for the symphony and provided major grants to CAPA to help complete the restoration and renovation of the Ohio Theatre by updating the various systems and enlarging the relatively small stage, which had been adequate for motion picture presentations but not for productions of opera, ballet, dance, or the symphony itself.

Through the late 1970s, then, BMIF was a major force in shaping the cultural milieu of Columbus with a series of grants intended to support various institutions in dance, such as Ballet Metropolitan, Dancentral, and the Zivili Kolo Ensemble. Grants were also made to the Players Theatre to permit expansion of the theater and its program, to the symphony to expand the number of permanent positions, and to the Columbus Museum of Art in response to a plan to renovate the new wing and to improve the museum's rapport with the community by providing support for a sculpture garden to be opened to the public.[5] In attempting to raise funds, organizations found that with a grant in place from BMIF, the community responded more enthusiastically to their solicitations than it might have otherwise. In other words, the effect of the BMIF grant program was to enrich the local arts community and, in turn, strengthen and promote it. The seven-year life of BMIF was of major importance not only to the arts and humanities but to organizations in the social services and health fields and to those in education and civic affairs.

This is not to say that BMIF was the only source of funding. Local organizations received grants from such groups as the NEA, the National Endowment for the Humanities (NEH), the Ford Foundation, the state of Ohio, and the city of Columbus. It is probably fair to note, however, that Columbus had not yet replicated the experience of Minneapolis, where major corporations commit a certain percentage of their taxable income to the cultural life of the community.

In March 1980, Rosemary Curtin Hite, then the art critic of the *Columbus Citizen-Journal,* reflected in a farewell column on the previous fifteen years of the arts in Columbus. She identified several major events as signaling the coming of age of the arts in the city. Included were the saving of the Ohio Theatre and formation of CAPA, the emergence of Ballet Met and the Zivili dance group, and the expanded and improved symphony. She acknowledged the importance of increased financial support for the arts from private individuals and institutions, as well as from the city, but she bemoaned the lack of more full-time professionals in the orchestra, the absence of a professional theater company, and the poor support for art education in the schools.[6]

By 1981, the NEA had carried out a study to assess the economic impact of arts and cultural institutions on their local communities. Columbus was one of six cities chosen for the study; the others were Minneapolis/ St. Paul, St. Louis, Salt Lake City, San Antonio, and Springfield, Illinois. A major objective of the six case studies was to determine how a subset of cultural organizations affected the economy in each city and how the role of such organizations may help to shape economic development policy in a community.

In Columbus, 6 of the more than 170 nonprofit arts and cultural institutions in the area were selected for the study: the Columbus Museum of Art, CAPA, Players Theatre, Ballet Metropolitan, COSI, and the Columbus Symphony. The study recognized that "the primary purpose of the arts and cultural institutions is to add to creative expression and quality of life, and not to generate dollars and jobs for the community. . . . The economic value of the arts should be viewed as a by-product and not the primary reason for their existence."[7] Nonetheless, the study revealed that almost $17 million was generated in the community by both direct spending and the secondary impact of the six organizations. Clearly, cultural and economic development may be complementary, and understanding the economic impact of cultural organizations in a community may provide incentives to advocate and support their role. The study also revealed that the "various arts events in Columbus . . . are supported by a large, diverse group of its citizens": nearly 700,000 patrons were drawn to the city in 1978–79 by the six institutions—largely from the Columbus Standard Metropolitan Statistical Area.[8]

In a talk in late 1986 to the Columbus Torch Club, a town-and-gown group of professional women and men, Andrew Broekema, then dean of the College of the Arts at OSU, reviewed the changes that had occurred in the art scene in Columbus in the previous decade and looked ahead to the future. He observed, "All along the way we have seen phenomenal growth in the number of arts events, in growth of audiences, in funding support, and in a general realization that we are just beginning." He also cited comments by John Christie, then president of the Chamber of Commerce, to the effect that the arts were "critical to the city's quality of life and developing economy. The entrepreneurial spirit is very much in force in Columbus now and it's especially evident in the arts."[9]

Broekema said that the arts schedule was now quite full and that there was concern about adequate stage space to satisfy demand, even with the Ohio and Palace Theatres, the Mershon and Veterans Auditoriums, and miscellaneous smaller facilities. He anticipated the near completion of the Riffe Center, with its three theaters, and the Martin Luther King, Jr. Center, and the future restoration of the Southern Theatre. And he noted with enthusiasm the excitement of the Short North, with its galleries, restaurants, and shops, and the Gallery Hop held there the first Saturday of every month.

By early 1987, the symphony had even reached the New York scene via the *New York Times,* albeit with a photo of striking Columbus Symphony musicians in an article discussing the financial straits that many orchestras around the country were then experiencing.[10]

In pushing its cultural envelope a bit further in 1989, Columbus could anticipate several attractions that Mel Dodge, then president of the Greater Columbus Convention and Visitors Bureau, called "long-running, blockbuster events . . . over the next few years." The events Dodge was talking about were, first, the Son of Heaven exhibition at Central High School, in which more than 225 "national treasures" of China were on display, and then, in 1992, AmeriFlora, an international horticultural event, and the Quincentennial Celebration of Columbus's voyage and discovery of 1492, the latter encompassing a variety of activities.[11] But the question was whether these events would "be the springboard that propels Columbus into the rarified heights of major league status?"[12]

By the end of 1992, the three events had run their courses, with financial losses for both public and corporate supporters and disappointment at the inability of these major events to draw tourists to the city. Worse yet, national press coverage of the events was largely negative, further confirming the disappointment. The *New York Times,* in a review entitled "An Odd Hybrid Called Ameriflora Struggles in Ohio," explained that the event "ended up costing millions and raising questions about its value as a horticultural event or as a boost to the city."[13] And the *Wall Street Journal* claimed that AmeriFlora would end up being one of the "biggest yawns" Columbus had experienced.[14] This despite earlier forecasts that suggested that AmeriFlora would be worth millions to the area economy. The effort did, of course, lose money, but area residents and local businesses responded well to it, and there is a legacy of improvements to the conservatory and parks where the event took place. Even so, the results indicated, it seems, that the city had not done very well at self-promotion.

In retrospect, it's possible that the opening of the Wexner Center for the Arts in 1989 was the major cultural achievement of the time. Certainly, Leslie Wexner helped to raise the ante in terms of community and corporate support for the arts and for the general well-being of Columbus. In so doing, a new standard was set in fund-raising, whether for arts organizations, COSI, or the United Way.[15]

In 1991, the community suddenly faced the closing of Opera/Columbus, founded in 1981, which had been called one of the fastest growing opera companies in the nation. Again, finances were at the heart of the decision. Happily, money was ultimately forthcoming— $50,000 in a gift from a local supporter, Professor Philip Jastram, which served to challenge other donors to respond to the need. It made it clear that private giving was vital to the success of the arts.[16]

The arts collectively may be in flux as familiar organizations and activities disappear and, we hope, new ones appear on the scene. The losses in the arts are usually attributable to financial problems—cost of productions, lack of community support, changing and declining markets for the "product"—and mismanagement or friction between boards, directors, and staff.

As noted earlier, certain of the symphony's problems were associated with inadequate finances, but there was also discontent with the director and management. Opera, one of the most expensive of the arts, was almost lost to the community due to lack of support, and the Players Theatre, which closed in late 1993, was beset by problems between management and staff and by lack of support for its move into the Riffe Center. With luck and good fortune, older activities continue with expanded enthusiasm, as in the case of Pro Musica, twenty years old in 1999, which has a new home in the restored Southern Theatre.

INTERLUDE, INTERMISSION, OR IS IT HALF-TIME?

As suggested earlier, the Columbus culture has always been divided between the arts and sports, but never more so than today. On the other hand, it may be argued that there is, at least to some extent, interest in and support for *both* the arts *and* sports. Might this not be the best of all worlds in this day and age?

I've had some experiences when attending the symphony at the Ohio Theatre that seem to support this notion. It's fairly clear that enthusiasts for fine music and the symphony orchestra may also be enthusiasts for various sports; in the past, this has especially been true for those associated with the university. It may not be commonplace, but it isn't uncommon either, to hear the intermission referred to as "half-time" by concert attendees. Even *Dispatch* critic Barbara Zuck, in her review of the Pavarotti concert at the Schottenstein Center, noted that "he sounded at the top of his form in the second half."[17] Recently, as I moved through the lobby at "half-time," I overheard an interesting exchange between two well-dressed businessmen. One asked, "Where are your seats?" The enthusiastic response of his friend, as he pointed upward, was "Oh, we're up in C-deck!" drawing a clear analogy between the upper balcony of the theater and the C-deck at Ohio Stadium.

A *Times* article in late 1996 raised some questions about the fact that "audiences these days are quick to rise to their feet, no matter how mediocre the show," and wondered, "Are they really praising themselves?"[18] I'm not sure why this practice occurs in New York City, but here in the home of the Buckeyes, I'm convinced that it's a manifestation of our football fever. One has to wonder if we aren't just enthusiastically cheering the score, whether it be of a musical masterpiece or of a touchdown at the stadium. There may be a rah-rah spirit present in both, and that might not be all bad.

This close relationship of the arts and sports is reflected, as well, in the use of a phrase such as "major league status" or "big league" to define a cultural event. And it doesn't come as a surprise to the citizenry when a civic leader such as Douglas Kridler, president of CAPA, heads up community drives to raise funds for both theaters and arenas and stadiums.

THE SPORTS CULTURE

Whatever understanding one might have had about the sports culture in Columbus fifty years ago, for many old-timers, Columbus sports came of age then. The dominant force was, clearly, Ohio State football, both because of its considerable successes and because of its reputation as a coach's "graveyard" until Woody Hayes arrived on the scene. The community and the press, locally and nationally, followed OSU football religiously and with fervor.

It's been said that even today, in a national polling of CEOs asked to identify the city, the major response is that Columbus is the home of the Buckeyes. If that remains true today, doesn't it say something about why other sports—and especially pro sports—are simply not as necessary to the local sports scene as they are in other communities?

OSU football and the Columbus Redbirds of the minor league American Association were the two sports teams that represented Columbus nationally fifty years ago. These, along with other intercollegiate sports teams at our numerous smaller universities and good sports programs in the high schools, served to satisfy Columbus sports fans. Ardent fans packed the stadium in the autumn and later the Fairgrounds Coliseum for basketball. The construction of the St. John Arena forty years ago was a community event, not just another OSU venture.

As the city grew and the culture changed somewhat, there may have been early thoughts about a professional major league baseball team. But the basic geography of the major leagues, which represented the then urban hierarchy of the country, and the presence in Ohio of two teams already in the "majors"—Cleveland and Cincinnati—was enough to convince proponents that major league baseball in Columbus was not to be. Absent then, of course, was the powerful influence of lucrative television market coverage and revenues and the "critical mass" of population to alter the situation. But how has this changed—if it has?

In early 1978, an article in the *Columbus Dispatch* headlined "Market Study Indicates City Could Not Support Arena" reported the conclusions of a consulting firm assessing the city's potential not only for an arena but for the necessary teams to justify it. The article suggested that there have to be "at least two major league franchises to make it [an arena] work, and even then it still needs a subsidy." At the time, only one metro area in the country smaller than Columbus had a major league team (San Antonio with a basketball team), and no city smaller than Columbus had a National Hockey League team.[19] Nonetheless, in response to what might be called the city's inferiority complex, the mania to have both an arena and a professional major league team continued, despite increasing evidence that cities tend to lose money when they get into the public financing of an arena or stadium, whereas the owners of the franchises profit from the gate receipts. In other words, tax dollars are used to subsidize a team, while payment goes to some of the richest investors in town.[20]

The issue resurfaced in Columbus in 1986, when voters defeated by a 54 percent to 46 percent margin a $691 million sales tax plan that had been advertised by proponents as a way "to transform Columbus into a *major league* city" (italics added). About half the figure would have helped to subsidize the Central Ohio Transit Authority; slightly less would have funded the Columbus New World Center, a convention center that would have allowed the city to compete for major conventions and would have had flexible seating of 15,000 to 65,000 "for football, basketball, soccer and other entertainments." John B. McCoy, then the Chamber of Commerce chair, was quoted as saying that "the center is among six projects that will make Columbus a *big league* city by 2000" (italics added).[21]

By 1989, some satisfaction was gained when professional basketball, albeit in the Continental Basketball Association, had its inaugural in November at the Ohio Expositions Center. By December, a sports arena (to seat 20,000) had been proposed by Downtown Columbus Inc., to be built on the former penitentiary site. In the spirit of the day, it was proposed that the arena would be linked in some fashion to the Central High School site as part of the commitment to bring increased activity into the Downtown.

Four years later, with neither an arena nor a major professional sports team in sight, it was argued that an arena was "a logical next step," especially as the new Convention Center had opened in mid-March. The same reasoning prevailed: an arena was needed to be part of the promotion of a larger vision of the Downtown, along with the expansion of COSI and development of the Peninsula site. Those supporting growth in the Downtown argued as well that "OSU would be a fine candidate to use a Downtown arena for such activities as basketball,"[22] but the university remained opposed to this idea, with the current president, E. Gordon Gee, supporting instead an arena on campus.[23]

In 1993, Charlotte, North Carolina, was selected by the NFL to be its twenty-ninth team. The syndicated columnist Bob Greene, in a column that appeared in the *Columbus Dispatch,* discussed Charlotte's excitement about landing the franchise but also suggested that "any *big league* may be our age's most overvalued concept"—an interesting point in Columbus. As if in response, a *Dispatch* article noted that the mayor was kicking off a search for a pro sports team by appointing a committee to recruit a team for the pro basketball and hockey leagues.[24]

Early in 1994, a *Columbus Monthly* article identified "seven reasons why Columbus will never have a big-league sports franchise." Whether written in jest or not, the seven included some serious issues: "money," and the willingness to spend it; "no arena, no stadium and no plan," which, with the third reason, "all talk and no action," may really be the major point; "it's too late" (i.e., the "big leagues" may already have reached their limits); "geography" and the recognition that our "critical mass" of population and our market territory may not justify a franchise, given the sixth reason, "Ohio State" and its great tradition of successful Big Ten sports and its hold on the market; and, finally, the suggestion that "we don't really want one," which for some folks is probably true.[25]

In late 1994, the city and the university announced plans for two separate arenas, although the pros and cons associated with the financing of an arena and the need for professional major league teams remained under debate. In its publication *Cross Section,* the Federal Reserve Bank of Richmond published a detailed article thoroughly reviewing Charlotte's experience with its team. Although some basic questions concerning the economic impact of the team and facility upon the community remained unanswered, there appeared to be general agreement that the image of the community and area had been enhanced nationally.[26]

A study conducted in the geography department at Ohio State in 1994 considered six U.S. cities as possible expansion sites for major league baseball—Columbus, Denver, Miami, Phoenix, Portland (Oregon), and Tampa—and predicted revenues for each. By the time the study was completed, Miami and Denver had already been chosen as sites. Since then, two other cities have attracted expansion teams, Phoenix and Tampa. Portland and Columbus, the two cities with the lowest projected revenues, have still not attracted a team. In a letter to Mayor Greg Lashutka, an offer was made to make the unbiased research available to the city and to meet with city officials to discuss it, but the offer was not accepted.[27]

A member of the General Assembly, E. J. Thomas, responding to the assembly's economic development initiatives, cautioned that there were lessons to be learned from other cities, especially in controlling the costs associated with arena or stadium development. Thomas stated frankly that "pro sports are big business with each franchise seeking the community with the best deal" and noted that "loyalty to any local community . . . will always be secondary."[28] Both the *Economist* and the *New York Times* explored the issues and came up with much the same conclusions: arenas or stadiums are almost always subsidized by the public sector—that is, you as taxpayer—whereas the profits derived from the revenues accrue to the "already wealthy professional sports team owners rather than the community."[29]

Even so, Columbus went ahead with its various committees formed to raise enthusiasm for arenas, stadiums, and professional sports teams *and* for funds to support the initiatives. By early 1997, a plan was put forth for a 0.5 percent sales tax increase to be voted on in the May election. The total cost for a 21,000-seat arena to be located near the Convention Center and a 30,000-seat stadium to be located on the penitentiary site, assuming demolition of the penitentiary, was estimated at $287 million. Despite support from the political and civic leadership and the media, voters defeated the proposal by a 56 percent to 44 percent margin. The general conclusion was that voters did not want a new tax and, especially, a tax that would subsidize private business in sports, where owners are often seen as "the new robber barons."[30]

After this defeat at the polls, and despite the fact that most arenas have been financed by public money, the mood in Columbus was such that Nationwide Insurance and the Dispatch Printing Company announced a plan to build a $125-million arena, to be owned 90 percent by Nationwide and 10 percent by the Dispatch Printing Company, to attract a National Hockey League expansion team.[31] On June 17, 1997, Columbus was awarded an NHL expansion team, justifying the optimism of Ron Pizzuti, developer and sports enthusiast, who, following the defeat of the tax issue, had predicted that "if there is some way an arena can be . . . built, the NHL will come."[32]

There was concern, however, about possible competition for attractions between the Nationwide Arena and the new Schottenstein Center with its Value City Arena at Ohio State, and also about the ability of the Convention Center to accommodate increased activity. An article in *Columbus Monthly* in July 1997 on "the town-gown battle" reviewed the sometimes acrimonious relationships between city leadership and that of the university over both the financing of the facilities and the question of competition over the scheduling not only of sports events but of other entertainment events, such as ice shows and concerts.[33] Not to be outdone, the mayor appointed the Greater Columbus Sports Commission to try to increase the number of amateur, collegiate, and professional sports activities in the community.[34]

By early 1998, plans for the Nationwide Arena and the Nationwide Arena District, a commercial-residential neighborhood mix with the arena as its central point, were made public. Groundbreaking occurred in May, with plans for completion of construction in time for the National Hockey League season in 2000 and play by the Columbus team, the Blue Jackets. A stadium for the Columbus Crew soccer team, then playing in Ohio Stadium, had been planned for Dublin, but that initiative too was defeated at the polls. In May 1998, plans were announced for a new soccer facility for the team at the Ohio Exposition Center, with a 22,500-seat, privately financed stadium. Groundbreaking occurred in July 1998, and the Crew opened its season to a capacity crowd on Saturday, May 15, 1999.

OVERVIEW

I would argue that the cultural milieu in Columbus is broad, ranging from the sports culture that seems to have such a strong grip on the community to that of the arts. Both are active. The question is, can both be supported effectively? Not long ago, two of our local television stations interrupted their programming at 10:30 on a Wednesday morning (January 6, 1999) to inform the community that an OSU football player had decided to turn pro! When did they last interrupt programming to announce, with bated breath, any activity associated with the arts? One can understand the concern of those who feel that our community culture is dominated by sports and the sports media.

Consider another matter—attendance at an event. We who attend the symphony have all noticed the array of empty seats, and even rows, at the theater despite fine programs, a young and improving orchestra, and an exciting conductor. Is it that corporate sponsors buy the seats to support the symphony but can't fill them? Can you imagine that at Ohio Stadium or at the Schottenstein Center? Of course not!

So at the beginning of a new millennium, Columbus has certainly come of age in "the arts culture" with the widening recognition of its symphony, an active Opera/Columbus, Pro Musica, Ballet Met, the several theaters, and other performing arts. Then, too, we have the Museum of Art with its innovative exhibits, an expanded and exciting new COSI, and the highly successful zoo, with worldwide recognition for its gorilla breeding program and its nationally known director emeritus, Jack Hanna.[35] These three institutions are among the major attractions for out-of-town visitors to Columbus. Finally, the Wexner Center for the Arts has brought Columbus international attention, and the Convention Center is now expanding and, with renovation of the Ohio Center facility, will serve the needs of an increasing number of convention groups, bringing visitors and revenue to the city.

Not to be outdone, the "sports culture" flourishes, even if we have not attracted the cluster of professional major league sports teams that many would like. But most of the world knows about Jack Nicklaus and golf at Muirfield, and still, for many, the intercollegiate sports programs associated with Ohio State and the other area colleges and universities satisfy their spectator sports needs. And with the Crew now playing in its new stadium and the arena underway, professional soccer and hockey on a major league level may go a long way toward bringing the kind of status to the sports scene in Columbus that many have sought.

13

Time and Change

O N NOVEMBER 3, 1956, I LED AN "URBAN-Industrial Field Trip of the Columbus, Ohio, Area" for a meeting of professional geographers from the Midwest. It was the first such field trip that I had presented, but in the years since, I have given scores of field trips to university classes, public officials, a variety of local agencies and organizations, and professional organizations such as the Real Estate Institute, the American Bankers Association, and Torch International. One of the prime purposes of the trips was to inform those involved about Columbus and the central Ohio region.

Recently, I provided another field trip for the same organization of geographers for whom the 1956 trip was prepared. The 1956 trip stressed the urban-industrial character of the city. Why this particular focus? The simple fact was that just a few years before I had completed dissertation research on the transition of Columbus, a traditional commercial or service center, into an industrial center—a transition that needed explanation, and the field trip provided some.

Now, more than forty years later, the same field trip *reexamined* provides interesting insights into changes that have taken place in various parts of the Columbus area. Obviously, despite my research arguments, Columbus was not to become a major industrial center, and this, along with the emergence of an even stronger role in the service economy, is part of the story. Certainly, some of the city's features that were rather exciting in 1956 now appear to be trivial, if not dull. And in many instances, it is difficult to ascertain the nature and impact of changes that have occurred in the forty-year time frame. One thing is clear: much of the physical character of individual parts of the community has changed relatively little in this period.

What is presented here is the text of the 1956 field trip, complete with mileage figures, with commentary relating to the features of the landscape as they were encountered at that time. This is followed by my current commentary, noting the changes that have taken place and considering the consequences of those changes. Obviously, the geographic spread of Columbus during the last forty-plus years—suburbanization of the city and its many activities—is beyond the purview of the 1956 field trip, so the focus here is just on the changes that have taken place in the city and its various parts as defined in 1956.

Important changes that are not readily apparent from the field trip experience include the relatively stable political activity in the region; the full impact of urban renewal upon the city, especially the core area; the impact of desegregation upon individual school districts and the region as a whole; the increasing vitality of neighborhood groups in shaping their own development and destiny; and Columbus's role as one of the nation's dynamic growth centers.

A 1956 URBAN-INDUSTRIAL FIELD TRIP
OF COLUMBUS WITH UPDATED
COMMENTARY TO 1999

0.0 miles   *Leave The Ohio State University campus (elev. 760'), pro-*
ceeding south on College Road to W. 12th; turn west passing student dor-
mitories (some under construction); proceed to Neil Avenue and turn north
passing Mirror Lake, the Library, and buildings of the old section of the Col-
lege of Agriculture; turn west on Woodruff.

► Obviously, the campus has changed. It was redesigned in the 1970s
in order to minimize automobile traffic on the Oval and to better accommodate pedestrians. New dormitories were under construction in 1956 to
meet the challenge of a growing student population; that is no longer an
issue. The buildings housing the College of Agriculture are now west of
the Olentangy River, and the farms that were once there are now gone.

0.5   *St. John Arena (to seat approx. 15,000) and the O.S.U. Fieldhouse are*
now being completed; to the south is the Stadium (seating capacity 80,000)
and in the distant south, the hospital center. Continue to and proceed west
on Lane Avenue.

► Changes are underway. Construction of the complex of six new
buildings housing the Fisher College of Business was completed by autumn 1999; stadium renovation continues; and the St. John Arena, a
state-of-the-art arena when built in 1956, has seen its last OSU basketball game.

To the north along Lane Avenue are a Holiday Inn for visitors and
high-rise apartments and coops, shops, and bars catering to student residents, a far cry from the days when students lived in campus dormitories.
In a sense, the academic university has become the corporate university.

1.0   *Olentangy River Road (a planned limited access highway). Ap-*
proaching the Road, Olentangy River is crossed as it flows thru campus. At
the juncture of Lane and the River Road may be seen the farm campus of
the University to the southwest. A new four lane road is now being com-
pleted from Arlington to the campus (a distance of about 1.5 miles).

► At the northwest corner of the Lane Avenue and Olentangy River
Road intersection is the new Schottenstein Center. It is larger and more sophisticated in its offerings than the old St. John, but the displacement of

the old by the new suggests that the life cycle of arenas may very well be forty years, although the Stadium survives even as it changes its basic format to house the corporate culture. On the northeast corner of the intersection is the memorial for cancer survivors, reminding us of the university's impact in medicine.

A new Route 315 just to the west has minimized traffic flow on the River Road, but commercial activity remains strong to the north. The "farm campus" of the university has been displaced by the extension of the campus to the west and by a further expansion of athletic facilities.

1.1 *Head north on the River Road. On the west are barracks and dormitories for married couples and single men; also, university research activities—the Institute of Geodesy, Photogrammetry, and Cartography and others—are housed here. Continuing north is an area of limited residential and commercial development restricted almost entirely to the River Road.*

▶ Many of the former university-related activities on the west side of the road have been displaced by expanded athletic facilities, including the Woody Hayes Athletic Center, with its indoor practice fields, a new baseball field, and other facilities. The Fawcett Center continues as a site for meetings and conferences to the east. Chemical Abstracts, which began its life in campus quarters in the 1940s, is a major organization that helps to account for Columbus's reputation as a growing information center. Its present site was a golf course and sports center forty years ago.

2.1 *Heavy commercial development emphasizes the failure of the limited access highway. The drive-in type of business has been established here creating traffic hazards.*

▶ The commercialization of River Road, including the University City complex with residential units to the west, continues to characterize the area, with hotels, restaurants, and drive-ins catering to both university trade and that linked to the area's hospitals and related service facilities. Traffic has been relieved somewhat on Olentangy River Road by the newer Route 315 highway.

2.7 *North Broadway. North of this, a suburban residential development is underway on the west; homes to the east in the river plain are new within the past two years, but to the west, as in Marburn, they are older and also more expensive.*

▶ The expanding Riverside Hospital complex (once the White Cross

Hospital, located in the Goodale area) at the North Broadway intersection and the presence of Route 315 through the area signify dramatic change over time. Both to the east and west of the old Olentangy River Road are expanding health care and retirement facilities that have displaced the farmlands of the past.

3.2 *In order to widen the highway to four lanes, the Olentangy River was altered in its course and straightened. Floods are no longer severe due to a storage dam in Delaware County to the north (hence, homes are safely built in the floodplain). The old highway, a two lane road, can be seen to the west above the former river bank.*

▶ Highway expansion has been one measure of change in the Olentangy Valley. The old River Road was a pleasant two-lane drive to the north that followed the course of the river. The four-lane improvement was in place by 1956. The completion of the Route 315 system responding to the suburban growth north into Delaware County reaches to north of I-270, the Outerbelt. There is continuing concern for the maintenance of the Olentangy River Valley to the north into Delaware County as upscale suburban development goes on unabated.

3.7 *Across the river is an older (1920's) residential area and the Columbus Park of Roses, a 13½ acre area developed with the intention of making the city a rose center.*

▶ The area to the east across the river is part of the Clintonville community. It remains a dynamic community of young homeowners in a neighborhood of older homes. The Park of Roses thrives, although Columbus has not evolved as a major rose center.

4.2 *Henderson Road. Turn east crossing the Olentangy River; new homes along the route are priced near $24,000. Moving into the older neighborhood, the homes are more substantial and higher priced; most of this area has developed since 1945.*

▶ At Henderson Road, the convergence of the several roadways results in considerable congestion. What was farmland has been replaced by highways, residential development to the southwest, especially, and some parkland along the river to the east. Henderson Road carries heavy traffic to and from High Street and beyond. The residential neighborhoods remain strong and well kept both to the south and north. Obviously, home prices have risen!

5.0 *Henderson and N. High Street. Turn north. Due east is a growing residential district new since 1949. Note the new schools—public and parochial.*

▶ To the southeast, the collection of buildings and shops remain active. The post office occupies what was a major chain grocery before the development of Graceland Shopping Center in the early 1950s. A modest commercial cluster serves the residential communities.

5.2 *On the west, a branch library. The small, modern facility has been built in many sections of the city to meet the demands of the growing, younger population. Continue north on High St. To the west is Old Beechwold with homes from approximately $25,000 and up. To the east, homes are in the $13,000–$20,000 class; lots in this area have a width of 40' to 60'.*

▶ In general, housing on the east side of High Street is now priced in the $90,000-plus range; to the west, prices typically exceed $100,000, and in Old Beechwold, homes are selling for over $350,000.

5.7 *Rathbone Road. Boundary of the city until recent annexation activities brought in scattered areas to the north. Approx. seven miles from Downtown.*

▶ The Morse (Rathbone) Road intersection with High Street has been widened to permit more efficient movement of traffic through the area to east on Morse. Still at issue, however, is the question of a possible bridge and connector roadway between Morse Road and Bethel Road west of the Olentangy River. The "connector issue" originally goes back to 1930s. In 1968 the affected communities used a referendum to defeat a city plan to build such a connector through the area.

5.9 *Graceland Shopping Center. In 1950, this was farmland. It is one of six centers built by the Don Casto organization. With few exceptions, these centers lack charm or graceful planning when compared to shopping centers in other cities. Access from the main thoroughfare is inadequate and difficult. Adjacent are some smaller centers one of which existed before the large unit was built, then closed, and are now reopened. Howard Johnson's Restaurant was here before the center; the motel has come within the past year.*

▶ Graceland Shopping Center, and others like it that were products of the 1950s, have suffered from the development of the larger regional shopping centers, such as the Northland Mall east on Morse Road in the 1960s, and currently from the evolution of the new and larger malls, such as the Mall at Tuttle Crossing and the Easton and Polaris developments. The Howard Johnson's is long gone, but restaurants and fast-food drive-ins continue in the area. Wesley Glen, a large retirement center, is operated by the Methodist Church.

6.2   *The Ohio State School for the Blind and Deaf. This new facility occupies a tract of land extending east approx. one mile and south about one-half mile, in part. This unit replaces the buildings originally constructed 75 years ago and situated in the near Downtown.*

▶ Currently, there is concern for the future of the old Blind School building on Parsons Avenue, given the city's history with respect to preservation. The Deaf School, on Town Street, was destroyed in the 1970s, and until recently the city has encouraged the destruction of other historic buildings in its fervor to serve the development interests.

6.7   *Continue north through an area developed since 1950. To the east is Colonial Hills, a development of basement-less homes priced from $12,500 to $17,500.*

▶ This remains an attractive residential community, with well-treed large lots and homes selling at modest prices, in the $100,000 range or more.

7.1   *Continue north to Worthington with a population in 1955 of over 5,300 which was a 148% increase since 1950 due largely to annexation. Worthington is desirous of city stature to better combat Columbus' annexation plans. The community is primarily residential, attracting a professional group. Note the old college building and the Masonic Building, constructed in 1820.*

▶ Worthington remains a fine residential community with a strong commercial core that preserves a sense of the community's history. The community has increased its area through annexation to the north and west across the Olentangy River in an attempt to minimize encroachment by Columbus. The population is about 15,000.

7.6   *Worthington Town Square (elev. 880'). Worthington was founded in 1803, nine years before Columbus. Turn west onto Route 161; note descent into the Olentangy River Valley of 120'–140'.*

7.9 *Worthington's schools are built on the campus plan with swimming pool, athletic fields, and a unified building plan. Worthington's schools are envied in this area although the tax rate is not.*

8.7 *Return east to the juncture of Rts. 23 and 161; continue east on Rt. 161. At the town square on the n.e. corner, note the Griswold Inn dating back to 1811; the Episcopal Church was constructed in 1827.*

▶ The juncture of Route 23 (High Street) and Route 161 has changed little except for the loss of the historic Griswold Inn. The heavy flow of traffic through the area is a concern as Worthington struggles to retain its park space in the square and its strong sense of community.

In 1956, the field trip route went no further north than this intersection, given that the northern edge of the community was just several blocks to the north and farmland lay beyond.

9.8 *Rt. 161 and Sinclair Road. Turn south on Sinclair Road through a suburban housing area that has developed slowly since 1950.*

▶ East of Sinclair Road, one encountered suburban housing and farmland in 1956. In recent years, Route 161 has become a major commercial artery to the east, somewhat akin to the Morse Road commercial mix to the south. Indeed, the number of fast-food outlets on this stretch of the highway led an Italian magazine, *Europeo,* to comment in September 1985, "La Route 161 . . . considerata la 'capitale mondiale del fast-food.'" Continuing suburban growth to the east and north supported much of the mix—giving credence to the claim of "world capital."

Housing immediately south on Sinclair Road typified suburban expansion of the 1950s onto fairly large residential lots on the edge of the city. These remain as mature, well-developed sites.

10.7 *New, low-cost housing units called by many "slums of the future." This development is all post-1954; it features cheaply constructed homes on very small lots, for the most part.*

▶ The low-cost housing units on small lots remain in good shape, surprisingly, a tribute to those who own and maintain them. Increased commercialization to the south, with distribution and warehouse facilities and office buildings, is related in part to access to and traffic generated by I-71 to the east.

11.1   *Bulk oil storage facilities of Pure Oil (opened in 1955) and Sinclair Oil (present for many years) lie adjacent to the main north-south tracks of the Pennsylvania Railroad.*

▶ The bulk oil storage facilities have long since disappeared, replaced in part by motels, hotels, and other service functions near the I-71 and Sinclair-Morse juncture.

11.4   *Morse and Sinclair Roads. This large tract was the proposed site for a Ford Motor Company plant. POSSIBLE STOP.*

▶ A surface railroad crossing on Morse Road was replaced with the construction of I-71. Before the highway's construction, a planned location of a Ford Motor Company plant in the northeast quadrant east of the tracks was rejected by residents of the north Columbus community. To the east, Morse Road was a two-lane road passing through farmlands and other low-density uses, such as the North Columbus Airport, an eighteen-hole golf course, a large church summer campground, and limited residential properties. Today, east of the tracks, Morse Road has become a symbol of good planning gone awry under pressure from development interests.

11.8   *Cross Pennsylvania Railroad and New York Central tracks. This is one of many such crossings in Columbus. Overpasses and underpasses are scarce.*

Continue west to Indianola Avenue; to the north is the Deaf and Blind institutions seen earlier from High Street.

▶ There was no reason in 1956 to head east on Morse Road; the trip headed west to Indianola Avenue and south into the Clintonville area instead. At the time, Indianola was a two-lane road that ended at Morse. The commercial development to the east, largely of distribution facilities, has grown, and the residential properties to the west have matured. It is a neighborhood of relatively modest but well-kept homes and yards. Continued development of the area has been affected by the presence of the north-south railroads and I-71. Construction of the interstate highway, in particular, has served as a barrier to east-west contacts through the north Columbus community and continues to shape development. Apartments and residential housing units were built in the area as I-71 improved access to the job markets in the Central Business District.

12.0   *Head south on Indianola Avenue. Most of the housing on the west is post-1950; much of it is post-1954. Commercial growth has occurred since*

1953 on the east. Housing is older as one nears High Street, the main north-south artery.

13.2   *Beginning of warehouse district new since 1954. Residential district continues to the west. Continuing south, housing is older and lower priced, currently. Neighborhoods change from owner-occupied dwellings to more rental units and some transient rentals.*

15.0   *Arcadia and Indianola avenues. West one-half mile is North High School, the only public high school to serve the entire north end of Colum- bus. This area is World War I in age.*

▶ With the passage of time and the changing political boundary of Columbus, the role of community schools has changed. The change was influenced further by school desegregation and the beginning of pupil bus- ing. This older neighborhood houses a mix of families, including many with ties to the university community to the south. Housing costs are in- creasingly in the $100,000-plus range.

15.2   *Continue on Indianola Avenue to Hudson; turn east one block.*

▶ This portion of Indianola appears much as it did in 1956, which is, in a sense, a tribute to the maintenance of the area as a viable residential community. The old stores and neighborhood movie house, which were vital to community life in 1956, are gone. Immediately to the east of In- dianola and north of Hudson Street is an area known as Glen Echo. In 1997, the Glen Echo community, whose homes retain their early twenti- eth-century character, was nominated to the National Register of Historic Places. It is a desirable neighborhood just north of the university neighbor- hood development district.

15.4   *Hudson and Summit streets. East on Hudson is another surface rail- road crossing. Beyond the crossing is the Columbus Auto Parts Company, northernmost of the city's manufacturing plants. It employs 400; markets are in Detroit. Turn south on Summit St., passing through an older residen- tial area consisting of owner occupied, rentals, and transient rentals. This area is declining in quality and value; first Negro families have entered the area within the past year.*

▶ The Columbus Auto Parts Company is no longer in production, and the building has fallen into decay. In late 1999, plans were underway for redevelopment of the site. Manufacturing activity now extends well beyond this northern limit of manufacturing in 1956, with much of it adjacent to or near the northern leg of I-270, such as the Anheuser-Busch Brewery and the Worthington Steel plants in Worthington.

16.2 *Summit and 17th. Turn east on 17th. To the south and west is the northeastern fringe of the campus fraternity and sorority district and the rooming house district. The rooming houses dominate to the east.*

▶ University area communities are not known for the high level of living provided, and the case is no different here in Columbus. Often, absentee ownership of rental units has a negative effect on the quality of the rental units and the overall upkeep of the neighborhood. Over time, deterioration of housing reaches a point where low-income residents, not students, are the norm. This has happened in and near the university neighborhoods. Currently, a major effort is underway to revitalize the entire community, with city government, the university, business interests, and homeowner residents joining forces to undertake the effort. Plans call for the "renewal" not only of the High Street corridor but of the residential neighborhoods as well.

16.5 *East on 17th. Northernmost railroad underpass. Continue to the Ohio State Fairgrounds.*

▶ I-71 is essentially the eastern boundary of the extended Ohio State Fairgrounds, with 17th Avenue dividing the older southern section from the open spaces to the north. Major occupants of the northern section include the Ohio Historical Society's museum (dedicated August 1970) and the Ohio Village, the State Highway Patrol Academy (opened 1965), and several exhibition buildings associated with the Fair. Much of the open space once housed trailer homes and a few small homes and since has been used for parking associated with the fair in August.

A new hockey arena was constructed in the northern part of the area in mid-1999, housing the Columbus Crew hockey team, a tribute to Columbus's quest to bring major sports into the region.

16.7 *Enter the Fairgrounds. This area is expanding north of 17th to include an acreage totaling approx. 350 acres. The outmoded area we pass through is scheduled to be revamped; about 150 acres are in this older section.*

▶ The Fairgrounds are no longer open to traffic. There has been considerable expansion of the site, with new activities added to the traditional agricultural focus of the fair.

17.3   *Leave the Fairgrounds and turn west on 11th Avenue.*

17.6   *Pass under railroad underpass turning south on Grant Street. This is an older manufacturing area (developed prior to World War I) as is evident from the homes and types of buildings present.*

▶ Many of Columbus's major manufacturing facilities have been lost through mergers, outright purchase and removal of the facilities, or management failures. One of the city's major industrial districts was this area north of the Downtown core on the adjacent railroad lines. In many cases today, all traces of a previous industry are missing, and rarely has new manufacturing industry taken its place.

17.9   *Columbus Coated Fabrics Company, world's largest manufacturer of coated materials including cloth, plastic, and mixed materials. The company located here in 1900 when the area was beyond residential Columbus. Employment is approx. 1,150.*

▶ The Columbus Coated Fabrics plant (450 employees) continues to function as a division of the Borden Company, but its days may be numbered, at least under present ownership. It was one of several Columbus-born and nurtured companies that produced a unique product—initially, oilcloth—that reached a national and international market.

18.1   *Grant and Fifth avenues. Turn east on Fifth Ave. In this area, an older industrial area, are Clark Grave Vaults Co. (1,000 emp.), since government contracts in World War II an auto parts supplier, Ohio Malleable Iron Co. (500 emp.), Kinnear Doors (400 emp.), and Timken Roller Bearings (3,000 emp.). Timken built here in 1919; at that time the plant was located on the n.e. edge of Columbus.*

▶ Clark Grave Vault continues in production, primarily of its original product, vaults. The Ohio Malleable Iron plant is gone, and Kinnear Doors operates at a different site. Continuing east on Fifth Avenue to Cleveland Avenue takes one past the former site of the large Timken Roller Bearing plant, which was recently torn down. This facility, on this site since 1919, had been a major employer of industrial workers. A reduced version of the plant continues in operation to the south on Cleveland Avenue.

18.4   *Continue east crossing Cleveland Avenue, a main north-south artery. Numerous small shops (primarily machine shops) and residences line Fifth Avenue.*

▶ With the decline of manufacturing in general, many of the small machine shops are no longer in operation.

19.1   *Truck depots developed in this area since 1950. From an access and traffic standpoint, the location is poor; to serve Columbus' industry, the location is reasonably well-centered.*

19.3   *Pennsylvania Railroad yards and surface crossing. This is one of the major traffic headaches in Columbus. Continuing east, note the amount of vacant land that has yet to attract any industry.*

▶ The construction of I-670, a direct connecting route between the Central Business District and the airport, has helped to change the character of this area. I-670 occupies, in part, former railroad right-of-ways of the Pennsylvania Railroad and the Norfolk and Western. As in 1956, increased economic development along the route continues to be sought.

19.7   *Many of the homes adjacent to Fifth Avenue and lying within one-half mile of the street are Negro-occupied. There is a heavy concentration of Negroes south of Fifth Ave. to Broad St. in east Columbus. East High School, which was once the prestige high school in the city, has a student enrollment today of which 70% is Negro.*

▶ The black population in Columbus today is concentrated in a series of census tracts essentially east of I-71 and north of I-70.

20.3   *Cross under Pennsylvania Railroad and B&O tracks.*

20.5   *Frey-Yenkin Paint Co. (30 emp.) is newly located here. The old building was on the site of the new Spring-Sandusky Interchange. Continue east on Fifth Ave. through a mixture of residential and commercial structures. Development has been haphazard at best.*

▶ Cross over I-670. To the north of Fifth Avenue is a large retirement center; to the south, the city of Bexley. Homes along Fifth are in good condition; this was once a workingman's community.

21.7   *South off Fifth Ave. may be viewed the extended structure which once housed the Ralston Steel Car Co., one of the city's larger firms prior to 1950.*

▶ The plant building and site are now the location of a series of small manufacturing operations and a variety of service activities.

22.7 *Fertilizer plant (130 emp.) is one of three such plants; all are on the east side of the city. The others have been surrounded by later residential development. Major markets for such firms are central Ohio farms.*
▶ One plant, IMC Agri-Business, remains the sole fertilizer plant in the area. A few small manufacturing shops are found along Fifth Avenue, where many machine shops produced items for the aircraft industry in earlier years.

23.1 *South of Fifth Ave. and beyond the railroad tracks is the beginning of the Columbus Army Depot, a government storage facility said to be the largest such facility in the world. It employs more than 3,000 civilians. To the north, a number of small plants developed since 1950.*

23.5 *On the north is the beginning of the huge North American Aviation plant which employs approx. 16,000 persons in the assembly of jet aircraft and guided missiles. Part of this structure was originally built by the Federal Government for a Curtis-Wright war-time operation. Later, part of the plant was occupied by the Lustron Corp. North American came here in 1950.*
▶ The Rockwell organization and, most recently, General Dynamics followed in this location. After the demise of the manufacturing operations, the office buildings have been occupied by the Defense Finance and Accounting Service's Columbus office, which recently located here with nearly 3,000 employees.

24.4 *Port Columbus. A bond issue passed this year will permit expansion of the port. Note the new 15-story control tower to the north. New runways and building are the immediate needs. Possible stop. Then, continue east on Fifth Ave.*
▶ The modern and expanding terminal for Port Columbus is to the north and west of the old facility on Fifth Avenue. The airport is now being enlarged to provide increased parking. Various warehouse and distribution facilities are present along Fifth Avenue, linked to both airport service and the railroads. Included is the city's produce terminal.

25.3 *Junction of Fifth Ave. and Hamilton Rd. Turn south on to Hamilton Rd.*

25.7 *Ebco Manufacturing Co. (200 emp.). This modern facility replaces a multiple-story structure formerly in a crowded, near Downtown in Franklinton. The old plant had no room for expansion or parking.*

Leave the Ebco site and enter a part of the Borough of Whitehall (pop. of 15,031 in 1955 for an increase of 208% from 1950). This is one of the two fastest growing areas in Columbus. Much of the growth is attributable to industry in the area. Shopping centers, two within one mile, lie to the south on Hamilton Rd.

▶ Whitehall remains a self-contained suburb whose greatest period of growth was the postwar years. It has a healthy employment base and strong commercial sector to the east. Its population, about 20,500, remains fairly stable.

26.1 *Hamilton Road and Broad Street, or Rt. 16. Turn west on Broad St., passing the Columbus Depot's main entrance at 26.8. Note new housing.*

▶ Much of the area north of Broad Street to the railroads and Fifth Avenue is occupied by the federal government's Defense Supply Center, Columbus (3,000 employees). It was located here about sixty years ago as a storage facility for military equipment and supplies. It was known locally as the Columbus Army Depot. The new high-rise structures house administrative operations of the Federal Defense Finance and Accounting Service.

27.2 *Town and Country Shopping Center (or the Miracle Mile) developed by the Casto group opened in 1949. This was the first shopping center in Columbus. Smaller centers have sprung up around it. An older elementary school is now badly located.*

▶ Town and Country Shopping Center continues to serve the eastside community. After nearly fifty years, it is showing its age as it faces increasing competition for the consumer market from the large new malls in northeast and northwest Columbus and from City Center. There is evidence of a considerable number of changes both in the Town and Country Center and in the adjacent community.

28.2 *Enter Bexley (pop. 13,147 with an increase of 6% since 1950). Bexley is the older, wealthy section of Columbus. Continuing west on Broad; much of Bexley's commercial activity and some newer residential development are present.*

At 28.5 is a modern Episcopal Church and at 29.0 a new Jewish Temple;

both suggest growth throughout the area. A local sociologist stated that a study shows that Jews move east in Columbus as well as in most large cities.

▶ Much of the commercial development is to the east of the Bexley city limits; Broad Street, as it passes through Bexley, is a residential street of fine homes and is maintained as such.

29.6 *Broad and Drexel. Turn south on Drexel Ave., passing through an area of expensive homes, large lots, and well-landscaped yards.*

▶ The southwest corner of Broad and Drexel is the campus of the Columbus School for Girls, the principal private school for girls in Columbus.

30.5 *Drexel and E. Main St. Directly south is Capital University, a Lutheran-supported college with approx. 1,200 students and a graduate seminary. Turn west on Main Street.*

▶ Capital University and Lutheran Seminary maintain their presence on Main Street. A group of upscale shops, restaurants, art galleries, and the original Drexel Theatre, now a small-scale "multiplex" theater, have developed here.

30.8 *Acro Mfg. Co. (emp. 250 of which one-half are females) makes highly machined parts for the electrical industry; it is housed in a multi-story structure which was once the home of the world's largest manufacturer of piano stools. Amusement park to the south is the only one in the city.*

▶ The manufacturing is gone, and there's no trace of the amusement park noted in 1956! The grain elevators mentioned in 31.0 are still present, but the character of the street to the west, where in 1956 there were antique shops and other facilities catering to tourists on old Route 40, has changed, as has the racial mix.

31.0 *Grain elevators storing grain from central Ohio farms.*

31.3 *E. Main and Fairwood Ave. Turn south on Fairwood passing through an old residential area (1920's). Newer housing is evident further south, but by no means in the quantity seen in the north and east. South and Southeast Columbus have not experienced residential or industrial growth comparable to many other sections of the city at this time.*

32.4 *Wesleyan University Press building; formerly located in Downtown Columbus. Opposite is a trailer park—more will be seen in this area indicating, to some extent, the more transient nature of the people and their closer ties to West Virginia, Kentucky, and the south.*

▶ South on Fairwood, the single-family homes have been well maintained after forty years. Further south, the Wesleyan University Press, which had located here out of the Downtown in the postwar years, is gone, but the buildings are now the city offices for the Regulation Division of the Trade and Development Department. The 1956 trailer park is still here, but anticipated growth did not materialize.

33.0 *Fairwood and Frebis Avenue. Turn west on Frebis. This area is beyond the city limits; note trailer parks again. To the east buildings of the Alum Crest and Benjamin Franklin hospitals (TB).*

▶ This area has well-maintained homes on fairly large lots, with mixed low-scale commercial and residential development to the south. The hospitals noted are no longer functioning units but are now a Franklin County Service Center and a rehab and nursing facility.

33.5 *Frebis Avenue and Lockbourne Rd. Turn south on Lockbourne.*

34.3 *Lockbourne and Marion Rd. Turn west on Marion Road and enter an industrial area dating from pre-1900. Plants include American Blower (emp. 600), Bonney Floyd (400+), Federal Glass (1,200), Hercules Box (230), and Bell Sound Systems (150). The area was developed outside the city to secure more favorable tax rates, but it is now a part of Columbus.*

▶ The cluster of major manufacturing plants in this old, large industrial sector on Marion Road has diminished. Only one or two holdovers remain, including Brown Steel and the buildings related to the Federal Glass and Hercules Box plants. These buildings now house "industrial parks."

35.3 *Marion Rd. and Parsons Ave. (elev. approx. 730'). Turn south on Parsons through one of the poorer sections of the city. Large Negro and foreign-born populations in this area; many cheap shops, bars, and a high crime rate.*

▶ South Parsons Avenue was crowded with shops and shoppers in 1956. Today, many of the storefronts are boarded up and the avenue is empty. The industrial jobs that employed thousands of workers are largely gone, and so are the businesses catering to them.

35.9 *Buckeye Steel Castings Co. (emp. 1,300) is a manufacturer of rail-road castings and the only example of heavy industry in the city. A blast furnace and steel plant operated in this area until 1927 using, at an earlier date, Ohio iron ore and coal.*

▶ Buckeye Steel Castings (1,360 employees), until recently a part of Worthington Steel, continues in production. Nearby, the old Chase Foundry is still in operation, and of course the extensive Chesapeake and Ohio Railroad yards are active.

36.5 *Parsons and Dering Road. Turn west on Dering. C&O railroad yards pass through the south side making it undesirable for residential, commercial, or industrial development. No new industry, other than small shops in homes, in the last 15 years and very little new housing. At Dering Rd. is a branch plant of the Keever Starch company, utilizing central Ohio farm products. At High St., greenhouses producing tomatoes for Columbus market.*

▶ West on Dering Road, Keever Starch is gone, but Keener Sand & Clay is an operation tied into the area's quarry industries. West to High Street, the small old homes remain, but the greenhouses at High Street are gone, and the large empty field remains. Just to the north, a relatively new stretch of Route 104 provides high-speed access to the west and east.

37.0 *Dering and High Sts. Turn north on High; to the west lakes occupy former gravel pits and quarries (elev. 700').*

▶ The old quarries along the Scioto River, and their lakes, are finding new uses as sites for residential and recreational housing as well as for office parks (see illustration on p. 13).

37.5 *Seagraves Manufacturing Co. (emp. 350) largest maker of fire engines and equipment in the world.*

▶ Seagraves was bought out by a group of New York investors a number of years ago and ceased production. To the south, two new German firms are engaged in manufacturing and distribution. The South Columbus industrial sector, once one of the dominant centers of manufacturing in the city, is in decline.

37.6 *From the top of the bridge, a view of the South Columbus industrial area. Continuing north on High St., note abandoned breweries (once there were more than a dozen active breweries in Columbus; today, there is but one). Occasional industrial plants are found usually a block west of High St.; representative industries include casket firms, foundries, machine shops. To the east, the residential area is tied to German settlement.*

▶ Two old brewery buildings remain, but the only active brewery in Columbus, other than small operations specializing in local brews, is the large Anheuser-Busch regional brewery in the Worthington area. Many of the other manufacturing firms are gone, but the old sawtooth-roofed plant that once housed early automobile production and casket production in 1956 continues as a site for industrial production. The AMTEKCO company (150 employees) manufactures wooden equipment (tables, stands, showcases, etc.) for supermarkets, bars, restaurants, and other establishments. The C&O Railroad is to the west in the Scioto Valley, carrying coal north to Lake Erie ports.

39.0 *Turn east on Deshler one block to City Park Avenue. Continue north to Whittier St., then head west to High. The small brick houses are representative of the many small German dwellings scattered through the area. Homes are usually neat, clean, and well-kept. The German labor force was once a vital location factor affecting industrial Columbus. North on High.*

▶ The area east of High Street was a German neighborhood where workers in South End industries established homes in the mid-1800s. Since 1960, when the German Village Society was founded and the German Village Commission was created by the city of Columbus to protect and control the area's architecture and development, a formally defined German Village exists. It is an area of 233 acres east of High Street, just south of the Downtown, in which more than 1,600 homes have been renewed since 1960. German Village is an example of a successful private sector renewal and restoration project. In recent years, it has attracted residents seeking the charm of the village and the kind of exclusivity that it represents. It is a neighborhood in which homes could have been purchased for less than $5,000 in 1956 but in which many homes sell for well over $100,000 today. Another German institution still associated with the area is the Columbus Maennerchor, a singing, eating, and drinking society on High Street.

39.8 *High and Sycamore. Turn west on Sycamore to Front St. At Front St. head north; the August Wagner Brewery, producer of Gam beer, occupies*

the n.w. corner. A variety of "downtown" firms are represented in the
multiple-story buildings along Front St.—a trouser manufacturer, paper
firms, branch operation of North American Aviation, and two large shoe
firms (low wages and a high % of female workers).

▶ The high-rise building is the Grange Mutual Insurance Company,
one of many insurance companies headquartered in Columbus, and to
the north on Front Street is the Brewery District. A statue of Gambrinus
marks the site of the old Gambrinus brewery. The cleared area is to house
a retail shopping center, a bit incongruous within this area. Several fine
old brewery buildings have been destroyed to make way for "progress," although several others remain to set the tone for an area that is a magnet
for both tourists and locals who seek fun and entertainment. North of Livingston Avenue and I-70 (below surface as part of the southern leg of the
old Innerbelt) are the city and county courts. As noted, a number of Columbus manufacturers were located in buildings along Front Street and
on Fulton Street to the east, but most of the firms *and* buildings are now
gone. The old armory has been preserved and restored as the Columbus
Cultural Arts Center. To its west, the high-rise Waterford Tower, an eigh-
teen-story residential building opened in 1987, overlooks Bicentennial
Park and the Scioto River, and construction of the Miranova Towers is
well underway. The headquarter offices of Columbia Gas of Ohio are located here as well. One exception to the loss of buildings is the large building at the northeast corner of Main and Front; it once housed the Walker T.
Dickerson Shoe Company (Columbus was still an important shoe-
manufacturing center in 1956) but now is a warehouse, Secur-It, for
household goods.

40.7 *North on Front St., note three parking garages operated by the Laza-*
rus organization; at Front and Town Sts. is the store. Continuing north on
Front, to the west is the State Office Building and small parks. Turn east on
State St. through the heart of Downtown Columbus. Continue east past the
State Capitol and the market area south on Fourth St. to the medical center
at Grant St.

▶ Continuing north is what remains of the Lazarus department store
complex. Lazarus successfully resisted movement from the city core early
on by building a series of garages with low per-hour rates to attract customers to its Downtown store. Today, only two of the garages remain, one
major building (the so-called Annex) is gone, and space within what appears to be the large Lazarus store has been sold or leased for government

offices. An elevated passageway above South High Street connects the main store with the City Center, now the focal point of the Downtown retail market. The old art deco State Office Building, recently renovated, and two other state office buildings are to the west. The Scioto River frontage has been improved through the years, and plans for alternative uses of the river valley continue to be debated. New high-rise buildings representing various aspects of private sector development—banks, insurance companies, and utilities—and of state government characterize growth in the Downtown. The luxurious new Riffe Center, a state office building, occupies the northwest corner of High and State Streets, and a new high-rise on the southeast corner links the Beggs Building and City Center. Ohio's State Capitol and grounds have been totally renovated, and much of the Capitol building has been restored. Private citizens responded to the idea of saving and restoring the Ohio Theatre, now home to the Columbus Symphony and other cultural activities. At State and Third Streets, the Hyatt on Capitol Square is a major addition on the site of the Hartman Building, which housed the old Hartman theater; on the southeast corner, the so-called "old, old post office" has been restored by the Bricker and Eckler law firm.

41.2 *State Street and Grant. Columbus Public Library. Turn north on Grant.*
▶ The expanded Columbus Metropolitan Library remains a major fixture, and to the south are the greatly expanded buildings of the Grant Medical Center complex. To the south, Town Street witnessed the construction of a number of low-rise office buildings after the extensive urban renewal activity that cleared the old farmers' market and wholesale fruit and vegetable markets from the area.

41.4 *At Broad St. turn west. To the east are several churches, the Columbus Gallery of Fine Arts, and many insurance firms. Continuing west are more insurance firms, the Catholic Cathedral, Columbus Club, and an exclusive shopping area.*
▶ On Broad Street, there are relatively new office buildings, including several insurance firm headquarters. COSI occupied old Memorial Hall, the former site of the Kelley Mansion, until its move in November 1999. At Broad and Fourth Streets is the building of the Borden Company, a national firm that moved its headquarters to Columbus from New York City, and the Columbus Club, the city's most prestigious private club.

41.9   *Broad and High. Continue west.*

▶ We pass the Bank One offices at Third Street and the state's Rhodes Office Tower on the north side of Broad, as well as a cluster of older office buildings.

42.0   *Civic Center (elev. 720') and AIU Tower (built in the late 1920's). Statue of Columbus presented to city on October 12, 1955, by the City of Genoa, Italy.*

42.1   *Turn north on Civic Center Drive. Across the Scioto River from south to north are the Health Center, Central H.S., and the Veterans Memorial. On the Drive are City Hall, police offices, and the Federal Building. At Gay St. is a multiple-story building now housing Internal Revenue, but once a shoe factory.*

▶ The tour heads north at the Lincoln-LeVeque Tower and City Hall. To the west is the new Broad Street Bridge and across the river the expansion of Central High School and COSI south of Broad and the Veterans Memorial to the north. The cluster of city government buildings is here, along with several former private office buildings now housing government offices. Missing is the old City Hall Annex building, now a parking lot just to the north of City Hall, an early victim of Columbus's lack of a sense of history. Several old warehouse and distribution sites have been renovated to other purposes.

42.5   *Turn east at Chestnut St. Columbus Bolt & Forging Co. (emp. 750) is to the west; it is Columbus' oldest factory, operating here since 1852. Continue east to the Nationwide Insurance buildings (formerly the Farm Bureau), the largest insurance firm in Columbus.*

▶ Chestnut Street west of High has disappeared, to be replaced by buildings of Nationwide Insurance and the state's Workers' Compensation building. Nationwide is one of the nation's largest insurance firms and the largest in the city. Columbus ranks as one of the leading centers for insurance company home offices. Continue north on High Street to Nationwide Boulevard and the Hyatt Regency Hotel. To the north is the Convention Center, designed by the Eisenman and Trott collaboration, and to the east are hotels, restaurants, and other shops, often in renovated older buildings. To the north on High is the area known as the Short North, a center for restaurants, galleries, small shops, and attractive apartment housing, although it was a derelict area of abandoned buildings and transient residents until 1985 when Sandy Wood and Company began renovation and restoration of the area. The development of the Convention Center, hotel, and other buildings is on the site of the old Union Station.

43.4 *West on Spring St., passing the Ohio Penitentiary, dating back to 1832. To the south may be seen evidence of construction on a branch of the Spring-Sandusky Interchange.*

▶ Proceed to the west and south, passing Arch Park, with the remaining arch saved in the demolition of the Union Station in the late 1970s. To the west along Spring Street, the old Columbus Bolt & Forging Company has been gone for quite some time, and, in early 1998, the Ohio Penitentiary buildings and site were leveled. The area is the site for the new civic arena and the development of an entertainment center.

43.5 *Spring and Dennison Ave. Turn north on Dennison. A number of industries lie to the west—Jaeger Machine (emp. 800), Belmont Casket (160), Surface Combustion (900), and others. This is an important truck transfer area.*

▶ Many of the old industrial buildings along Spring and north along Neil Avenue and interior streets still stand, but most of the manufacturing activity is gone. Several buildings continue to house warehouse and distribution activities, whereas others have been converted into artists' studios and galleries, loft spaces, and the like. The old city power plant still functions in the area, there is a police substation, and the Olentangy River can be accessed for boating. But the future of the area known now as Pen West will surely be affected by what happens with the penitentiary site and its surroundings.

44.0 *At Goodale Blvd. turn west entering an area scheduled for redevelopment (public). If Columbus has slums in the sense that other large cities do, this is one example. A recent bond issue supports the program.*

44.4 *Demolition activity may be seen in this area.*

▶ At this point, construction of parts of the Spring-Sandusky Interchange, of I-670, and of Route 315 compounds traffic problems in and through the area. The current highway construction, building upon work begun just about forty-two years earlier, attempts to improve flow of traffic through the area.

44.6 *Goodale Blvd. and Olentangy River Road. Turn south onto the Road towards the Spring-Sandusky Interchange. The tour skirts the heart of the Interchange.*

45.0 *To the west are a TV station, Coca-Cola bottling, and the area for proposed Sears store (warehouse and retail outlet).*
  ▶ Within the old interchange system, the TV station was erected and still operates, along with the city's major post office building. The proposed Sears operation was never developed on this site, but Sears did build a warehouse on what is now the west Outerbelt and a major retail outlet in Northland Shopping Center.

45.3 *City Water Works which draws water from Scioto River and reservoirs. To the north, Ohio Division of Natural Resources.*

46.0 *Dublin Road and Grandview Ave. Turn south off Dublin Rd. Bridge crosses quarrying operations. Further on is railroad crossing and New York Central roundhouse. (NOTE: Follow the route described below. Mileage figures may be off slightly as a result of current rerouting.)*
  ▶ Traffic routing is quite different from that followed in 1956 as we make our way to McKinley Avenue. Gone are the roundhouses and tracks of the New York Central and Pennsylvania Railroads. Occupying much of the vacated area between McKinley Avenue and the river are the buildings of COTA (Central Ohio Transit Authority), as one transportation facility replaces another, at least in part. Other older buildings in the area are primarily engaged in distribution, with one or two minor manufacturing shops.

46.5 *Grandview and McKinley Ave. Turn east on McKinley. Housing project on south side of McKinley was Federally-sponsored in the early 1940's.*

47.0 *McKinley and Central. Turn south on Central through a lower middle class housing area, largely workers' homes.*
  ▶ This old neighborhood of small worker homes remains intact in the main. Job orientation has changed with time, however.

47.5 *Central and West Broad St. Move west on Broad. The large expanses of land are devoted to State institutions (mental health and juvenile correction) constructed in the late 1800's. Property values in Columbus show that*

12% of the value is in State-held property and 2% in Federal property, neither of which is taxable. On the north, while still in "the flats," is a mound which may be a glacial remnant or an Indian mound (the Mound-dwellers were present in Ohio from 800 B.C. to 1,000 A.D. The mounds were usually burial plots.)

▶ Most of the state institutions associated with mental illness and related services are now closed, and the old buildings that represented the state's commitment to social service in the nineteenth century are gone. Their loss reflects changing attitudes and theories as to how the mentally ill should be treated. The Ohio Department of Public Safety and the Ohio Department of Transportation both have large facilities on the Hilltop. Several small facilities continue to care for a subset of the mentally ill, and there are juvenile correction operations here as well.

48.6 *On the north, the Juvenile Diagnostic Center. The area is known as the Hilltop (elev. 800+', or 80' above Broad and High). The Hilltop is a residential area with many state employees concentrated here. Broad St. is the main commercial artery.*

49.9 *Westgate. This residential area, new in large part since 1950, houses a large number of GM and Westinghouse workers. Many rental units are available.*

▶ It is difficult to ascertain where the Hilltop ends and where Westgate begins. Broad Street—old Route 40—has suffered the loss of small businesses and their customers, as have other communities on major traffic arteries, to the shopping centers and malls further to the west and beyond the area. Nonetheless, the street remains a commercial retail strip. The residential neighborhoods have not changed drastically in forty years, and home prices remain relatively modest.

50.4 *Westgate Shopping Center and the "Walk of Wonders." This Center is also Casto developed; its unique feature is the "Walk" which replicates some of the world's wonders. Leaving the Center, an extensive oil storage can be seen to the north.*

▶ Westgate Shopping Center is still functioning, with its exceptionally large parking area, but the "Walk of Wonders" has long been gone. It remains a typical example of the Casto-developed shopping center in Columbus, one that is facing more competition from newer centers and malls. Furthermore, within a short distance to the west, several centers built around stores such as Consumer Square, Target, and Kmart provide more competition. The experience here is no different from that in many other parts of the city, but the retail activity seems to be especially intense.

51.5 *Columbus City limits. Major industrial units here remain beyond the city limits although questions of annexation are now in court.*
▶ The city boundary has been extended as part of the city's aggressive annexation program, part of Columbus's development policy since the 1950s.

52.0 *To the south on Georgesville (Phillipi) Road is the Ternstedt Division of General Motors (emp. 4,100+); to the north is the Westinghouse plant (emp. approx. 4,000). GM came to Columbus in 1946 as the first postwar national industry; this division makes hardware for national distribution. Westinghouse came in the last five years originally to manufacture aircraft engines (never undertaken) but now producing refrigerators, dishwashers, and other appliances. Both firms are representative examples of the decentralization of industry to meet markets, materials, and labor more satisfactorily.*
▶ The General Motors plant continues to operate, although at reduced rates of production. The Westinghouse plant remains, but the company has been gone for many years. These two giant plants, along with what were quite successful "home-grown" industries, were the basis for postwar optimism concerning the industrial development of Columbus. Today, various facets of the service economy explain the employment mix in the area.

52.4 *Continue west on Broad St. to Lincoln Village.*
▶ Beyond Phillipi Road, the large Westland Shopping Center, a center that sought to reach a regional market, dominates the retail market of this area, with Lazarus and J.C. Penney providing key stores in the center. But today, Westland is feeling the impact of the Tuttle mall to the north on I-270. The J.C. Penney store has already decided to vacate Westland, and the future of the Lazarus store is not certain.

53.6 *Lincoln Lodge, a Nationwide Insurance–Peoples Development Corp. operation. At the Lodge, turn into Lincoln Village "a suburban community planned for easier living." Here are sections awaiting development with*

*roads, sewers, and utilities already established. As the tour continues, the
housing types, ranging from a minimum of $18,000 up to $40,000, may
be seen.*

▶ The trip now passes under I-270, just two-tenths of a mile to the
west of Westland, to reach Lincoln Village, which was a planned 1,180-
acre residential community developed by Nationwide Insurance in the
mid-1950s. The homes attracted a middle- to upper-middle-class homeowner. In 1954, there were thirteen separate models available, priced from
$12,000 to $32,000. The development provided for the needs of its residents and for tourists along old Route 40. The entrance today is almost
lost, with Lincoln Lodge gone since the early 1990s and the area surrounded by commercial activity, but the residential areas remain attractive
and well maintained.

55.7 *East on Broad St. (U.S. Rt. 40) to Phillippi Road and thence north,
passing the Westinghouse plant (approx. .7 of a mile in length) and a part
of the Lincoln Village Industrial Area.*

▶ The Consolidated Stores Company (4,040 employees) now occupies the Westinghouse plant, which serves as a warehouse and distribution
center adjacent, essentially, to the interstate system. Modest manufacturing shops and distribution facilities are still on the west side of the road.

57.6 *Bulk oil storage area located here to be near rail and pipe-line
facilities.*

▶ The bulk oil farms present in 1956 remain and are quite extensive
to the north of major rail lines and with I-270 a short distance away. Located here and on the south side of Fisher Road are Marathon, Ashland,
Clark, and Shell oil terminals. On the north side are a range of distribution facilities, offices, and light manufacturing operations, with an occasional truck terminal.

57.9 *Turn east on Fisher Road to Wilson Road. Turn north through a suburban commercial and residential area. Some area homes are very expensive. On the west is the beginning of a continuous farming belt.*

▶ Evidence of any farming activity is now missing. The area has been
built up heavily to the north of the overhead above I-70. Many offices and
apartment complexes and new homes have been built. Extensive construction of new sewer lines parallels Wilson Road.

60.4 *Turn east on Trabue Road. On the north is a municipal golf course once the home of Gebhardt Jaeger, Columbus industrialist and inventor of the concrete mixer.*

▶ At the northwest corner of the juncture of Wilson with Trabue Road is a large plant of Roxane Labs (634 employees). Nearby is an office park, and beyond is new suburban housing. To the east on Trabue, the old estate on the southeast corner is undergoing renovation; the public golf course is active to the north.

61.4 *San Margarheta, originally an Italian neighborhood housing quarry workers.*

▶ San Margherita has some commercial property but remains primarily a small Italian residential neighborhood. Some of the extensive gardens are now gone, but several homes continue to nurture vineyards and vegetable patches.

61.8 *Quarries.*

▶ The quarry lands are now being reclaimed for residential development on both sides of the Scioto River. This recognizes the fact that these once-quarried sites have potential for development. One site is called Marble Cliffs Crossing and promises luxury homes.

62.4 *Turn north on Dublin Road passing the Scioto Country Club (scene of a PGA tournament a few years ago) on the east and then enter an attractive residential area. The widespread use of limestone slabs in construction of walls and homes is common.*

▶ Once east of the Scioto River at Trabue and Dublin Roads, we abut or pass through the growing residential communities of Arlington that were noted in the 1956 field trip. In general, these upscale communities have aged gracefully. Commercialization has increased, but not within the residential neighborhoods as such.

63.9 *Leave Dublin Rd. entering a city metropolitan park to see Griggs Dam, oldest of the city's reservoirs on the Scioto River. Waters are used for recreation—boat docks may be seen upstream. This is a popular picnic area. Continue north.*

▶ The park space along the river has been maintained and expanded as demands of recreation seekers for park space and for water-related activities have grown.

65.0 *Turn east on Fishinger Rd. passing homes new since 1955 which are utilizing the more "rugged" topography for tri-level and split-level homes. The prices are well above $20,000. The entire area, the northern extent of the Upper Arlington residential area, is new since 1950. It has recently been annexed by Arlington to keep Columbus from encroaching. Upper Arlington's population in 1950 was 9,024; in 1956 it was 21,179 for an increase of 135%.*

▶ The population of Upper Arlington today is approximately 35,000, representing, in part, the areal expansion of the community since 1956. In general, the residential properties in the Arlington community have maintained their prestige and their value. Prices range from over $300,000 for large homes in old Arlington to homes starting at $125,000 to the north. Arlington has relatively little undeveloped land, but the pattern of development has preserved open space with large lots and numerous recreational areas that are well maintained.

66.2 *Fishinger and Redding Rd. Turn south on Redding Rd. passing still another area of new homes in the $17,000+ class. For the most part, these are basement-less two-bedroom homes.*

67.3 *Redding and Northam Rds. The Tremont Shopping Center was developed primarily to serve the new homes; note the modernistic Episcopal Church. Turn west on Northam and enter Canterbury. House prices are considerably higher and continue so as we proceed west into the area of ranch homes many priced in excess of $50,000.*

▶ The Tremont Shopping Center was a novelty in 1956 and is still an active retail center, although it has faced competition for many years from Kingsdale Center, just about a mile to the northeast, and from the Lane Avenue Shopping Center to the south. The small size of the Tremont facility means it cannot meet the demands of a large market; it currently appears to be struggling to retain the market it has.

69.0 *Turn into Abington and follow to Asbury continuing to Lane Ave. and the northwest corner of the Scioto Country Club.*

69.4 *Lane Avenue. Turn east into Lane passing the Country Club and some very expensive homes to the north. Lane Ave. is the dividing line between older Arlington, to the south, which was developed prior to World*

War II, and the newer areas developed since 1940 and principally since the war.

70.5   *The Lane Shopping Center is one of the smaller, older centers which developed in the area since 1950. The eastern-most unit has never been successfully operated; it was planned for a department store.*

▶ The Lane Avenue Center dates to 1949. It has gone through several refurbishings and remodeling, as well as expansions. It is an example of a competitive shopping center without a major "name" store as its focus. The north side of Lane has a mix of remaining residences and stores; to the south side of the shopping center, the residential area is well developed.

71.0   *Leave Lane Ave. turning south onto North Star Rd. To the east may be seen the University Farms and campus. If the day is clear, Downtown Columbus may be seen to the southeast. Much of land in the foreground is University-owned, but some remains in private hands. (Elev. 800+' to 720' in the Olentangy Valley.)*

▶ At North Star Road, a commercial intersection with Lane Avenue, head south. Once again, note that the university farms have all but disappeared; to the west, a pleasant residential area looks over the university open space. The area to the east is now all university property housing the university's West Campus and a number of its major research facilities. The major facility on Lane Avenue to the east is the State of Ohio Computer Center, a supercomputer operation, and just beyond it is the Edison Joining Technology Center. Both are linked to the university's research interests. Continuing south on North Star, the Satellite Communications Facility may be seen; it was one of the initial operations in contact with space. The fields are still being planted.

71.6   *Turn east on Kinnear Road.*

71.7

▶ As we head east on Kinnear Road, we pass the Prairie Grasses Reserve, a site for preserving prairie grasses once native to the central Ohio region. Kinnear Road is the major site for numerous research-related activities of the university today.

71.8   *OSU Research Labs, including the Antenna Research Lab, were housed in a facility that was originally a saw manufacturing plant. The area* *is part of an industrial unit developed by the C&O Railroad. Most firms in the unit are distributors, not manufacturers.*

▶ What was a modest effort by the C&O years ago to establish an industrial park in the area has been taken over by the university. Here are the ElectroScience Lab, the Van de Graaff Lab, the Museum of Biological Diversity, a Business Technology Center, the Research Foundation, and the Center for Mapping, among others. Further on are several private companies. At the juncture of Kinnear and Kenny Roads, the high-rise J. Camera Industrial Rehabilitation Center, along with the university's Wellness Center, Sports Medicine and Family Health Center, and other facilities, can be seen. The Center on Education and Training for Employment and the Eisenhower National Clearinghouse are here as well. Further east and to the south, a neighborhood of smaller homes is a reminder of housing built in the post–World War II period for faculty and students. Private sector businesses and an apartment complex are to the north.

72.7 *Lennox Furnace Co. (emp. about 500) is representative of the many firms engaged in heating and cooling equipment manufacture in Columbus; it is located on a large tract fronting on Olentangy River Road.*

▶ A surface crossing of the C&O tracks remains a hindrance to the easy movement of traffic in this now highly developed retail and entertainment area on the edge of the university. The Lennox Furnace Company plant is now gone; it was demolished in 1996, another example of the decline of local manufacturing. This large tract, more than 1.2 miles in circumference at its edge, adjacent to the university and not far from affluent residential neighborhoods, has become the center for a 24-screen theater and a variety of stores and restaurants. To date, it appears to be a very successful endeavor.

72.9 *Turn south on Olentangy River Rd. The University is to the east; the river in the foreground. Continue south through a commercial stretch which includes the city's largest restaurant, the Jai-Lai, which moved here from cramped quarters and limited accessibility on High St.*

▶ Commercial activity in this area increasingly seeks to cater to the large university student body and those who attend athletic activities in the university area. One example is the new, self-proclaimed largest restaurant in the city, the Buckeye Hall of Fame, catering primarily to the sports crowd.

73.5 *Turn east on Fifth Ave., crossing the Olentangy River.*

73.7 *Ranco, Inc. (emp. 900) is a manufacturer of heating controls. Origi- nally developed and owned by Columbus natives, it is now a part of Ameri- can Motors. Across from Ranco is the Battelle Memorial Institute, one of the oldest industrial research institutions in the nation and one of the largest. Taconite processing was developed here.*

▶ The Ranco plant was taken over by Battelle many years ago, but Ranco North America continues to operate north of I-270. Battelle, still said to be the largest private research institution in the world, continues to expand in Columbus and beyond. Its research has broadened over the years to include economic, educational, and social research.

74.1 *Turn north on Perry St. (formerly a residential area of many Univer- sity faculty), continuing to the entrance to University Hospitals. Older homes are bringing $20,000+ in this area. The University Hospitals in- clude a TB hospital, Cancer Clinic, The Columbus Receiving Hospital, Den- tal Clinic, and the major wing for general hospital care. The center has been expanded in the last six years.*

▶ The Ohio State University Medical Center has grown to become a major medical institution. Much of the growth has occurred to the south of the old established university campus, taking over former residential streets and homes and some open spaces. Neil Avenue remains oriented to the university, with Victorian Village, a historic neighborhood, several blocks to the south.

76.0 *Return to Campus.*

▶ This chapter on "time and change" has used the two field trips to provide examples of how the city and region have changed after more than forty years and suggests some reasons why. It has also revealed how some aspects of the community were little changed during this time.

14

The Changing Geography of Columbus

S O HERE WE ARE FIFTY YEARS LATER. AMONG
some souvenirs of earlier days, I found an Ohio State football program
for October 7, 1950, for the game between Ohio State and my alma mater,
Pitt. In looking through it, I was reminded of some of the changes that
have occurred both locally and nationally since then.

In the program were advertisements by six local hotels seeking to attract
visitors to the city—the Chittenden, Fort Hayes, Virginia, Seneca, Neil
House, and, of course, the Deshler-Wallick. Not to be outdone were the
restaurants. Seven offered enticing ads, including the Jai-Lai Cafe, the Maramor, the Meadowbrook Inn, Grandview Inn, Mills "19" and Mills Quick
Self-Service, and the Ionian Room of the Deshler-Wallick Hotel. Fifty years
later, these memorable institutions have ceased to exist!

More significant are social changes on the football field. Photographs
of thirty-six players from each team appear in my program—the OSU boys
natty in tie and jacket, the Pitt players in T-shirts. But more typical of the
great social changes that were to occur in the second half of the twentieth
century is the fact that only one of the seventy-two players was black, or
"Negro," as would have been said then—Warren Walton, a halfback for
Pitt. There were also photos of the Marching Band in a half-time segment
as it formed a "diamond-shaped Ohio" and played "The Buckeye Battle
Cry." (Where was "Script Ohio" and "Sloopy"?) Ohio State went on to

win the game, 41 to 10. The coach was Wes Fesler, whose Pitt team had beaten Ohio State a few years earlier. This Ohio State team finished with a 6–3 season.

What else have we learned in these fifty years of time and change? For one thing, that *change* is the constant; for another, that neither Columbus nor the larger society stands still. Columbus is growing and expanding physically, economically, and culturally, and at the same time it is experiencing increased regional competition within the central Ohio region.

Today, the old bounds of Central City Columbus have been expanded not only by the enlargement, through annexation, of its political area but by the increased economic and social activity in the adjacent counties of the metropolitan area. In other words, much of the story of Columbus at the end of the twentieth century lies beyond the city in the suburban areas where growth in population and jobs exceeds that in the city and where much of the excitement of the urban-suburban interaction is located.

Yet despite the many positive changes that have occurred in the city and region, several issues that confront the Columbus area in 2000 are much the same as those that confronted the much smaller city fifty years ago. At that time, we were faced with deterioration and obsolescence, and related parking problems and congestion, in the urban core of Central City Columbus. There was also an array of incentives that encouraged the movement of business and industry, as well as residential development, out of the core to the suburban region. And the economy was still responding and adjusting to the burst of industrial growth brought about by World War II and the postwar boom.

So what's new? In a rather perverse way, these same three issues continue to confront and challenge: we remain concerned about reversing the prospect of a declining core or Downtown; the dynamic suburban expansion of the region has created its own kind of problems, notably in sprawl and traffic congestion; and we have successfully made the transition into a full-blown and diverse service economy.

The health and well-being of the Downtown has been a challenge to our leadership throughout these fifty years, but several major events in the past decade have been encouraging as far as the enrichment of the Downtown experience is concerned. In 1989, the plan by Eisenman and Trott for the new Convention Center was approved and construction begun; that same year, City Center opened its doors. These events and related developments in the Downtown led the city's Development Department to suggest in 1990 that "our goal of re-establishing Downtown Columbus as the mag-

This view of the riverfront, with the display of flags of the fifty states above the flood wall, suggests more intensive use of the river setting. More effective use of land in the Scioto Valley for parks, recreational purposes, and public buildings, as well as high-rise residential units, is currently underway.

net for shopping, entertainment, commerce and tourism in Central Ohio is being achieved."[1] If the goal was not yet fully reached then, the potential seemed to be there, and greater attention was focused on the Downtown.

The recent call to "grow inward" and other initiatives addressed to the core city in response to continued suburban expansion seek to re-create and maintain a Downtown as the continuing dynamic center of the region, hopefully one with a strong residential component. The latter vision especially—increased housing in the Downtown—represents a challenge to reverse continuing suburbanization, but a challenge that has gone unheeded until recently.

Central High School, with its "Peninsula" site on the west bank of the Scioto River, has been a prime focus for development, along with creative plans for the improvement in and use of the riverfront. By November 6, 1999, the new Center of Science and Industry (COSI) had opened what the *New York Times* called the city's "jazzy new science center" on the Scioto Peninsula, promising an expanded tourist industry in the region.[2] And not

By 2000, the new COSI building was open on the West Bank of the Scioto River. The photo captures the sweep of the new structure as it blends in with the old Central High School building. The heart of Downtown Columbus is to the east. (Reprinted, with permission, from *The Columbus Dispatch*.)

far behind, the new Nationwide Arena and the development of its associated entertainment and retail areas have added to that promise.

At the other extreme, expanding suburbanization and urban sprawl, accompanied by increased traffic gridlock and what some regard as the despoliation of the countryside, also demand society's attention today in Columbus, as they do in many other urban centers. In retrospect, it appears that we—the national society—got it all wrong. The computer-based information society of which we are an integral part promised greater flexibility as to where the home and the workplace might be—the idea of the "cottage industry" reborn. The conveniences inherent in a communication system—the e-mail, Internet, faxes, home offices, and portable telephones, for example—were to help overcome distance and distance costs in terms of time and money, when time had become the scarce resource. Peter Drucker argued that "in the mental geography of e-commerce, distance has been eliminated."[3] Implied was the notion that reliance on the automobile would be minimized and the traffic problems of the past eliminated or greatly reduced. One model of the urban region of the future assumed that the development of communities would consist not only of "living clusters" but of "working clusters" as well, with other amenities that would relieve the reliance on the automobile. Our society, unfortunately, bought only half of the argument—it was ready to disperse to the residential suburbs to be free of core area problems of aging and congestion, but it was not prepared to give up the car and the mobility it offers.

It didn't surprise anyone that by late 1998, Columbus had reached the point as an urban area wherein "the number of cars meets or exceeds the road capacity" of the community, and it was judged then to be one of five urban areas in the nation "to have experienced the greatest growth in congestion."[4]

With the interstate highways I-70 and I-71 cutting through the heart of the region and with the increase of traffic moving *within* the city on I-270 and I-670, an efficient highway system has become essential to the sense of well-being in the community, but an inefficient system adds increasingly to its discomfort. The system has, in a sense, helped to shape the changing geography of the region.

A typical problem in Columbus, and one not unique to the city, relates to the construction of large malls in peripheral areas, in our case across the city's northern bounds, resulting in, perhaps, the "overmalling" of the area. The Interstate Highway System has been altered so that its original purpose—to move regional traffic expeditiously *through* the area—has been superseded by privately financed interchanges catering to the malls. The system does not necessarily increase access and freedom; rather, it causes congestion and overcrowding on a large scale. Consequently, these actions have created problems similar to those that the Downtown faced fifty years ago. The generic issues remain the same, but their geographic location has changed.

The industrial growth in the area economy fifty years ago encouraged efforts early on to expand manufacturing activity in the region. It was not evident at that time that both nationally and locally, we were in transition to a society and economy in which the various entities of the service sector—government, education, retail and wholesale trade, finance, insurance, real estate, research and development, transportation and communication, and others—were to stimulate change both in the workplace and in how the society lives and functions.

An advantage of large and growing urban regions such as Columbus, with major universities and R&D establishments, is the potential for the development of creative new ideas, of inventions, innovations, and adaptations to technological change. Columbus experienced such change as its manufacturing industry—the product of early innovation and invention in the industrial economy—declined in the face of the new challenges of the so-called postindustrial and computer-oriented communication and information revolutions. The call to create a "Tech Town" is optimistic, but it doesn't minimize in any way the fact of the city's current success in information generation, use, and distribution. Along the way, a clear transition has been made from what has been called a "production machine" economy to an "information or knowledge machine" economy in which knowledge and human capital are major resources.

Columbus, then, was well positioned to prosper within a service economy and, in many ways, was a leader in its evolution. Its historic role as a service center was reinforced as the information-intensive activities associated with the evolution of the new communication technologies came into play. The creativity inherent in its universities and research institutions and the involvement by its banks, insurance companies, and related service organizations led to growth in the service economy.

So where are we in 2000? Well, Columbus is now the fifteenth-largest city in the nation, and its metropolitan region is increasing in size at a faster pace than the political city. The city's area has been extended to more than two hundred square miles, providing opportunities for growth by and within the political city even as the metropolitan areas continue to grow. And we have evolved into a major information and service center with the promise of continuing growth. The quality of life for most of our people is satisfying and is a factor in shaping future growth. The cultural base has been broadened in both the arts and the sports cultures, and with COSI and the new arena in the core area of the city, there is the expectation of a more dynamic and livable Downtown. The culture assumes that growth is good and that more is better. Having become the fifteenth-largest city in the nation, can Columbus continue to be an "easy" place to live and to work? That's the challenge of 2000!

NOTES

CHAPTER 1

1. Roderick Peattie edited *Columbus, Ohio: An Analysis of a City's Development* (Columbus: Industrial Bureau of Columbus, 1930). Nine authors provided short chapters on the region's history, geology, weather and climate, original vegetation, agriculture, mineral resources and industries, human resources, transportation, foreign trade, and air commerce. Peattie was better known for a number of other books, such as *The Incurable Romantic* and *Geography and Human Destiny*, written for the general population.

2. The genesis of the production of ALL was, apparently, in an agricultural laboratory on Milton Avenue in Clintonville. In due course, the formula was sold to Monsanto, who was producing it in Columbus in 1949.

3. Henry L. Hunker, "Columbus, Ohio: The Industrialization of a Commercial Center" (Ph.D. diss., Ohio State University, 1953). This was published in a slightly revised form as *Industrial Evolution of Columbus, Ohio* (Columbus: Ohio State University, Bureau of Business Research, 1958).

4. George Sessions Perry, "Columbus, Ohio," in the "Cities of America" series, *Saturday Evening Post*, May 3, 1952, pp. 22–23, 96–100.

CHAPTER 2

1. C. E. Sherman, *Original Ohio Land Subdivisions*, vol. 3 of *Final Report, Ohio Cooperative Topographic Survey* (Mansfield: Press of the Ohio State Reformatory, 1925), p. 20. Virginia also received 150,000 acres of land in southern Indiana on behalf of George Rogers Clark and his soldiers.

2. Osman C. Hooper, *History of the City of Columbus* (Columbus: Memorial Publishing, 1920), pp. 11–12.

3. Data are from the Division of Geological Survey, Ohio Department of Natural Resources, *1998 Report on Ohio Mineral Industries* (Columbus: Ohio Department of Natural Resources, 1999).

4. In 1945, the Columbus Chamber of Commerce sponsored and published *Water for Columbus*, a study that considered the then current state of the city's water supply and anticipated the metropolitan district's needs to the year 2000. More recently, *Water Beyond 2000* (Columbus: Division of Water, City of Columbus, 1990) has extended the time frame to the year 2025.

5. Much of the early research on microclimates has been done in the central Ohio region and at Ohio State University. Professor John N. Wolfe began early work on microclimates in what is known as the Neotoma Valley in the Hocking Hills in the 1940s. He was so well known for the research that it was assumed that the "N" of his middle name stood for Neotoma! This valley was also home to Edward Thomas, a well-known nature writer of the time. Today, it is part of the Columbus and Franklin County Metropolitan Park District.

6. See "Climate Control Project," *House Beautiful,* October 1949, pp. 129–77ff.; further citations are in the text. The series of articles report on the project in general and about the specific nature of the central Ohio climate.

7. The American Institute of Architects, in conjunction with *House Beautiful,* "Regional Climate Analysis and Design Data," *Bulletin* of the American Institute of Architects, September 1949, pp. 15–36. As stated in the *Bulletin,* the project, which consisted of "a series of climatological charts and paralleling design data for various areas of the U.S.," was "officially designated '*The House Beautiful Climate Control Project.*' Nontechnical interpretations will be published monthly in *House Beautiful. . . .* The technical versions for the various regions will be published in the same sequence in the *Bulletin*" (p. 15).

8. In addition to St. Stephen's Episcopal Church, Brooks and Coddington designed the Education Wing of First Congregational Church and a number of fine homes and office buildings throughout the region.

9. Some of my observations are based on a conference paper that I completed in 1951, "South Columbus: An Area of Retarded Development," reflecting research and interviews that I had carried on in the South Columbus community.

CHAPTER 3

1. "A Survey of Communications: The Death of Distance," *The Economist,* September 30–October 6, 1995.

2. The reference is to *Annexation: Issues and Recommendation. Prepared by Arthur D. Little, Inc., Consultants to the Dept. of Development, City of Columbus,* "Implementation Study no. 6" of *The Columbus Plan: 1970–1990* ([Cambridge?, Mass.], 1970).

CHAPTER 4

1. Data from Bureau of the Census, *1980 Census of Population and Housing* (Washington, D.C., March 1981), and *1990 Census of Population and Housing* (Washington, D.C., March 1991).

2. "Columbus Growing Up: City Is Nation's 15th Largest," *Columbus Dispatch,* June 30, 1999, p. 1.

3. Bureau of the Census, *Metropolitan Areas and Cities. 1990 Census Profile,* no. 3 (Washington, D.C., September 1991), p. 4, table 2.

4. Ibid.

5. Bureau of the Census, "Area Classifications," *1990 Census of Population. General Population Characteristics. Ohio* (Washington, D.C., 1992), p. A8.

6. The Chamber of Commerce's current title as the Greater Columbus Chamber of Commerce was confirmed in a conversation with a chamber official on May 3, 1999.

7. Bureau of the Census, *1980 Census of Population and Housing*, and *1990 Census of Population and Housing*.

8. Peter Drucker, well-known business consultant and visionary, has stated that "the greatest change the 20th century has wrought . . . is the change in demographics." See "Peter F. Drucker—Chronicler of Social Change," *Beta Gamma Sigma News*, Fall 1997, p. 1.

9. George W. Knepper, *Ohio and Its People* (Kent, Ohio: Kent State University Press, 1989), p. 317.

10. *New York Times*, February 20, 1991.

11. Carl A. Klein, Burell T. Charity, and Barbara Brugman, *Growth Statement 1993* (Columbus: Department of Development, April 1993), table G-3.

12. Kelvin Pollard, "More than Black and White," *Population Today* 27, no. 7 (July/August 1999): 7.

13. In an article discussing efforts to reach the Hispanic market, the *New York Times*, March 21, 1997, noted that "the *Banc One* Corporation, the country's 10th largest bank, has become the financial services sponsor" of a film about a popular Latin singer, Selena Perez, in an attempt to reach the Latin market.

14. Klein, Charity, and Brugman, *Growth Statement 1993*, table G-3.

15. Ibid., table P-5.

16. Ibid., tables P-3, P-4.

17. James Breiner, "Inner City—Without Change, Future Bleak," *Columbus Dispatch*, September 18, 1983.

18. Stephen R. Holloway et al., "Race, Spatial Redistribution of Population, and the Concentration of Poverty in Columbus, Ohio, 1980 to 1990," unpublished research report, Department of Geography, The Ohio State University.

19. Stephen R. Holloway et al., "Exploring the Effect of Public Housing on the Concentration of Poverty in Columbus, Ohio," unpublished research report, Department of Geography, The Ohio State University.

CHAPTER 5

1. See Roderick D. McKenzie, "The Neighborhood: A Study of Local Life in the City of Columbus, Ohio," *American Journal of Sociology* 27, no. 2 (1921).

2. My own doctoral dissertation at Ohio State (see chap. 1, n. 3) reported research that suggested Columbus had indeed come of age in terms of industrial growth at this time.

3. Ohio Bureau of Employment Services, Division of Research and Statistics, "Non-agricultural Wage and Salary Employment in the Columbus MSA," *Ohio Labor Market Information* (Columbus, April 1981), data for 1960; data to 2000 are from the December 1999 issue.

4. Mark N. Dodosh, "Hello, Columbus: Thriving Ohio Capital Seems to Shed Its Image as a Country Bumpkin," *Wall Street Journal*, December 8, 1980.

5. Ohio Bureau of Employment Services, Labor Market Information Division, *Columbus MSA Job Outlook: 1994–2005* (Columbus, 1996).

6. Ohio Bureau of Employment Services, Labor Market Information Division, *Columbus MSA Job Outlook to 2006* (Columbus, 1999).

7. Ohio Bureau of Employment Services, Labor Market Information Division, "Non-agricultural Wage and Salary Employment in the Columbus SMSA," *Ohio Labor Market Information, Labor Market Review* (Columbus, December 1999).

8. Quoted in P. R. Warner, "OCLC: Impressive Helper for Librarians," *Columbus Dispatch,* September 13, 1981, p. J1.

9. "The Third McCoy," *Ohio Magazine,* April 1993, pp. 27–31, 75–76; *The Economist,* March 26, 1988, pp. 31–32.

10. Rodney Washington, "Among the Educated, We Rank Near Top," *Business First,* February 13, 1995, p. 5.

11. Ohio Bureau of Employment Services, *Labor Force Estimates, February 1999* (Columbus, 1999).

12. Jean Gottmann, a French geographer, created the concept of the "megalopolis" in his book *Megalopolis: The Urbanized Northeastern Seaboard of the United States* (New York: Twentieth Century Fund, 1961). His continuing interest in the changing city resulted in *The Coming of the Transactional City* (College Park: University of Maryland, Institute for Urban Studies, 1983).

CHAPTER 6

1. "Hello, Columbus," *Town & Country,* January 1975, pp. 81–94ff., quotation on p. 82.

2. Eric Solomon, "Free Speech at Ohio State," *Atlantic Monthly,* November 1965, pp. 119–20.

3. Mike Curtin, "Columbus Growing Rapidly, But Direction Unknown," *Columbus Dispatch,* January 11, 1976.

4. "Columbus: The Largest Small Town in America," *Columbus Citizen-Journal,* November 27, 1978.

5. David Lore, *Columbus Dispatch,* October 9, 1977, in a series on Columbus that ran from October 9 to October 16, 1977.

6. Ibid., October 16, 1977.

7. David Lore, "Columbus Lacking Venture Capital, Some Claim," *Columbus Dispatch,* October 17, 1977.

8. "Columbus's Inferiority Complex," *Columbus Monthly,* 1978.

9. "Columbus, We're Making It Great," *Columbus Citizen-Journal,* October 5, 1979.

10. "Mid-America Still in Business," *Columbus Citizen-Journal,* September 14, 1979.

11. Paul Gapp, "The American City, Challenge of the '80's," *Chicago Tribune,* March 29, 1980; a series of articles on eleven cities, including Columbus, which is defined as "quintessentially Middle American."

12. Mark N. Dodosh, "Hello, Columbus: Thriving Ohio Capital Seeks to Shed Its Image as a Country Bumpkin," *Wall Street Journal,* December 8, 1980.

13. "Jeffers, Lazarus: Their Perspectives from High Street," *Columbus Dispatch,* August 2, 1981, p. J1.

14. "Louisville Envies Us," *Columbus Dispatch,* January 17, 1982.

15. "Business Climate Here Superb," *Columbus Dispatch,* November 10, 1985. The assessment appeared in Rand McNally's *Places Rated Almanac.*

16. "Columbus's Livability Rating Not So Lively," *Columbus Dispatch,* January 6, 1982.

17. "America Discovers Columbus," *Chicago Tribune,* October 30, 1986.

18. "The Selling of Columbus," *Columbus Dispatch,* May 31, 1987.

19. "City's Image Poor," *Columbus Dispatch,* May 12, 1988. Macris was the featured speaker at the Columbus Landmarks Foundation's Recchie Awards program.

20. "Hot Cities—America's Best Places to Live and Work," *Newsweek,* February 6, 1989, pp. 42–49. The piece on Columbus was entitled "The Gleam along the Rust Belt," pp. 48–49.

21. "New Yorkers Visit Columbus: Find Intelligent Art, No Life," *Columbus Monthly,* June 1989.

22. "The Best Cities for Business," *Fortune,* October 22, 1990; "Lighting Up Main Street," *The Economist,* January 20, 1990.

23. "Where Is Columbus Anyway?" *Columbus Dispatch,* March 19, 1990.

24. "Hello, Columbus: Trendies Discover Unlikely New World," *Wall Street Journal,* August 23, 1990.

25. "Columbus' 'Energy and Vitality' Impress Visiting Housing Expert," *Columbus Dispatch,* June 6, 1991.

26. See "City Image Still Draws Blanks, Survey Finds," *Columbus Dispatch,* November 24, 1998.

27. Eugene Van Cleef, *Trade Centers and Trade Routes* (Boston: Appleton-Century-Crofts, 1937), pp. 53–55. The original article by Van Cleef on this topic appeared as "The Urban Profile," *Annals of the Association of American Geographers* 22 (1932): 237–41, which contained silhouette profiles of eight Ohio cities. If Van Cleef was not the originator of the concept, he was its major proponent.

28. Feinknopf quoted in "How Should Our City Grow?" *Columbus Dispatch Magazine,* January 2, 1983.

29. Edna Maria Clark, *Ohio Art and Artists* (Richmond: Garrett & Massie, 1932), p. 368.

30. "Discovering Columbus," *America West Airlines Magazine,* June 1992.

31. Jeff Long, "The Go-to Guy," *Columbus Monthly,* February 1997, pp. 51–55, quotation on p. 55.

CHAPTER 7

1. C. Wright Mills, *The Power Elite* (New York: Oxford University Press, 1956).

2. Delbert C. Miller, *Leadership and Power in the Bos-Wash Megalopolis* (New York: John Wiley & Sons, 1975), p. 56.

3. Related to the issue of leadership in Columbus is the role of Leadership Columbus, which has operated in the city since 1974, first as the Columbus Area Leadership Laboratory, later as the Columbus Area Leadership Program (CALP), and since 1992 with its present name. Its genesis was in a similar program in Atlanta that was created to meet the challenge of having lost many civic leaders in an airplane crash near Paris. Atlanta found itself without an echelon of informed top leaders and with a secondary level of

individuals who were not yet prepared to accept leadership roles. Leadership Atlanta sought to resolve that problem by providing an "educational" experience for potential leaders so that the knowledge of the city and its various operations could be gathered. Similar programs, including the one in Columbus, were later developed in many other U.S. cities.

4. John Gunther, *Inside U.S.A.* (New York: Harper Brothers, 1947). The quotations in this paragraph and the next are all from pp. 451–52.

5. *Point of View* 3 (May–June 1971).

6. Christopher A. Amatos, "City's Chamber Had Many Roles in Past 100 Years," *Columbus Citizen-Journal,* January 24, 1984.

7. Henry L. Hunker, *Industrial Evolution of Columbus, Ohio* (Columbus: The Ohio State University, Bureau of Business Research, 1958).

8. Max Brown, "Power in Columbus," *Columbus Monthly,* February–March 1976. Quotations in this paragraph are from pp. 24–30. Note that reference is made repeatedly to this magazine in the next few pages of text. The magazine has continued to rank the power elite and others in Columbus; rankings have been done in 1976, 1980, 1985, 1989, and 1996.

9. David Lore series on Columbus, *Columbus Dispatch,* October 16, 1977.

10. Julia Osborne, "Corporate Gunslingers," *Columbus Monthly,* December 1978, pp. 50–60.

11. Julia Osborne, "The Directors," *Columbus Monthly,* September 1979, pp. 57–62, 166–174.

12. Paul Gapp, "The American City, Challenge of the '80's," *Chicago Tribune,* March 29, 1980.

13. Max Brown, "Power: The More Things Change . . . ," *Columbus Monthly,* March 1980, pp. 50–59. This article also listed "The Power Pods," leadership in certain areas of the community such as arts/culture, labor, academe, women, and blacks.

14. The Editors, "The Titans: Six Men Who Rule Columbus," *Columbus Monthly,* June 1989, pp. 29–37.

15. John Grogan, "Power in Columbus: The Wolfes Have It and Plan to Keep It," *Kiplinger Program Report,* Spring 1986.

16. William H. Meyers, "Rag-Trade Revolutionary," *New York Times Magazine,* June 8, 1986, pp. 41–43ff.

17. "Lighting Up Main Street," *The Economist,* January 20, 1990.

18. Richard D. Hylton, "A Real Estate Fortune Dissolves," *New York Times,* March 6, 1991.

19. Ray Paprocki, "The End of an Era," *Columbus Monthly,* August 1994, an issue entitled "Death of the Titan."

20. The Editors, "Power Shift," *Columbus Monthly,* April 1996, in an issue entitled "Power in Columbus."

21. Jennifer Steinhauer and Edward Wyatt, "The Merlin of the Mall Looks for New Magic," *New York Times,* December 8, 1996.

CHAPTER 8

1. The quotation is taken from a 1957 brochure of the Casto organization which described the seven centers built between 1948 and 1957.

2. A "taxpayer strip" is defined as a commercial building with a single row of store-fronts, occasionally capped by one or two stories of lofts or offices. The strips were, apparently, related to speculative real estate developments and were intended to generate revenue to pay taxes and to hold for later development. See Chester H. Liebs, *From Main Street to Miracle Mile* (Boston: Little, Brown, 1985).

3. "An American Original: The Evolution of the Shopping Mall," *New York Times*, December 21, 1997. Some of the facts and comments concerning the Bank Block Building reflect statements contained in a National Register of Historic Places Registration Form used to submit the nomination of the building to the National Register. The Bank Block Building was entered on the Register on September 15, 1997.

4. The Lane Avenue Shopping Center was constructed in 1949 by the F & Y Construction Company and opened in 1950.

5. From the Casto organization brochure cited in n. 1.

6. Jonassen's initial research focused on Columbus, Ohio. A final report of the research was made to the Highway Research Board of the National Research Council by The Ohio State Research Foundation in 1952 under the title *Downtown versus Suburban Shopping: A Study of Attitudes toward Parking and Related Conditions.* This same report, except for a change in the title, was the basis for the publication *Downtown versus Suburban Shopping: Measurement of Consumer Practices and Attitudes in Columbus, Ohio* (Columbus: Ohio State University, Bureau of Business Research, 1953). This was followed by C. T. Jonassen, *The Shopping Center versus Downtown* (Columbus: Ohio State University, Bureau of Business Research, 1955). As noted in the foreword to the third publication, "The present study is a further testing of the methodology developed and results found in [the] earlier study." In this book, data related to consumer attitudes and practices were gathered for two other metropolitan areas in addition to Columbus—Seattle and Houston—to test the validity of methods used and the results gained by the initial study.

7. Jonassen, *The Shopping Center versus Downtown* (1955), quotations from introduction, pp. 1–3.

8. On June 1, 1962, Charles Lazarus, then president of the Lazarus store in Columbus, was inducted as an honorary member into Beta Gamma Sigma, the honorary business fraternity at Ohio State University. In the course of the evening, I introduced Mr. Lazarus to Professor Jonassen. Lazarus immediately recognized the Jonassen name and recalled his research on Columbus and the issues it dealt with. He acknowledged that the findings presented by Jonassen's research concerning shopping habits and parking in the Downtown had played an important role in limiting the Lazarus stores' entry into the suburban shopping center market.

9. Kenneth Meckstroth, "Order $3-Million Parking System," *Ohio State Journal*, December 3, 1949, p. 1.

10. Ronnie Jauchius and Bob Dishon, "Plans for Redevelopment Launched," *Columbus Dispatch*, December 24, 1950.

11. Henry L. Hunker, *Industrial Evolution of Columbus, Ohio* (Columbus: Ohio State University, Bureau of Business Research, 1958).

12. The Northland area is currently under study once again, with respect to both the large Northland residential community of over 70,000 residents and the future of the Northland Mall and other commercial services on Morse Road.

13. Molly O'Neill, "Hello, Columbus," *New York Times Magazine*, May 18, 1997, pp. 97, 98.

14. "City Center Mall: The Showpiece of Capitol South Redevelopment," *Columbus Development News,* October 1989, p. 1. This Columbus Department of Development newsletter provides a concise summary of the Capitol South project.

15. See Donald Borror, "Capitol South Is Columbus' Future," *Columbus Economic Review,* Summer 1981. Borror took over the leadership of the project in 1980. In this article, he noted that there were a number of small shops in the three-block area that were demolished but that they only employed about 500 persons and generated tax revenues of about $250,000 a year. Of course, a number of the small shop owners were driven out of business as a result of the demolitions.

16. Michael Grossberg, "Architect Whyte Likes Style Here," *Columbus Dispatch,* November 19, 1987.

17. "Urban Expert Praises New City Center," *Columbus Dispatch,* August 18, 1989.

18. See "Goodbye to Mall Envy," *Columbus Monthly,* March 1997, pp. 109–12.

19. The Limited sold its interest in the Tuttle Mall to the Taubman interests in 1997. Taubman then sold his interests in the Tuttle Mall and City Center to the GM Pension Trust in 1998.

20. See "Wexner Has Vision for Northeast," *Columbus Dispatch,* March 5, 1995, pp. 1–2.

21. The Casto organization published a 1997 calendar carrying the title "We've Got You Covered, Columbus!" and listing the eighteen Casto shopping centers then in operation in the city-region.

CHAPTER 9

1. I have excerpted certain phrases and ideas in this section from a research paper, "The Franklinton Area: Alternatives for Development," that I prepared for the Franklinton Area Commission in 1975.

2. Richard Bangs, then president of the Board of Trade, quoted in Jane Ware, "Franklinton Eldest of All," *Columbus Monthly,* August 1991, p. 48.

3. A publication celebrating Franklinton's bicentennial in 1997 provides a fine glimpse into the community and especially of its people. See "The Faces of Franklinton, 1797–1997, A Special Anniversary Section," *Columbus Dispatch,* March 2, 1997.

4. Charles W. Minshall, "A Model of Residential Site Selection: The Jewish Population of Columbus, Ohio" (Ph.D. diss., Ohio State University, 1971). Minshall had approached me about undertaking a dissertation about the black population in Columbus, but as a number of similar studies of blacks were already underway, I suggested that he consider Rabbi Folkman's remark concerning the eastward movement of Jewish populations in American cities.

5. Ibid., p. 18.

6. Comments here are taken from an article in *According to Hoyt: 50 Years of Homer Hoyt, 1916 to 1966* (Washington, D.C.: n.p.), a collection of Hoyt's writings on urban growth and structure, urban land values, real estate cycles, the sector theory, and economic and political issues. The material on the sector theory is from "Forces Underlying City Growth and Structure," pp. 296–305.

7. Minshall, "A Model of Residential Site Selection," pp. 21–23, quotation on p. 22.

8. Ibid., p. 20.

9. Aminah Robinson, *A Street Called Home* (New York: Harcourt Brace, 1997), unnumbered pages. Here are recorded Robinson's memories of life in the expanding black community of the 1930s and 1940s, captured with vivid verbal and visual imagery.

10. Ibid.

11. "The Southside: A Tradition of Economic Strength, Attractive Development Opportunities, and Determined People," *Columbus Development Notes,* Columbus Department of Development, November 1991.

12. Henry L. Hunker, "South Columbus, Ohio: A Study of Limited Urban Development," paper presented at the Ohio Academy of Science meeting, spring 1952.

13. Daniel J. Prosser and Jeffrey T. Darbee, *German Village Handbook* (Columbus: Department of Development, 1982).

14. Roderick D. McKenzie, "The Neighborhood: A Study of Local Life in the City of Columbus, Ohio," *American Journal of Sociology* 27, no. 2 (1921): 151.

15. "German Village, Urban Renewal through Private Enterprise," *Columbus Business Forum,* June 1965.

16. Mary-Dixon Sayre Miller, "The Effect of Preservation on Residential Real Estate Tax Values" (master's thesis, Ohio State University, 1981), pp. 107–8. The thesis used a sampling technique, with the Clintonville neighborhood serving as a control area for comparison purposes.

17. Jon A. Peterson, "From Social Settlement to Social Agency: Settlement Work in Columbus, Ohio, 1898–1958," *Social Service Review* 39, no. 2 (1965): 191–208. This is a fine account of the establishment and growth of the Godman Guild and of conditions in the early Flytown.

18. The data are derived from a study I conducted in 1950, "Northeastern Columbus: Geographic Factors Affecting Industrial Settlement," unpublished research paper.

19. Herb Cook, Jr., Nancy Richison, and Laura Pienkny Zakin, "Best Neighborhoods: 20 Great Places to Live," *Columbus Monthly,* October 1998, pp. 34–54; Old Beechwold is discussed on pp. 47–49.

20. Ellen Rose, *Beechwold, 1800–1975* (Old Beechwold Association pamphlet, 1975). This is a four-page pamphlet written by a longtime resident of Old Beechwold and distributed to members of the Old Beechwold Association.

21. Beechwold Realty Company, *Beechwold the Beautiful* (brochure, ca. 1915).

22. "Old Beechwold Historic District," *Keystone,* Fall 1998, pp. 1–3. *Keystone* is the newsletter of the Columbus Historic Preservation Office.

23. See "Developer Examines Lifestyles," *Clintonville-Beechwold This Week,* September 2, 1991, pp. 1ff.

24. Quoted in James Breiner, "The Legacy of Tom Moody," *Capitol Magazine,* January 1, 1984, p. 14, under "The Moody Wit."

CHAPTER 10

1. Information about Alfred Kelley and his home may be found in Abbot L. Cummings, *The Alfred Kelley House of Columbus, Ohio* (Columbus: Franklin County Historical Society, 1953), p. 52. The account reviews Kelley's life and documents and the building of the house. There are photos and drawings of the house as well as Mrs. Kelley's written recollections and family letters.

2. Robert E. Samuelson, Pasquale C. Grado, Judith L. Kitchen, and Jeffrey T.

Darbee, *Architecture Columbus* (Columbus: Foundation of the Columbus Chapter of the American Institute of Architects, 1976).

3. In his grant proposal letter of September 30, 1977, to the Columbus Foundation, James Keyes, the first president of Columbus Landmarks Foundation, identified the other participants as the local chapter of the American Institute of Architects, the Ohio State University Architecture Department, the Mid-Ohio Regional Planning Preservation Office, and the Ohio Historical Society.

4. Memo from Paul Young to Columbus Landmarks Foundation board members on October 31, 1977.

5. "Landmarks Law Clears Court," *Citizen-Journal,* July 15, 1978.

6. Quoted in letter from James Keyes to the Columbus Foundation, September 30, 1977.

7. Letter from James Keyes to the Columbus Foundation, September 30, 1977, p. 3.

8. Letter from the Columbus Foundation to the Columbus Landmarks Foundation, November 22, 1977.

9. "Task Force Assignments," October 24, 1977, internal document prepared by Paul Young for Columbus Landmarks.

10. See "Negotiating the City's Future," *Nation's Cities Weekly,* June 26, 1979. Included are seven articles by different authors that explain the concept as "an experimental plan for pooling urban investments and bargaining to coordinate policy goals." See also Henry L. Hunker, "Shaping Public Policy: The Negotiated Investment Strategy," paper presented at the annual meeting of the Association of American Geographers, Los Angeles, April 22, 1981.

11. These three quotations are taken from Dick Campbell, "Is City Hall Annex Worth Saving?" editorial, *Columbus Citizen-Journal,* December 22, 1979.

12. In his obituary in the *New York Times,* November 3, 1998, Weese was described as "a major figure in Chicago architecture and planning since the 1950's . . . [who] specialized in historic preservation as well as new buildings" and as the designer of Washington's metro system, which ranks "among the greatest public works of this century."

13. See Henry L. Hunker, "The Role of Historic Preservation and Restoration in Economic Development," Issue Paper no. 11, Mayor's Economic Development Council, February 1980.

14. "Why Tear It Down?" editorial, *Columbus Citizen-Journal,* January 14, 1980.

15. "City Hall Annex Debate Termed 'Good for the City,'" *Columbus Dispatch,* January 20, 1980.

16. Lee Stratton, "Demolition Dust Clouds Columbus," *Columbus Dispatch,* June 8, 1980, p. B3.

17. Bohm, "Influencing World Architecture from Columbus," *Business First,* September 5, 1997, p. 36.

18. Columbus Landmarks Foundation, *Feasibility of the Adaptive Use of the Ohio School for the Deaf as a Congregate Retirement Community,* March 1, 1979.

19. "Landmarks Foundation Endorses Hotel Sale," *Columbus Citizen-Journal,* November 18, 1980, p. C1.

20. Columbus Landmarks Foundation, *An Inventory and Evaluation of Historic Buildings in the Columbus, Ohio, CBD, September 1980,* p. 10.

21. The paragraphs that discuss the inventory are taken in part from a letter from Henry L. Hunker, Columbus Landmarks Foundation, to Joseph Imberman, Director, Columbus Foundation, October 1, 1980.

22. Jack W. Giljahn and Thomas R. Matheny, *A Guide for the Adaptive Use of Surplus Schools* (Columbus: Columbus Landmarks Foundation, 1981).

23. Letter from Henry L. Hunker, Chair of the Historic Resources Commission, to Mayor Tom Moody, November 24, 1982.

24. Columbus Landmarks Foundation, "Position Paper—Central High School," March 15, 1982.

25. Columbus Landmarks Foundation, "Comments about the Beggs Building," October 12, 1983.

26. Columbus Landmarks Foundation, *Preservation Means Economic Development: A Report of the Columbus Landmarks Foundation* (Columbus: Office of Management and Budget, June 1985); and *Historic Preservation: The Investment Alternative* (Columbus: Department of Development, 1986).

27. Columbus Landmarks Foundation, *Goals for a Better Built Environment in Columbus* (Columbus: Columbus Landmarks Foundation, 1988).

28. Columbus Landmarks Foundation, *Landmark Decisions: Visions of Our City* (Columbus: Columbus Landmarks Foundation, 1989).

29. Nancy Recchie and Jeffrey Darbee, *Historic District Evaluation for the City of Columbus,* September 1989; and *Historic Property Evaluation for the City of Columbus,* September 1990, both issued by the City of Columbus, Department of Development.

30. See *Reinvest-Reuse-Renew* (Columbus: City of Columbus, Department of Trade and Development, 1992).

CHAPTER 11

1. David Lowenthal, *Environmental Assessment: A Case Study of Columbus, Ohio* (New York: American Geographical Society, 1972), p. iii. This is one of eight reports, five of which described and compared urban milieus in Columbus, New York, Boston, and Cambridge, and three of which analyzed and interpreted the images of the environment.

2. House Committee on Banking and Currency, *The Quality of Urban Life,* Hearings, 91st Congr., 1st and 2nd sess. (Washington, D.C.: Government Printing Office, 1970).

3. Byron Munson, *Changing Community Dimensions: The Interrelationships of Social and Economic Variables* (Columbus: Ohio State University, College of Administrative Science, 1968), p. 105.

4. The definition was provided in a letter Minus sent out to council members to announce the annual meeting of the Council for Ethics in Economics in 1988.

5. For a fuller discussion of the various aspects of the quality-of-life concept, see David Ley, "The Quality of Urban Life," in *A Social Geography of the City* (New York: Harper & Row, 1983), chap. 10.

6. See Ben Chieh Liu, *Quality of Life Indicators in U.S. Metropolitan Areas* (New York: Praeger, 1976). The data were for 1970 and followed research at the Midwest Research Institute completed earlier by J. O. Wilson, using 1960–66 data for the fifty states.

7. Philip M. Burgess, *Aspects of the Quality of Life in Metropolitan Columbus,* Bench-

mark Social Reports, no. 1, Columbus Area Social Profile (Columbus: Benchmark, 1974). This was the first in a series of reports dealing with the subject.

8. See Susan L. Cutter, *Rating Places: A Geographer's View on Quality of Life* (Washington, D.C.: Association of American Geographers, 1985).

9. Liu, *Quality of Life Indicators.*

10. "Best Cities to Bet On," *Time,* November 9, 1998, p. 123.

11. Brad Edmondson, "The Place-Rating Game," *Attache,* November 1998, pp. 72–76, 78.

CHAPTER 12

1. *The Columbus Area Economy, Structure and Growth, 1950 to 1985,* vol. 1, *Employment, and Value Added by Manufacture* (Columbus: Ohio State University, Bureau of Business Research, 1966), p. 36. The research was carried out by a team of university faculty consisting of James C. Yocum, Richard A. Tybout, Henry L. Hunker, Gilbert Nestel, and Wilford L'Esperance. Vol. 2 of this study was *Income, Trade, Housing,* and vol. 3 was *Population and Labor Force.* The three-volume study was completed in 1967.

2. Thomas H. Langevin with Robert H. Bremner, Henry L. Hunker, Lucia B. Findley, Carole J. Rogers, et al., *The Battelle Memorial Institute Foundation 1975–1982: A History and Evaluation* (Columbus: Ohio Historical Society, 1983), chap. 4, pp. 72–95.

3. Ibid., chap. 2, pp. 13–60. Battelle Memorial Institute Foundation (BMIF) was incorporated as a charitable corporation under the nonprofit corporation laws of Ohio in 1975 in response to a lawsuit that challenged how the institute was meeting its responsibility to charitable causes in the area.

4. Ibid., p. 78.

5. In 1977 Budd Bishop, then director of the museum, contacted Russell Page, the great British landscape designer who in 1973 had designed the garden for the Frick Collection in New York, to design the sculpture garden on the east side of the museum. The Columbus Museum garden is one of his two works in Ohio. The other is a series of eight gardens at the home of Thomas Vail, publisher and editor of the *Cleveland Plain Dealer.* Page, ever protective of his work, wrote to the museum and "admonished the museum staff not to change the 'anomalies and asymettrys' [*sic*] of his carefully calculated plans." Marina Schinz and Gabrielle van Zuylen, *The Gardens of Russell Page* (New York: Stewart, Tabori & Chang, 1981), p. 230.

6. Rosemary Curtin Hite, "Arts in Columbus Have Grown in 15 Years—Farewell: It's Been Fun, But . . . ," *Columbus Citizen-Journal,* March 13, 1980, p. 8.

7. National Endowment for the Arts, *Economic Impact of Arts and Cultural Institutions: Case Studies in Columbus, Minneapolis/St. Paul, St. Louis, Salt Lake City, San Antonio, and Springfield* (Washington, D.C.: National Endowment for the Arts, 1981), section on Columbus on pp. 29–40, quotation on pp. 10–11. The organizations that were selected for the study were Ballet Metropolitan, Columbus Museum of Art, Columbus Symphony Orchestra, Center of Science and Industry, Players Theatre of Columbus, and Columbus Association for the Performing Arts (Ohio Theatre).

8. See David Cwi, *The Economic Impact of Six Cultural Institutions on the Economy of the Columbus SMSA* (Baltimore: Johns Hopkins University, Center for Metropolitan Planning and Research, 1979). This report reviewed the study procedures, the direct

effects and secondary effects of the institutions upon the community, and their impact with respect to government expenditures and revenues.

9. Andrew Broekema, "The Arts in Columbus or a Gamut of Games," paper presented at the Columbus Torch Club, December 11, 1986, pp. 4, 6.

10. "Many U.S. Orchestras Are in Financial Straits," *New York Times,* January 19, 1987, p. 14. Columbus Symphony president Edward Moulton was cited in the article, noting that "society's dilemma is how it chooses to support the arts" and who among it make the choices. He noted further that the average age of the symphony audience was well over fifty years and that something needed to be done to reach a younger audience. A *Columbus Dispatch* article dealing with community support suggested that "orchestras mirror civic status" and that "going to the symphony is simply not a way of life in Columbus." See Christopher Amatos, "Columbus Symphony Enjoys Community Support," July 12, 1988, p. C6.

11. "Columbus Official Visitors Guide—Spring/Summer '89," p. 3.

12. Ray Paprocki, "Can AmeriFlora Work?" *Columbus Monthly,* April 1990, p. 37.

13. "An Odd Hybrid Called Ameriflora Struggles in Ohio," *New York Times,* August 6, 1992, p. B1.

14. Quoted in *The Booster,* October 21, 1992.

15. Ray Paprocki, "Les Wexner's Impact," *Columbus Monthly,* March 1994, pp. 30–39.

16. Emily Foster, "Season on the Brink: The Rescue of Opera/Columbus," *Columbus Monthly,* May 1991, pp. 34–38.

17. Barbara Zuck, "Tenor in Top Form in Benefit Concert," *Columbus Dispatch,* March 1, 1999.

18. Peter Marks, "Standing Room Only (And That's Not Good)," *New York Times,* December 8, 1996, p. H5. The article discusses some of the reasons why standing ovations have become commonplace and even a bit embarrassing.

19. Mike Curtin, "Market Study Indicates City Could Not Support Arena," *Columbus Dispatch,* January 5, 1978, p. B2.

20. See *Newsweek,* "Rx for Cities: Build a Dome," December 28, 1987.

21. Robert Sohovich and Robert Ruth, "Debate over Tax Proposal Heats Up," *Columbus Dispatch,* February 23, 1986, p. B2.

22. Darris Blackford, "Leaders Believe an Arena Should Be in City's Future," *Columbus Dispatch,* April 18, 1993, p. D3.

23. "Is That the Ticket? City Leaders Ponder Arena Development," editorial, *Columbus Dispatch,* May 5, 1993, p. A8.

24. Bob Greene, "Cities without Big-League Sports Are Luckier than They Know," *Columbus Dispatch,* October 8, 1993; Barbara Carmen, "Mayor Kicks Off Search for Pro Sports Team," *Columbus Dispatch,* October 20, 1993. It should be noted that, in contrast to Columbus, Charlotte had little competition within its market territory and had the "critical mass" to support a major league team. See Peter Applebome, "Regional Configuration Gets Pro Football Team," *New York Times,* October 28, 1993.

25. Jeff Long, "Seven Reasons Columbus Will Never Have a Big-League Sports Franchise," *Columbus Monthly,* February 1994, pp. 39–45.

26. Steven Taper and San Tutterow, "The Panthers: Charlotte's Gold Mine or Fool's Gold?" *Cross Section* (Federal Reserve Bank of Richmond), Winter 1994/95, pp. 18–25.

27. Eric S. Schmid, "Determining Major League Baseball Fan Regions and Predicting Total Revenues" (master's thesis, Ohio State University, 1994).

28. E. J. Thomas, "Columbus Should Learn Stadium Lessons from Rival Cities," *Columbus Dispatch,* August 28, 1995.

29. "The Stadium Game," *The Economist,* May 4, 1996, p. 26; "Picking Up the Tab for Fields of Dreams," *New York Times,* July 27, 1996.

30. Richard Sandomir, "The Name of the Game Is New Stadiums," *New York Times,* June 4, 1997, pp. 23, 25. Seven paragraphs explain the rejection of the sales tax referendum in Columbus as well as Peter Karmanos's well-publicized, if offensive, role in the city, which may have affected the vote.

31. Scott Powers and Steve Wright, "Not Many Privately Built Arenas in Medium Cities," *Columbus Dispatch,* June 5, 1997, p. C30.

32. Steve Wright, "Developer: Time for Private Arena Plan Is Now," *Columbus Dispatch,* May 22, 1997, p. C6.

33. Greg Davies, "The Town-Gown Battle," *Columbus Monthly,* July 1997, pp. 122–28.

34. Doug Caruso, "Mayor Wants New Panel to Lure Sporting Events," *Columbus Dispatch,* December 27, 1997.

35. See Jeff Lyttle, *Gorillas in Our Midst: The Story of the Columbus Zoo Gorillas* (Columbus: Ohio State University Press, 1997).

CHAPTER 14

1. Columbus Development Department, *Columbus Development Notes,* June 1990, p. 1.

2. Bruce Weber, "Two Cities, Two Leaps of Faith: Columbus Pins Its Dreams on a Jazzy New Science Center," *New York Times,* November 14, 1999.

3. Quoted in Fred Andrews, "The Sage of Value and Service," *New York Times,* November 17, 1999, pp. C1, C14.

4. Population Reference Bureau, *The United States Population Data Sheet* (Washington, D.C., 1998).